THE LAW OF FREEDOM OF INFORMATION

FIRST CUMULATIVE SUPPLEMENT

THE LAW OF FREEDOM OF INFORMATION

FIRST CUMULATIVE SUPPLEMENT

by

John Macdonald QC

With

Ross Crail

Colin Braham

OXFORD
UNIVERSITY PRESS

OXFORD
UNIVERSITY PRESS

Great Clarendon Street, Oxford OX2 6DP

Oxford University Press is a department of the University of Oxford.
It furthers the University's objective of excellence in research, scholarship,
and education by publishing worldwide in

Oxford New York

Auckland Cape Town Dar es Salaam Hong Kong Karachi
Kuala Lumpur Madrid Melbourne Mexico City Nairobi
New Delhi Shanghai Taipei Toronto

With offices in

Argentina Austria Brazil Chile Czech Republic France Greece
Guatemala Hungary Italy Japan Poland Portugal Singapore
South Korea Switzerland Thailand Turkey Ukraine Vietnam

Oxford is a registered trade mark of Oxford University Press
in the UK and in certain other countries

Published in the United States
by Oxford University Press Inc., New York

First published 2006

British Library Cataloguing in Publication Data
Data available

Library of Congress Cataloging in Publication Data
Data available

Typeset by Newgen Imaging Systems (P) Ltd., Chennai, India
Printed in Great Britain
on acid-free paper by
Antony Rowe Ltd., Chippenham, Wiltshire

ISBN 0–19–928806–2 978–0–19–928806–9

1 3 5 7 9 10 8 6 4 2

The authors would like to thank those who contributed to the main work for their help and encouragement. The law is stated as at 15 September 2005

CONTENTS—SUMMARY

F FREEDOM OF INFORMATION AND THE COMMERCIAL WORLD

G PRIVACY, CONFIDENTIALITY, AND HUMAN RIGHTS

H DEVOLUTION

APPENDICES

II: Materials

INTRODUCTION

Three sets of rules

From 1 January 2005 public authorities became subject to the full effect of the Freedom of Information Act 2000 ('the 2000 Act'). On the same day, they became subject to the Environmental Information Regulations 2004 ('the EIR'), which came into effect on 1 January 2005. They continued to be subject to the Data Protection Act 1998, which had been amended and extended by the 2000 Act.

For the public authority faced with a request for information the first question must be: which set of rules applies? Are we being asked for private information, or environmental information, or public information? This introduction is intended for those who have to answer these questions. It states shortly the definitions of 'personal information' or more accurately 'personal data', and 'environmental information', explains the extent to which the three sets of rules fit together, and indicates the main differences between them.

Personal data

A person is entitled to receive information relating to himself or herself under the Data Protection Act 1998 ('the 1998 Act'). The applicant is called the *data subject*. 'Data' includes information stored automatically (that is, on a computer), manually processed data stored in a structured form (for example, a handwritten card index system) and, under an amendment introduced by the 2000 Act, processed data in an unstructured form. Data is 'personal' if it enables a living individual to be identified from it, or from it and other information in the hands of the data controller.

One of the exemptions to the right to information under the 2000 Act, in section 40, is for personal information. The purpose of the exemption is not to prevent the release of such information, but to recognize that a regime governing the processing, including the release, of such information already exists under the 1998 Act.

Where the applicant is the data subject, section 40(1) creates an absolute exemption. The effect of this is to remove such applications entirely from the regime of the 2000 Act, leaving them to the existing regime of the 1998 Act. The effects of that regime, considered in detail in the Main Work in chapter 10, are essentially threefold. First, to give 'data subjects' rights of access to, and certain other rights of control over, personal information which concerns them. These rights are subject to the exceptions contained in the 1998 Act. Second, to regulate the use that is made of information contained in personal data through the application of 'data protection principles'. And third, that there should be impartial supervision of those who hold the data (now undertaken by the Information Commissioner and the Information Tribunal, whose jurisdiction extends across the fields of both freedom of information and data protection).

Where the applicant is not the data subject, but a third party seeking personal information, matters are a little more complicated. Such applications should be dealt with under the 2000 Act, but because the release of personal information to a third party raises issues of data protection, very broad exemptions apply to such requests, and these exemptions are defined by reference to the 1998 Act.

Wherever an application for 'personal data' is made by someone other than the 'data subject', the information to which it relates will be exempt from disclosure under the 2000 Act where either of two conditions is satisfied. Their general effect can be described as follows. Where disclosure by the public authority of the data would contravene any of the 'data protection principles' it is absolutely exempt. Where the data falls within the original form of section 1(1) of the 1998 Act (that is, it is information stored in a computer or is manually processed data stored in a 'structured' rather than an 'unstructured' form) then disclosure is also prevented if it would contravene the data subject's right to prevent processing likely to cause damage or distress (pursuant to section 10 of the 1998 Act). The exemption is not, however, in such a case absolute, but is subject to the public interest test. The same is true if the information in question is exempt from the data subject's own right of access under the 1998 Act: it is again exempt, but the exemption is subject to the public interest test. Further, the duty to confirm or deny under the 2000 Act is excluded where an application is made by someone other than the data subject if compliance would contravene any of the data protection principles, or section 10 of the 1998 Act, or where the data is exempt from disclosure to the data subject under the 1998 Act.

Environmental information

Section 39 of the 2000 Act provides that information is exempt information if an authority is required to make it available in accordance with the EIR (or would be so required but for an exception within the EIR). This is not a true exemption: it means that environmental information is available under the different regime established by the EIR. This regime applies across the European Union.

Under regulation 2(1) of the EIR *environmental information* has the same meaning as in Article 2(1) of Council Directive 2003/4/EC, namely any information in written, visual, aural, electronic, or any other material form on:

(a) the state of the elements of the environment, such as air and atmosphere, water, soil, land, landscape, and natural sites including wetlands, coastal and marine areas, biological diversity and its components, including genetically modified organisms, and the interaction among those elements;
(b) factors, such as substances, energy, noise, radiation, or waste, including radioactive waste, emissions, discharges, and other releases into the environment, affecting or likely to affect the elements of the environment referred to in (a);
(c) measures (including administrative measures) such as policies, legislation, plans, programmes, environmental agreements, and activities affecting or likely to affect the elements and factors referred to in (a) and (b) as well as measures and activities designed to protect those elements;
(d) reports on the implementation of environmental legislation;
(e) cost–benefit and other economic analyses and assumptions used within the framework of the measures and activities referred to in (c); and
(f) the state of human health and safety, including the contamination of the food chain, where relevant, conditions of human life, cultural sites and built structures inasmuch as they are or may be affected by the state of the elements of the environment referred to in (a) or, through those elements, by any of the matters referred to in (b) and (c).

This is a very broad definition and includes, for example, many of the activities undertaken by local authorities. Requests for information which fall within this definition would have to be dealt with under the EIR.

Differences between the EIR and the 2000 Act

The definition of *public authorities* in regulation 2(2) is wider than the definition in the 2000 Act and includes bodies such as privatized water authorities and power companies. The main differences between the substance of the two regimes are first, that a public authority is required to apply a presumption in favour of disclosure under the EIR: there is no such presumption under the 2000 Act. Second, the exemptions in the EIR are narrower; there is, for example, no express exemption for information the disclosure of which would be likely to be prejudicial to the economic or financial interests of the United Kingdom. Third, none of the exceptions in the EIR are absolute—they are all subject to the public interest test; and fourth, all the substantial exceptions under the EIR only apply to the extent that disclosure would adversely affect the interest protected; in contrast, prejudice is only required to be shown in about half the qualified exemptions under the 2000 Act. Applicants will therefore be keen to have their requests considered under the EIR rather than under the 2000 Act.

HOW TO USE THIS SUPPLEMENT

This is the first supplement to the first edition of Macdonald and Jones on *The Law of Freedom of Information*, and has been compiled according to the structure of the main volume.

At the beginning of each chapter of this Supplement is an abbreviated table of contents from the main volume. Where a heading in this table has been marked by the symbol ■, this indicates that there is relevant information in the Supplement to which the reader should refer.

Within each chapter, updating information is referenced to the relevant paragraph in the main volume. Wholly new paragraphs can be identified by a paragraph number followed by a letter, eg 58Y.

TABLES OF CASES

United Kingdom

A *v* B Plc [2002] EWCA Civ 337, [2003] QB 195, CA (Civ Div) 21.38
A *v* Secretary of State for the Home Department [2004] UKHL 56, [2005] 2 AC 68, HL. 21.19
American Cyanamid Co (No1) *v* Ethicon Ltd [1975] AC 396, HL. 21.60
Attorney General *v* Barker (Civil Proceedings Order) [2000] 1 FLR 759 . . . . 5.102

Bowman *v* Fels [2005] EWCA Civ 226, [2005] 1 WLR 3083, [2005] 2 Cr App R 19, [2005] 2 CMLR 23, CA (Civ Div) 14.34A

Campbell *v* Mirror Group Newspapers Ltd [2004] UKHL 22, [2004] 2 AC 457, HL 10.04, 20.93B–20.93E, 21.69A-21.69C
Cream Holdings Ltd *v* Banerjee [2004] UKHL 44, [2005] 1 AC 253, HL 21.60
Criminal Proceedings against Lindqvist (C101/01) [2004] QB 1014 . . . . 10.08A

Darnton *v* University of Surrey [2003] ICR 615, [2003] IRLR 133, EAT 13.29, 13.37
Derbyshire CC *v* Times Newspapers Ltd [1993] AC 534, HL 20.89A
Douglas *v* Hello! Ltd (No1) [2001] QB 967, CA (Civ Div) 20.89A
Douglas *v* Hello! Ltd (No 6) [2005] EWCA Civ 595, CA (Civ Div) 20.99C
Dunnachie *v* Kingston upon Hull City Council [2004] UKHL 36, [2005] 1 AC 226 . . . . 13.67(g)
Durant *v* Financial Services Authority (Disclosure of Information) [2003] EWCA Civ 1746, [2004] FSR 28 . . . . . 6.62C, 10.04, 10.08B–10.08H, 10.09, 10.44, 22.92

Harrow LBC *v* Knight [2003] IRLR 140, EAT 13.73

Jagger *v* News of the World, 10 March 2005, QBD 20.50, 20.93F
Johnson *v* Medical Defence Union [2004] EWHC 2509, [2005] 1 WLR 750 . . . . 10.35

Kaye *v* Robertson [1991] FSR 62, CA (Civ Div) 20.89A
Kraus *v* Penna plc [2004] IRLR 260 (EAT) 13.26

Marcic *v* Thames Water Utilities Ltd [2003] UKHL 66, [2004] 2 AC 42, HL 21.27
Melia *v* Magna Kansei Ltd [2005] ICR 874, [2005] IRLR 449, EAT. . . . . 13.67(g)

European Court of Human Rights

Australia

Canada

Ireland

United States of America

TABLE OF LEGISLATION

TABLE OF TREATIES AND CONVENTIONS

4

FREEDOM OF INFORMATION UNTIL JANUARY 2005

C. The Ombudsman's Investigations

The following new paragraphs come at the end of section C of the Main Work:

4.89A The rest of this section examines key decisions Ann Abraham, the Parliamentary Ombudsman, has made recently.

Legal advice

4.89B The Ombudsman's investigation into the refusal of the Cabinet Office to release the Attorney-General's legal advice on the legality of military intervention in Iraq is case no A.35/04. The full reports of the Parliamentary Ombudsman can be downloaded from the Ombudsman's website: http://www.ombudsman.org.uk.

4.89C On 16 October 2003 Mr Evans wrote to the Cabinet Office and asked, under the Code, for complete copies of all the documents drawn up by the Attorney-General that gave the Prime Minister advice on the legality of military intervention in Iraq. He said that he did not believe that Exemption 4 of the Code (*information covered by legal professional privilege*) could be held to apply in this case, and he drew attention to the written answer given in the House of Lords on 17 March 2003 (*Hansard*, HL (series 5) vol 646, col WA2 (17 March 2003)) in which the Attorney-General had set out a version of that legal advice. Mr Evans said that he believed it to be illogical to make public a summary of the Attorney-General's advice but not to make available a fuller version of it given that it was a matter of public importance.

4.89D The Cabinet Office replied on 22 October 2003. It said that it could do no better than refer Mr Evans to the Lord President of the Council's statement in the House of Lords (*Hansard*, HL (series 5) vol 653, col 600 (13 October 2003)) in which she said 'My Lords, there is a long-standing convention adhered to by successive governments, and reflected in paragraph 24 of the Ministerial Code, that legal advice from the Law Officers is not publicly disclosed. This is consistent with paragraphs 2 (*internal discussion and advice*) and 4(d) of the code.'

4.89E On 24 November 2003 Mr Evans asked the Cabinet Office to reconsider its decision. In its reply, the Cabinet Office adhered to its decision that the information was exempt under both Exemption 4 and Exemption 2 of the Code. In providing his comments on the complaint the Managing Director of the Cabinet Office said that it did not accept Mr Evans' argument that the privilege relating to this information had been waived by the Government. He said that he had been advised that the Attorney-General's statement to Parliament on the legal basis for the use of force in Iraq did not amount to such a waiver.

4.89F The Ombudsman in her assessment said:

> There was some unfortunate initial confusion with the Cabinet Office, in particular the Prime Minister's Office, about whether or not my Office had an entitlement to

> see the information requested by Mr Evans. I am pleased to say that I was able to clarify that matter and I am satisfied that I have now seen all of the information that falls within the scope of this request.

One of the very satisfactory things about the way the Ombudsman has overseen the Code is the firmness with which she has treated Ministers and the very senior levels of civil servants in Whitehall in politically sensitive cases. Her predecessor was equally firm in his investigation into the *Hinduja* case in which a journalist sought information contained in a telephone conversation between Peter Mandelson and Mike O'Brien at the Home Office regarding the naturalization application of one of the Hinduja brothers. The Ombudsman reported that the Cabinet Office appeared to be withholding papers, which it readily acknowledged existed, from his investigation. He prepared a draft report and as a result of that the Secretary of the Cabinet wrote, with the agreement of the Prime Minister, to say that the Cabinet Office was now content for the Ombudsman's staff to inspect the papers made available to Sir Anthony Hammond's inquiry into Mr Hinduja's application. (For more details, see Main Work para 4.44.) It is to be expected that the Information Commissioner will be as robust, now that the Act has come fully into force.

There is no doubt that the fact that the Ombudsman's staff have looked at the information which is sought has been a great reassurance to people who are probing the Government machine, even when their requests for information have been refused. **4.89G**

In the Iraq case the Ombudsman said that she had very carefully examined the information sought by Mr Evans. She continued: **4.89H**

> Having done so I am satisfied that the sole purpose of that information was to provide legal advice to the Prime Minister on the legality of military intervention in Iraq. The information I have seen does not include any other assistance that a lawyer might provide to a client such as presentational or policy advice. I am satisfied therefore that all the information...can reasonably be said to be covered by legal professional privilege.

She accepted that the Cabinet Office acted properly in citing Exemption 4(d) and she did not therefore have to consider Exemption 2.

The Ombudsman said that the question of waiver was a question of law which it was not her function to determine. Her own legal advisers told her that in deciding this point the questions which would need to be considered include whether, in the absence of an express waiver, there has been a waiver by implication; whether disclosure of extracts of privileged information means that the privilege in respect of the whole information is waived; and whether the summary information has been 'deployed' in such a way as to waive privilege by implication over the full version. The Ombudsman, somewhat surprisingly, did not consider that it was necessary for her to decide these questions in order to determine the complaint before her, which she did not uphold. **4.89I**

4.89J A further request for the Attorney-General's advice was made under the Act on 1 January 2005. A significant part of the advice was leaked to the newspapers in April 2005 during the run-up to the General Election held on 2 May 2005. The Government then released the advice. Although the matter had been raised with the Information Commissioner, he had not ruled on the application when the Government published the advice.

The public interest test

4.89K Case no A.21/04 concerned the refusal to release a copy of the London Resilience Team (LRT) report. This investigation involves the application of the harm test. Following the attacks in New York and Washington on 11 September 2001 a major review of London's resilience was commissioned by a Cabinet Sub-Committee. The outcome was the London Resilience Team report, which was presented to Ministers in March 2002 and contained 143 detailed findings and recommendations for improving the emergency planning and response arrangements across London for coping with a catastrophic incident. These findings and recommendations subsequently formed part of the basis of a continuing programme of multi-agency work involving the Government, the emergency services, local authorities, and other key front-line responders, to strengthen London's preparedness to deal with a major disaster.

4.89L On 6 December 2002 Tom Brake MP requested a copy of the LRT report. The Minister for Local and Regional Government replied in January that because of the sensitive nature of the material it contained, the Department had not circulated the report widely and had no plans to do so, but he said he would be happy for Mr Brake, who is the MP for Carshalton and Wallington, to be briefed confidentially on the key findings and recommendations that had been implemented following the report. Mr Brake asked if he could read through the report. The Minister replied that the Government had concerns that the disclosure of the report could have a damaging effect on London's security and that it had therefore decided to withhold the report under Exemption 1(a) of the Code (*national security or defence*). He also said that it would rely on Exemption 2 (*internal discussion and advice*). By this time Mr Brake had received a briefing from the Director of the London Resilience Team and the Minister said that he would be pleased to answer any questions Mr Brake might have regarding the continuing efforts across the capital to strengthen London's resilience.

4.89M On 23 April 2003 Mr Brake wrote to the Permanent Secretary at the Department and said that while he recognized that some sections of the report might have to remain confidential, he questioned the necessity of withholding the whole report. He asked the Permanent Secretary to investigate whether an all-embracing restriction was appropriate. She replied that the great majority of the report could be withheld under Exemption 1(a) of the Code and that the entire report could be withheld under Exemption 2. On 4 August Mr Brake wrote back and said he intended to refer the matter to the Ombudsman as the decision effectively prevented any independent scrutiny of the progress the Government and other parties were making in preparing emergency plans for London.

The Ombudsman concluded that although the report was two years old it did contain information that would be valuable to groups and organizations wishing to cause death and destruction in London, and therefore fell within Exemption 1. **4.89N**

She also noted that the London Resilience Team collected information from several public and non-public bodies and collated it into one report that provided advice and recommendations to the Cabinet Sub-Committee which commissioned it. She accepted the general principle that the value of such advice depends upon candour for its effectiveness and that it would be substantially less effective if it were thought that it would be made available to a wider audience. She was therefore of the view that the advice and recommendations in the report were covered by Exemption 2. **4.89O**

That is not the end of the matter: the Ombudsman had to decide whether the harm that could be caused to national security and/or the frankness and candour of internal discussion was outweighed by the public interest in making it available. She said: **4.89P**

> There can be no argument that the public interest in any matter that has the potential to cause harm to the security of London is very strong. The public want, and need to be assured that, the Government are taking the security risks seriously and that the development of London's resilience is being managed efficiently and effectively. Moreover, independent scrutiny of such an important matter is a necessary part of the process by which the Government should account to, and be held to account by, Parliament and the public. While the disclosure of the LRT report would go some way towards meeting the demand for information about London's preparedness for a catastrophic incident I nevertheless consider that the benefits of disclosure are outweighed by the potential harm that could be caused, particularly to the security of London. In reaching this decision I have taken account of the steps that ODPM [Office of the Deputy Prime Minister] has taken to keep Parliament and the public informed of the work being done in relation to London's resilience.

The Minister had been questioned for over two hours by the House of Commons Defence Select Committee on the efforts being made to strengthen London's resilience and he and the team leader had both appeared before London Assembly members.

The Ombudsman concluded that this was not a case in which it would be either helpful or wise to disclose a redacted version of the report. **4.89Q**

The London Resilience Report case can be contrasted with case no A.12/03 in which the Ministry of Defence refused to release information about accidents involving nuclear weapons. **4.89R**

4.89S In July 1996 the Minister for the Armed Forces, in answer to a Parliamentary Question, stated that nuclear weapons accidents were divided into two categories: Category 1 being accidents where there has not been a release of radioactive material, and Category 2 being where a release of radioactive material has been detected, or the nature or severity of the occurrence is such that the possibility of a release cannot be excluded. The Minister said that there had been seven category 1 incidents reported since 1966.

4.89T On 19 December 1997 Mr Evans asked the Ministry of Defence for the following items of information in respect of each of the seven accidents: the date of the accident; the location; the cause; a description of the accident; the results of any inquiry into the accident; the recommendations from any such inquiry; and the progress made in implementing the recommendations. On 17 February 1998 Mr Evans wrote again to the MoD about 20 weapons-related incidents referred to in a 1992 report by Professor Oxburgh, the MoD's Chief Scientific Adviser. Mr Evans asked for a definition of a 'weapons-related incident' and the same information about the *incidents* which he had sought in relation to the *accidents*.

4.89U The MoD told Mr Evans that it was Government policy neither to confirm nor to deny the presence of nuclear weapons at any particular time or place. It refused to give the information, relying on Exemption 1 (*defence, security and international relations*). The MoD then carried out a review of the answer given to Mr Evans in conjunction with the Department's Strategic Defence Review. This was completed on 17 July 2001 when the Department renewed its objections to disclosure, but provided Mr Evans with some information in the form of a table relating to the seven Category 1 incidents already disclosed. The table was placed in the House of Commons Library.

4.89V The Ombudsman accepted that Mr Evans' requests fell within Exemption 1, so the substantive issue for her to consider was the harm test. The Ombudsman made three points. The first was that the information sought did not in any way relate to current nuclear capacity. The most recent accident about which Mr Evans asked occurred in January 1987 and the most recent incident in October 1996. All the information sought, whether as to accidents or incidents, involved obsolete weapons. On point (i) the Ombudsman concluded that it was difficult to envisage that the release of information about events that happened some time ago to weapons that no longer existed could cause harm if made more widely available.

4.89W Point (ii) was that the principle of not releasing information of this kind had already been breached by the MoD. The information disclosed to Mr Evans in 2001, while brief, did at least include the year of the accident (in most cases the actual month), the approximate location (except in those cases which occurred at sea) and brief details of what happened. No harm had resulted from the release of this information and the Ombudsman did not see why releasing the more detailed information which Mr Evans sought should cause any harm either.

Point (iii) was that while the MoD had released information about the seven accidents, it had refused to release information about the 20 incidents which it defined as: **4.89X**

> An unexpected event which has been reported so that we can draw from it any broader lessons for safety policy and practice, or because the event itself may come to the public attention.

The Ombudsman said it was hard to accept the logic of an argument which permitted the release of information about serious matters but refused the release of information about less serious ones. The argument put forward by the MoD was that these incidents posed no threat to public safety, therefore there was no public concern needing to be alleviated. That did not seem to the Ombudsman to be the issue and she concluded that the release of the information which Mr Evans sought would not cause any harm.

The Ombudsman concluded by recalling that the previous Ombudsman had said that the public interest in disclosure is particularly strong where the information in question would assist public understanding of an issue currently the subject of public debate. The whole question of weapon safety is such a subject. **4.89Y**

The economy

Case no A.3/04 concerned the Treasury's refusal to release the eighteen supporting studies which informed the five economic tests that need to be satisfied before the UK can join the Economic and Monetary Union. This was a third high-profile case in which the Ombudsman came down on the side of Whitehall, in relation to the Treasury's five tests for joining the euro. **4.89Z**

Gordon Brown, in his Mansion House Speech on 26 June 2002, said that when the assessment was complete, the 18 supporting studies would be published alongside it. **4.89AA**

Michael Howard wrote to the Chancellor on 15 April 2003, saying that there would be a huge amount of material to digest and asking him to reconsider his stance on the timing of publication in the interests of transparency and open debate. On 19 May Mr Howard wrote again to the Chancellor, saying that in light of the fact that the Chancellor's statement had been delayed until 9 June and leaks of the 18 studies had already begun to appear and would doubtless continue, there was an urgent need to publish the studies. **4.89AB**

The Permanent Secretary, in offering his comments on Michael Howard's complaint, relied on Exemptions 2 (*internal discussion and advice*), 6 (*effective* **4.89AC** *management of the economy*), and 10 (*information which is or will soon be published*). The Ombudsman criticized the Treasury for not treating Mr Howard's letters as information requests under the Code, but she held that Exemption 10 applied.

Parliamentary privilege, defence, security, and international relations

4.89AD Case no A.10/04 concerned the refusal by the Foreign and Commonwealth Office to release a National Audit Office report and other information relating to the Al Yamamah project. This is another case in which the Ombudsman substantially upheld the Whitehall position.

4.89AE In 1992 there was a National Audit Office report on the Saudi Arabian Airforce project, known as the Al Yamamah project. The project was an arrangement for the sale and maintenance of military aircraft, naval vessels, and associated weapons infrastructure to Saudi Arabia. At the outset both Governments had agreed that details of this arrangement should be regarded as secret. The programme, which is still in existence, has generated many thousands of United Kingdom jobs and significant export earnings, in addition to aiding closer political co-operation and future defence projects, both in Saudi Arabia and more widely in other states participating in the Gulf Co-operation Council.

4.89AF On 3 February 2003 Mr Evans wrote to the Ministry of Defence and the Foreign and Commonwealth Office (FCO) requesting information about the 1992 Audit Report. He asked for complete copies of all the documents held by their respective departments relating to the audit report.

4.89AG The National Audit Office Report was a report to the Public Accounts Committee. The Chairman of the Public Accounts Committee had decided in 1992 that it should not be published and that it should be handled on a very restricted basis. The Ombudsman was satisfied that the report was covered by Parliamentary privilege and that the decision as to whether or not to disclose the report was a matter for Parliament and was therefore covered by Exemption 15 (*Parliamentary privilege*). The Ombudsman, however, took the view that she should ask the current Chairman of the Committee for his comments.

4.89AH The Chairman said that the Committee and the Government had consistently argued against its disclosure. He said that many of the reasons were summarized in a written answer to Harry Cohen MP by the then Chairman on 13 February 2002:

> 10 copies of the 1992 National Audit Office report on the Saudi Arabian Airforce Project—known as project Al-Yamamah—were produced.
>
> The report looked at the use of taxpayers' money in relation to the project. It referred to confidential arrangements between the governments of the United Kingdom and

> Saudi Arabia. The report was not published because publication would have breached that pledge of confidentiality.
>
> The then PAC chairman (now Lord Sheldon) was quoted as saying after he and the then senior Conservative member of the PAC had considered the report in private in February 1992: 'I did an investigation and I find no evidence that the MoD made improper payments. I have found no evidence of fraud or corruption. The deal...complied with Treasury Approval and the rules of government accounting.'

The Ombudsman then asked: what of the remaining information held by MoD and FCO? She set out the type of information to which she was referring: **4.89AI**

(a) advice, comment, opinion by MoD and NAO about the confidentiality of the NAO report and how it should be handled;
(b) information about how to handle enquiries from the media and other interested parties about the NAO report once it had been issued;
(c) correspondence between MoD and FCO about the handling of the NAO report, including its restricted nature and how to respond to enquiries about it;
(d) discussion about who should appear as the Accounting Officer before the Committee;
(e) copies of Parliamentary Questions;
(f) briefing papers for Parliamentary Questions and Prime Minister's Questions;
(g) papers setting out MoD's policy on the handling of the NAO report;
(h) information received from the British Embassy in Riyadh on the Saudi reaction to the NAO report and media speculation about the Al Yamamah project.

In refusing to provide this information the Departments relied on Exemptions 1 (*defence, security and international relations*) and 2 (*internal discussion and advice*). The Ombudsman concluded that some of the information, such as the Parliamentary Questions and the proposed responses to enquiries about the NAO report, was either already in the public domain or was intended to be put in the public domain, even if it was never used, and she saw no reason why this information should not be made available to Mr Evans. **4.89AJ**

She decided that the rest of the information fell within the exemptions and considered whether any harm arising from disclosure was outweighed by the public interest in making information available. It was common ground that there was a strong public interest in the report and the Al Yamamah project itself. In weighing the interests the Ombudsman took into account the fact that although the report was 10 years old the project was still very much an ongoing concern, the harm to relations between the United Kingdom and Saudi Arabia, the harm to the project itself, and the benefits to the economy, which were indisputably significant. On balance the Ombudsman came down against disclosure. **4.89AK**

Internal discussion and advice

4.89AL The Cabinet Office, in case no A.25/03, refused to provide information contained in background briefing for Parliamentary Questions.

4.89AM On 18 March 2002 Mr Rob Blackie wrote to the Cabinet Office requesting information relating to the briefings prepared by officials in response to Parliamentary Questions asked by Matthew Taylor MP since 1 September 1999. The Cabinet Office replied saying that the background notes written as briefing contained opinions, advice, and recommendations, and were exempt from disclosure under Exemption 2 (*internal discussion and advice*). The Cabinet Office said on 9 October 2002 that it was not just the content of individual briefing notes which was at issue; it was the principle of whether or not officials were able to offer opinions and advice to Ministers in the knowledge that they were not likely routinely to be made public.

4.89AN It is worrying that as recently as October 2002 the Cabinet Office was seeking to apply a crude class test inappropriately and was not considering the harm that disclosure of the actual information sought might cause.

4.89AO It was accepted that much of the information sought was factual. Exemption 2 does not apply to factual information and the Ombudsman recommended that it should be disclosed.

4.89AP While the Cabinet Office reserved the right to consider any future cases on their merits, it nevertheless agreed to provide some comments contained in the briefing, the release of which would be unlikely to jeopardize the quality of future advice. The Ombudsman considered this to be a satisfactory outcome to a partially justified complaint.

Effective management and operations in the public service and third party's commercial confidences

4.89AQ Cases nos A.21/03 and A.15/04 were ones in which the applicants succeeded in getting information about ministerial meetings by limiting their request to factual information about what meetings had been held and not asking for details of the discussions which had taken place. In case no A.21/03 the Cabinet Office refused to provide information about the contact that had been made between Ministers and representatives of a trade association. In case no A.15/04 the Treasury refused to provide details of external meetings attended by the Chancellor of the Exchequer, Treasury Ministers and special advisers.

4.89AR In the first case Mr Evans wrote to 18 government departments, including the Cabinet Office, requesting information relating to any contact that had been made between Ministers in each of those departments and a particular trade association. He asked for:

(a) the number of meetings that had taken place between the Prime Minister and/or Ministers in each department and representatives of the trade association since 1 November 2000; when and where each of these meetings took place; and which Ministers attended each of these meetings;
(b) the number of times that representatives of the trade association had written to the Prime Minister and/or Ministers in each department since 1 November 2000; on what dates each of these letters had been written, and to which Minister each of these letters had been addressed;
(c) the number of times that the Prime Minister and/or Ministers in each department had written to representatives of the trade association since 1 November 2000; on what dates each of these letters was written; and which Minister wrote each of these letters;
(d) the number of representations that had been made since 1 November 2000 by the Prime Minister and/or Ministers on behalf of the trade association to other parties; on what dates each of these representations had been made; and to whom they were made.

The answers to these simple questions would give a good idea of the extent to which the trade association was lobbying the Government. **4.89AS**

In the second case Matthew Taylor MP asked the Chancellor of the Exchequer, by means of Parliamentary Questions, for information about meetings between Treasury Ministers and special advisers and the representatives of private companies. The companies included Citigate, Chevron, Texaco, Phillips Petroleum, IMC, Global, TXU, and CMS. He also asked for details of those the Chancellor had met on official business in July 2001. The Chancellor said that it was not the Government's practice to release such information. **4.89AT**

Both departments relied on Exemptions 7(b) (*effective management and operations of the public service*) and 13 (*third party's commercial confidences*). The Ombudsman said that the Cabinet Office approach to the release of the information requested by Mr Evans was to refuse to provide it, without either establishing whether they had it, or if they did, without assessing its individual merits on the grounds that, by implication, it was the kind of information for which a class exemption existed under the Code. The Ombudsman emphasized that the Code did not recognize class exemptions. The Treasury said that the decision to withhold information was taken on the basis of central guidance prepared by the Cabinet Office. The Ombudsman told the Treasury that the Cabinet Office's guidance was currently being revised as a result of the Ombudsman's recommendations in the other case. **4.89AU**

The Ombudsman upheld the complaints in both cases. **4.89AV**

The Silverstone Bypass and smallpox vaccine cases

4.89AW In the following two cases the Department of Transport and the Department of Health relied on Exemption 2 *(internal discussion and advice)*. In case no A.37/03 the Ministry of Transport refused to release information about the construction of the Silverstone Bypass.

4.89AX On 28 February 2002 the then Secretary of State for Transport issued a Ministerial Directive accelerating the construction of the Silverstone Bypass. Subsequently, Mr Edward Davey MP asked what advice had been received by Ministers, and from whom, that the wider national interest would be best served by the acceleration of this project.

4.89AY The Department of Transport provided Mr Davey with an explanation of the factors which had contributed to the Government's belief that the wider national interest would be best served by speeding up the project, but declined to release two submissions made to the then Secretary of State (one by the Minister of State and one by the then Permanent Secretary), citing Exemption 2 of the Code (*internal discussion and advice*). The Department took this position notwithstanding that copies of the Ministerial Direction and a submission from the Highways Agency Operation Director had been placed in the House of Commons Library.

4.89AZ The Ombudsman concluded that the two undisclosed submissions formed an integral part of the decision-making process: that there was an undoubted public interest in the availability of information about expenditure of an additional £8.064 million of taxpayers' money on the acceleration of the Silverstone Bypass construction project; and that the Government recognized this by publishing two out of four key documents. The Ombudsman could see no case for selective disclosure and concluded that there would be no harm in publishing the remaining two documents. She upheld the complaint.

4.89BA In case no A.14/03 the Department of Health refused to provide information about the awarding of a contract to supply smallpox vaccine.

4.89BB This was an extremely complex case. On 29 April 2002 Ms Branigan, a journalist, asked the Department of Health for information relating to the award of a contract to PowderJect Technologies plc to supply a stock of smallpox vaccine, as a defence to a possible terrorist attack. On 30 April 2002 she asked 17 government departments, including the DoH, for information relating to contacts between respective Ministers and representatives of PowderJect. Finally, on 29 May 2002 she asked the DoH for information relating to the work of the sub-group of the Joint Committee on Vaccination and Immunisation, which had given advice on the choice of the particular smallpox vaccine strain.

4.89BC The DoH declined to release most of the information sought by Ms Branigan and relied on Exemptions 1(a) (*defence and security*), 2 (*internal discussion and advice*),

7 (*effective management and operations of the public service*), and 13 (*third party's commercial confidences*). On 9 April 2003, following Parliamentary and media concerns about possible links between donations made by the Chief Executive of PowderJect to the Labour Party, the National Audit Office published a report entitled *Procurement of Vaccines by the Department of Health*. The report put some of the information Ms Branigan sought in the public domain.

After a protracted investigation beset by DoH delays, the Ombudsman recommended that almost all the information sought by Ms Branigan be released. Following a further exchange of correspondence, the DoH agreed to the release of information which had already entered the public domain but either refused to address the remaining recommendations or refused to release the information recommended for disclosure. This will not, or at any rate should not, be an option open to Whitehall now that the Freedom of Information Act has come fully into force. The Ombudsman concluded her report by saying: **4.89BD**

> This is a matter of great concern. I am deeply disappointed by the manner in which DoH have handled Ms B's initial information requests. I am equally disappointed by the way in which they have refused to engage effectively with my own subsequent investigation. Both have been beset with delays and a basic lack of understanding of the Code that does not augur well for the treatment of similar complaints under the forthcoming Freedom of Information legislation. I regret that DoH continue to refuse information for which, in my opinion, they have provided no adequate justification under the Code.

5

ACCESS TO INFORMATION HELD BY PUBLIC AUTHORITIES

A. Introduction

The following new paragraphs come at the beginning of section A of the Main Work:

5.00A The Department of Constitutional Affairs ('the DCA') and the Information Commissioner have both issued extensive guidance on the application of the Freedom of Information Act 2000 ('the Act'). The DCA's guidance is primarily aimed at officials in government departments.

5.00B The DCA's guidance is in four parts:

(i) *an introduction to exemptions*, published at: http://www.foi.gov.uk/guidance/exintro/index.htm (13 June 2005);
(ii) *procedural guidance*, published at: http://www.foi.gov.uk/guidance/proguide/index.htm (13 June 2005);
(iii) *summaries of exemptions*, which summarizes sections 21–44, published at: http://www.foi.gov.uk/guidance/exsumm/index/htm (13 June 2005); and
(iv) *full exemptions guidance*, detailed advice on the individual exemptions contained in sections 21–44, published at: http://www.foi.gov.uk/guidance/exguide/index.htm (13 June 2005).

5.00C The Information Commissioner has published a series of 28 guidance notes on his website, entitled *awareness guidance*. The notes are in two groups: (i) *procedural guidance*, and (ii) *exemptions guidance*. The notes can be downloaded at: http://www.informationcommissioner.gov.uk/eventual.aspx?id=8261.htm (8 June 2005). The Commissioner has also published notes entitled *casework guidance* on audit exemptions, court records, and the economy.

5.00D In this Supplement under chapter 5, significant points of the procedural guidance issued by the DCA and the Commissioner are noted and analyzed.

C. Public Authorities

Information held by public authorities

5.27 The DCA's guidance states that if a public authority only holds information on behalf of someone else, for example a department holding trade union information on its computer system, then that authority may not have to provide the information in response to a Freedom of Information Act request: see DCA's *procedural guidance*, ch 2.

The Information Commissioner's *awareness guidance no 12* deals with when information is caught by the Act. It is in the form of answers to frequently asked questions, including the following:

> Q. Is non-official information in the possession of public authorities caught by the Act?
> A (i) *Trade union communications*
> The trade union is a separate legal entity, and although it will represent the employees of a public authority, it does not have a role in respect of the functions of that public authority. The public authority has neither created this information nor does it retain the materials for its own purposes. The public authority simply holds the information on behalf of, and as a service to, the trade union. As such, these communications would not be held for the purposes of Freedom of Information.
> The only kind of trade union information that would be caught by the Act is that which is held by the public authority for the purposes of its official dealings with the trade union, and is therefore held for the purposes of its functions as a public authority. Examples include minutes of joint meetings between management and the union and a public authority's trade union recognition agreement. Copies of such information in the possession of the trade union itself would not be subject to FOI unless they were being used on behalf of the public authority.
> A (ii) *Personal written communications (emails, etc)*
> Even if the private use of emails in the workplace were monitored, the public authority would still not *hold* this information as it has no interest in it, unless disciplinary action were taken against particular members of staff. Problems may arise in terms of hybrid emails, which contain a mixture of personal content and that relating to the duties of the employee. The information which falls within the latter classification is potentially disclosable, and so as part of good email management the formulation of such emails should be avoided.
> A (iii) *Party political communications*
> A common example of party political communications would be emails between councillors which discuss party political matters. In this context the authors will be communicating in their party political capacity and the emails would not relate to the functions of the public authority. These communications would therefore not be held for the purposes of FOI.

As to the general treatment of emails, the DCA's guidance states that it is important that email messages that form part of the official record are saved for as long as business needs require and are moved from email accounts and personal folders and stored corporately in accordance with departmental record management procedures. Email messages that do not form part of the official record should be managed within the mailbox in the short term, but permanently deleted when no longer required: DCA's *procedural guidance*, ch 2.

Another frequently asked question raised by the Information Commissioner in *awareness guidance no 12* is whether information is 'held' by a public authority when it has 'read-only' access to it.

An example would be a central electronic repository containing information created by a number of public authorities. Each public authority would be able to access each other's information from it but on a 'read-only' basis.

In this case, it is the public authority which created the information and provided it to the repository that *holds* it for the purposes of FOI. This means that if a public authority receives a request for information located in the repository that it has not created, it should at the very least refer the applicant to the authority that *holds* the information.

Government departments

5.55 The DCA guidance makes clear that the Act does not apply to information held by the Security Service, the Secret Intelligence Service, the Government Communications Headquarters (GCHQ), the Special Forces, or any unit of the Armed Forces providing assistance to GCHQ; they are not public authorities for the purposes of the Act: see DCA's *full exemptions guidance*, introduction, ch 2, para 2.4. However, other access regimes, including the Data Protection Act and the Environmental Information Regulations, do apply to these organizations.

D. The Information

The request

5.60 The DCA guidance states that the Act does not apply to unrecorded information which may be known to an authority or to information which an authority has held in the past but which has been destroyed in recorded form before a request for it is received: see DCA's *exemption guidance*, introduction, ch 2, para 2.6.

Form of the request

5.65 The Welsh Language Act 1993 confirms that Welsh and English are equal in Wales, as a matter of law. It places an obligation on the public sector to treat the Welsh and English languages equally in the provision of services to the public in Wales. The DCA's guidance makes clear that any request received in the Welsh language should therefore be translated into English if necessary and processed as normal. Public authorities should also consider, the department says, whether it is appropriate to translate the response back into Welsh in the interests of good customer service. The translation of text to and from Welsh is not chargeable under the costs regime since it fulfils a pre-existing statutory obligation: see DCA's *procedural guidance*, ch 4.

The following new heading and paragraph come after paragraph 5.67 of the Main Work:

Assessing requests for information—The Clearing House

The Clearing House set up in the DCA will act as the central point of expertise, guidance, and advice for all FOI requests which raise sensitive issues and have Whitehall-wide implications: see the DCA's *procedural guidance*, ch 5. **5.67A**

The Clearing House will, according to that guidance: **5.67B**

(a) ensure a consistent government-wide position on round-robin cases and on those that have the potential to set precedents;
(b) provide guidance on all sensitive cases with a potentially high profile;
(c) align responses, where necessary, with government policy and guidance;
(d) revise government guidance in the light of emerging case law and new policy; and
(e) be a source of expert advice and guidance to departments on the Act, data protection, and the Environmental Information Regulations.

The DCA's guidance suggests that the following range of matters should be seen by a department's FOI specialist and should, if he or she considers it appropriate, be referred to the Clearing House: **5.67C**

(a) requests which obviously involve Whitehall issues;
(b) round-robin requests, such as those relating to departmental financial information;
(c) requests raising difficult issues about the application of sensitive exemptions, for example those relating to policy-making process (advice to Ministers, Ministerial letters), Cabinet correspondence or papers, national security or international relations, commercial confidentiality, or legal advice;
(d) requests for which Ministerial certificates may have to be considered; and
(e) particularly difficult mixed requests.

The Clearing House will not answer requests on behalf of departments. It will provide advice on difficult cases, but the responsibility for answering the requests will still lie with the department which holds the information requested. This is important, because while it is obviously sensible to have a central point of reference and advice, it would be unfortunate if central control led to an over-defensive reaction. It is noteworthy that the Cabinet Office and the Prime Minister's Office have had the greatest difficulty in complying with the Ombudsmen's requests under the Code: see Main Work and Supplement ch 4 section C. **5.67D**

E. Advice and Assistance

The section 45 Code

The second edition of the section 45 Code was laid before Parliament on 25 November 2004. The paragraphs of the second edition which deal with advice **5.75–5.79** and assistance comprise paras 3–15 of the Code. They are in substantially the same terms as the first edition but arranged under useful headings:

– advice and assistance to those proposing to make
– requests;
– clarifying the request;
– limits to advice and assistance;
– advice and assistance and fees.

The second edition of the Code is reproduced in full in Supplement Appendix D1 and is discussed further at Supplement paras 5.132–5.159.

The following new paragraphs come at the end of section E of the Main Work:

The Information Commissioner's guidance

5.79A The Information Commissioner's *awareness guidance no 23* deals with advice and assistance in the form of answers to frequently asked questions.

5.79B How does a public authority judge what is a reasonable provision of advice and assistance? The Commissioner says that the authority should adopt a flexible approach and treat each application on a case-by-case basis. The duty to provide advice and assistance will be fulfilled much of the time by the delivery of the authority's usual customer service standards.

5.79C It is good practice for a public authority to keep a record of the advice and assistance that has been provided: *IC awareness guidance no 23*, para 4.

5.79D If an authority has informed an applicant that it requires further information in order to be able to identify and locate the information requested, it is not obliged to comply with the request, but it should still offer advice and assistance so that the request can be clarified: *IC awareness guidance no 23*, para 9.

5.79E Where an applicant makes a request which relates to more than one piece of legislation, for example a request involving the Freedom of Information Act and the Data Protection Act, the authority should tell the applicant that this is so, and explain the consequences, for example differences in timescale and possibly fees: *IC awareness guidance no 23*, para 11.

5.79F If the authority estimates that complying with the request will exceed the cost limit, the authority is not obliged to comply with the request but it would be appropriate to offer advice and assistance in refocusing the request, together with an indication of the information that would be available within the cost limit: *IC awareness guidance no 23*, paras 12–14; and see Supplement para 5.87L.

F. Fees and Costs

The draft fees regulations

The draft fee regulations have been replaced by the Freedom of Information and Data Protection (Appropriate Limit and Fees) Regulations 2004, SI 2004/3244, which are very different from the draft which was circulated. For the text of the regulations, see Supplement Appendix J1. **5.87**

The following new paragraphs come after paragraph 5.87 of the Main Work:

The appropriate limit

Section 12 of the Act allows public authorities to refuse to answer requests for information if the cost of complying would exceed *the appropriate limit prescribed in the regulations*. Section 9A of the Data Protection Act 1998 (inserted by section 69 of the Act) makes a similar provision in relation to subject access requests to public authorities insofar as they relate to *unstructured* personal data; no limit applies to any other forms of personal data. **5.87A**

Regulation 3 of the Appropriate Limit and Fees Regulations 2004 ('the 2004 Fee Regulations') sets the appropriate limit for both Acts at: **5.87B**

(a) £600 for an authority which is listed in Part 1 of Schedule 1 to the Act, ie central government, Parliament, and the armed forces; and
(b) £450 for other public authorities, including local authorities, police, and authorities in the health service and education.

The appropriate limit has to be applied separately to the duty to confirm or deny (*section 1(1)(a)*) and the duty to communicate (*section 1(1)(b)*). A similar distinction is made in the Data Protection Act by section 9(4)(a).

The regulations set out what may be taken into account when public authorities are estimating whether the appropriate limit will be exceeded. The costs are limited to those that an authority reasonably expects to incur in: **5.87C**

(a) determining whether it holds the information requested;
(b) locating the information, or a document which may contain the information;
(c) retrieving the information, or documents; and
(d) extracting the information from a document containing it.

The DCA's fees guidance makes it clear that (d) includes editing or redacting the document, and can include the first time an individual working in the authority reads the information to establish what is contained within a file or document: see the DCA's *fees guidance*, para 2.3.2 and endnote 4 at http://www.foi.gov.uk/feesguide.htm (27 June 2005).

5.87D Regulation 4(4) provides that staff costs shall be estimated at the rate of £25 per person per hour, when an authority is estimating whether the appropriate limit will be exceeded. The DCA's *fees guidance* makes clear that the authority may not take into account the expected costs of:

(a) the time taken to check that a request for information meets the requirements of the Act;
(b) considering whether the information requested should be withheld in reliance on an exemption under the Act; this includes any costs incurred through seeking legal advice about whether exemptions apply;
(c) considering whether a request is vexatious or a repeated request;
(d) obtaining authorization to send out the information;
(e) the time taken to calculate any fee to be charged; or in providing advice and assistance under section 16 of the Act.

Estimating the costs of complying with a request—aggregation of related requests

5.87E The costs of answering more than one request can be added together for the purpose of estimating whether the appropriate limits would be exceeded in relation to any one of those requests. This can be done where:

(a) two or more requests have been made to the same authority;
(b) they are from the same person, or from different persons who appear to the authority to be acting in concert or in pursuance of a campaign;
(c) the requests relate to the same or similar information; and
(d) they have been received by the authority within the space of 60 consecutive working days. Working days do not include weekends, Christmas Day, Good Friday, and public and bank holidays.

See regulation 5 of the 2004 Fee Regulations.

5.87F The DCA's *fees guidance*, para 2.4.3 says that as a matter of good practice authorities should exercise caution when considering whether requests can be aggregated. There should usually be strong grounds for believing that requests have been framed precisely in order to circumvent the appropriate limit, before they are aggregated. Some worked examples of aggregation are described in the annex to the DCA's *fees guidance*.

Fees if the appropriate limit has not been reached

5.87G If the appropriate limit has not been reached, the maximum fee for requests for personal data subject access requests is £10 and this is so whether or not they include unstructured personal data. Credit reference agencies can only charge £2 and education records and manual health service records attract a maximum fee of £50: Data Protection (Subject Access)(Fees and Miscellaneous Provisions) Regulations 2000.

Regulation 6 provides that the maximum fee that can be charged under the Act is based on the authority's estimate of the costs that it reasonably expects to incur in informing the person making the request whether it holds the information and communicating the information to the person making the request. This includes the costs of: **5.87H**

(a) putting the information in the applicant's preferred format;
(b) reproducing any document containing the information, eg photocopying or printing; and
(c) postage and other forms of communication.

No account can be taken of staff time in undertaking these activities. Authorities can charge for the actual costs incurred, but charges are expected to be reasonable. The DCA's *fees guidance* says in para 3.5.1 that where the maximum fee would be very low—say less than £5 or £10—public authorities are encouraged to consider waiving the fee altogether.

The recommendation in the guidance to consider waiving fees is given added weight by the fact that on 18 October 2004 the Lord Chancellor, Lord Falconer, stated that 'no individual should be priced out of the right to know'. **5.87I**

Fees where requests cost more than the appropriate limit

If the request would cost more than the appropriate limit, the authority can turn the request down (section 12(1) of the Act); answer and charge any permitted fee; or answer it and waive the fee. **5.87J**

The power to charge a fee in these circumstances is in section 13(1) of the Act. The maximum charge (see regulation 7 of the 2004 Fee Regulations) is the sum of: **5.87K**

(a) the costs which the authority was entitled to take into account in calculating that the appropriate limit would be exceeded; and
(b) the costs of informing the requester whether the information is held, and of communicating the information to the requester.

These costs under both (a) and (b) can include the cost of staff time at £25 per person per hour in carrying out these activities.

The authority should always advise the applicant how he can rephrase or cut down his request so as to remain within the appropriate limit. The Information Commissioner so decided in the case of *Ferryhill Town Council*, case reference FS5005378 (14 July 2005). For further discussion of this case, see Supplement para 7.77G. **5.87L**

5.87M Section 13 of the Act introduces a new power for authorities to charge fees when they choose to reply to a request that they did not have to answer because the cost to them exceeds the appropriate limit. However, section 13 does not displace any existing legal power, statutory or otherwise, to charge for the disclosure of such information. If the authority has such a power it can use it and will not be subject to the restrictions of section 13, though it will of course be subject to any restriction on the power being exercised.

VAT

5.87N The DCA's *fees guidance* says at para 6.1 that HM Customs and Excise does not consider that the release of information under the Act constitutes an economic activity. As such, any fees charged will be outside the scope of VAT. This means that no VAT should be added to the fees. The position is different if the information is also held by organizations that are not public authorities. Then, any fees would attract VAT. This distinction is made so as not to distort competition between the public and private sectors.

Mixed requests

5.87O The three regimes (freedom of information, data protection, and environmental information) have different fee provisions. Public authorities can usually charge no more than £10 for subject access requests made under the 1998 Act. The fees regime under the Environmental Information Regulations is similar to that for FOI requests, although there is no appropriate limit above which public authorities can refuse requests. Public authorities must separate out the constituent parts of a request for the purpose of calculating what fees may be charged. Maximum fees must be determined according to each separate regime.

G. Time for Compliance and Transfers

Time for compliance

5.91 The DCA's guidance identifies *working days* as all days except Saturdays and Sundays, Christmas Day, and Good Friday, and all Bank Holidays anywhere in the United Kingdom as set out in the Banking and Financial Services Act 1971. Civil Service *privilege days* do count as working days: DCA's *procedural guidance*, ch 6.

In eight of the first sixteen decision notices issued by the Information Commissioner he found that the authorities were in breach of section 10 in that they had failed to reply within 20 working days. In six of the eight cases the authority had replied by the date of the decision notice. In the other two, *Rushden*

Town Council, case reference FS50069103 (16 May 2005), and *Westminster City Council*, case reference FS50059852 (18 February 2005), the Commissioner gave the authorities 30 days from the date of the notice in which to comply. The Information Commissioner publishes his decision notices on his website at: http://www.informationcommissioner.gov.uk.

The DCA's *procedural guidance* at ch 6 lists four cases which have been identified as meriting an extension of time under section 10(4) of the Act, which allows the Lord Chancellor by regulation to extend the time from 20 up to 60 working days:

(a) school holidays, since schools will not be staffed at that time;
(b) when frontline units of the armed forces are impossible to reach for operational reasons;
(c) if a public authority needs to consult posts, governments, or companies abroad to obtain information; and
(d) when the National Archives need to determine whether requested information in a transferred public record that has not been designated as open information is exempt, or whether the duty to confirm or deny is excluded under Part II.

See SI 2004/3364, which has made this change.

It is important that requests are logged for management monitoring purposes. **5.97**
Whilst there is no requirement in the Act to produce statistics of the number or type of requests received, or indeed to keep a log of requests, the DCA's guidance says that public authorities will find it is good business practice to keep a log: DCA's *procedural guidance*, ch 6.

Transferring requests

The second edition of the section 45 Code was laid before Parliament on **5.98–5.99**
25 November 2004. The paragraphs of the second edition which deal with *transferring requests* are in substantially the same terms as the first edition: see Supplement para 5.144. For the text of the second edition of the section 45 Code, see Supplement Appendix D1.

H. Vexatious and Repeated Requests

Vexatious requests

The Information Commissioner's *awareness guidance no 22* says that the case of **5.102**
Attorney-General v Barker [2000] 1 FLR 759 suggests that it may be reasonable to treat as vexatious a request which is designed to subject a public authority to inconvenience, harassment or expense: *IC awareness guidance no 22*, Part A, para

2. What Lord Bingham of Cornhill said in that case was this:

> The hallmark of a vexatious proceeding is in my judgment that it has little or no basis in law…; that whatever the intention of the proceeding may be, its effect is to subject the defendant to inconvenience, harassment and expense out of all proportion to any gain likely to accrue to the claimant; and that it involves an abuse of the process of the court, meaning by that a use of the court process for a purpose or in a way which is significantly different from the ordinary and proper use of the court process.

5.103 The Information Commissioner in his *awareness guidance no 22* has said that he considers that the exception in the Act for vexatious and repeated requests is important, especially as no fee will be charged for most requests. His approach, he said, will be influenced by the desirability of keeping compliance costs to a minimum and avoiding damage to the credibility or reputation of the Freedom of Information framework: *IC awareness guidance no 22*, Introduction, para 2.

The use of threatening, offensive, or abusive language or behaviour may be strongly indicative of a vexatious request: *IC awareness guidance no 22*, Part A, para 5.

A communication may be so rambling or impenetrable as to make vexatious any request which it may contain: *IC awareness guidance no 22*, Part A, para 6.

The DCA guidance points out that the fact that the motives of the applicant are irrelevant means that a public authority is not entitled to know the reasons for a request or to impose conditions on disclosure or on the use which may be made of information following disclosure. This, the guidance says, is an important part of the context in which decisions on disclosure fall to be made; it means that in principle the same information should be provided to any person who makes the same request, and that when information has been disclosed it must be assumed to be available in the public domain: see DCA's *exemption guidance*, Introduction, ch 2, para 2.10.

Regulation 12(4)(b) of the Environmental Information Regulations 2004 provides that a public authority may refuse to disclose information to the extent that the request for information is 'manifestly unreasonable'. The Information Commissioner says that a request which is manifestly unreasonable is equivalent to a vexatious or repeated request under the Act: *IC awareness guidance no 22*, annex, para 1.

Repeated requests

5.107 Even though a request may be repeated, the Information Commissioner's *awareness guidance no 22* says that there will be cases where a positive response should be considered. The following are examples given in the guidance:

(a) in the request, the applicant states that he or she lost the information but still requires it;

(b) the applicant states that he or she disposed of the information but has subsequently discovered that it was still required;
(c) the applicant reasonably requires another copy of the information previously sent to him, for instance because he has been obliged to supply the original to another body;
(d) cases where some of the information requested is new, but the rest has previously been supplied to the applicant. In such hybrid cases, it might be easier to comply with the request but supply only the information which has changed and classify the remainder of the request as repeated.

See *IC awareness guidance no 22*, Part B, para 5.

I. Refusal of the Request

Section 17

In his decision notice in the case of *Bridgnorth District Council*, case reference FS50065282 (17 May 2005), the Information Commissioner held that the Council was in breach of section 17 because it had not given the applicant details of its complaints procedure in its refusal notice. However, this did not have any consequences because the Commissioner held that the Council had correctly applied the absolute exemption in section 32, which covers court records. **5.117**

K. The Lord Chancellor's Code of Practice

The Code

The second edition of the Code was laid before Parliament on 25 November 2004. The Code has been recast and is now arranged under six sub-headings; an introduction, and sections on each of the five matters specified in section 45(2) of the Act. The Code (including the foreword) is reproduced in full in Supplement Appendix D1. **5.132**

I. Introduction

The aims of the Code have been transferred from the introduction to the foreword.

II. The provision of advice and assistance to persons making requests for information

This section now comprises paragraphs 3–15 of the Code. It is in substantially the same terms as the first edition but arranged under useful sub-headings: **5.133**

- advice and assistance to those proposing to make requests;

- clarifying the request;
- limits to advice and assistance;
- advice and assistance and fees.

III. Handling requests for information which appear to be part of an organized campaign

5.140 This section does not appear in the second edition of the Code.

IV. Timeliness in dealing with requests for information

5.141 This section does not appear in the second edition of the Code. The Act normally requires public authorities to respond to requests for information promptly and in any event within 20 working days. However, where a decision on disclosure involves the public interest test this time limit does not apply and responses can be made within such time as is *reasonable in the circumstances*. The fact that the public interest test has to be considered does not mean that some complex issue is necessarily involved. During the passage of the Act through Parliament Lord Bach, then a Government whip, said that the Code would refer to the desirability of:

> making all decisions within 20 working days wherever possible
> (*Hansard*, HL (series 5) vol 619, col 250 (14 November 2000)).

The first edition of the Code did this. There is now no suggestion that authorities should attempt to deal with such requests within 20 working days where possible. Nor is the point reflected in the DCA's *procedural guidance*, which merely states that where the public interest test is involved the 20 day limit 'is extended by a reasonable period': DCA *procedural guidance*, ch 6. The Campaign for Freedom of Information complained about this in a letter to the Lord Chancellor dated 29 November 2004.

Despite this change in the Code it remains good practice to attempt to deal with all requests, including cases where a public authority needs to consider the public interest test, within 20 working days. The Information Commissioner is unlikely to be sympathetic to an authority which delays, without good reason.

V. Charging fees

5.143 This section is omitted from the second edition of the Code. The fees position is dealt with in the Freedom of Information and Data Protection (Appropriate Limits and Fees) Regulations 2004: see Supplement paras 5.87A–5.87N.

VI. Transferring requests for information

5.144 Paragraphs 17–24 of the second edition of the Code are in substantially the same form as paras 24–30 of the first edition. The introductory para 16 in the second edition is pithier than paras 21–23 of the first edition.

VII. Consultation with third parties

This section has been recast in the second edition of the Code, which starts by saying that there are many circumstances where requests for information may relate to and affect the interests of third parties. **5.145–5.146**

Public authorities are *highly recommended* to take steps to ensure that third parties and those who supply information to public authorities are aware that under the Act information will have to be disclosed unless an exemption applies: para 26.

The guidance is that it will be good practice to consult, directly and individually with third parties where a public authority proposes to disclose information relating to third parties, or information which is likely to affect their interests. Third parties should be given advance notice, or, failing that, the disclosure should be drawn to their attention afterwards: para 27. This is the guidance which is provided in response to the provision in section 45 of the Act which requires the Code to provide guidance on consultation with persons to whom requested information relates or persons whose interests are likely to be affected by disclosure. Telling third parties after disclosure hardly amounts to consultation. It is clear that the government does not think it is enough to tell other government departments after the event because para 29 states that no decision to release information which has been supplied by one government department to another should be taken without first notifying, and where appropriate consulting, the department from which the information originated. This is the standard which prudent public authorities should apply to all third parties.

Where information to be released relates to a number of third parties and they have a representative organization the authority may consider whether it would be sufficient to notify or consult the representative organization.

VIII. Freedom of information and public sector contracts

This section has been replaced by a new section V: *Freedom of information and confidentiality obligations*. The advice in the second edition on the approach to confidentiality clauses is more tentative than in the first edition. For further discussion of this, see Supplement para 6.81G. **5.147–5.149**

The new section V states that public authorities should have their obligations under the Act clearly in mind when preparing to enter into contracts which may contain terms relating to the disclosure of information by them. If they are asked to accept confidentiality clauses they should carefully consider the compatibility of such terms with their obligations under the Act: paras 31–32.

Where there is good reason to include non-disclosure provisions in a contract, public authorities should consider the desirability of making express provision in the contract, identifying the information which should not be disclosed and the reasons for confidentiality. They should also consider including in the contract provisions stating when consultation with third parties will be necessary and appropriate before the information is disclosed. Similar considerations will apply to the offering or acceptance of confidentiality obligations by public authorities in non-contractual circumstances: paras 34–35.

IX. Accepting information in confidence from third parties

5.150 This section has been omitted from the second edition. The Campaign for Freedom of Information is critical of this change. The guidance in the first edition seems unobjectionable and the sort of advice that prudent public authorities will still want to follow. For further discussion of this, see Supplement para 6.81I.

X. Consultation with devolved administrations

5.151 This section has been omitted from the second edition of the section 45 Code.

XI. Refusal of request

5.152–5.153 This section has been omitted from the second edition of the section 45 Code.

XII. Complaints procedure

5.154–5.159 This section has been recast but covers much the same ground. For the DCA's guidance on complaints procedure, see Supplement para 7.63.

L. The Code of Practice on Record Management

The Lord Chancellor's Code of Practice on record management

The following new paragraphs come after paragraph 5.168 of the Main Work:

The Information Commissioner's guidance

5.168A The Information Commissioner's *awareness guidance no 8* deals with record management. It is in the form of answers to frequently asked questions, which include the following:

5.168B Q. What is the status of information held on back-up servers?

A. Information on a back-up server is not regarded as being held by a public authority for the purposes of FOI. Such information must have been deleted *twice* in order to claim that it falls outside the scope of the Act:

(a) The information should have been sent to the recycle bin; and
(b) the information should have been deleted from the recycle bin to the back-up or non-live system.

This means that information located in desktop recycle bins would be subject to the Act as this has been deleted only once. On the other hand, information sent to the back-up server is no longer readily retrievable for business purposes, and unscrambling it would be *unreasonable* for the purposes of FOI. When sending information to back-up servers, the intention should be that it is never to be accessed again: *I.C. awareness guidance no 8*, p 5, question 3.

Q. What are my obligations if I receive a request for information that is due for destruction? **5.168C**
A. If the information is contained within a record that is due for destruction within 20 days of the request being received, there is no requirement to release the information. [It is difficult to see how this guidance can be reconciled with the wording of the Act and with para 9.9 of the section 46 Code.] However, [the guidance continues] it may be worth considering the following points of best practice:
(a) Delay destruction until disclosure has taken place;
(b) Under the duty to offer advice and assistance, identify whether another authority holds the information, and inform the applicant accordingly;
(c) Offer to provide similar or related information if this is appropriate: *IC awareness guidance no 8*, p 6, question 4.

Q. How does the Act apply to records held in remote storage? **5.168D**
A. No distinction is made between information held by an authority in its head office and in other locations: *IC awareness guidance no 8*, p 6, question 5.

Q. Should environmental information be managed differently?
A. The principles and policies relating to records management under the Act also apply to environmental information: *IC awareness guidance no 8*, p 6, question 6. **5.168E**

Q. How does Records Management under the Act interface with the Data Protection retention and fair processing principles? **5.168F**
A. The Data Protection Act relates to personal information. As long as you have clearly identified the personal information, data protection principles are not applicable to the other information that you hold. However, good records management is likely to assist in compliance with the data quality principles, including the requirements that personal data is adequate, relevant and not excessive for the purpose for which it is held, that it is accurate, and that it is kept for no longer than is necessary for the purpose for which it is held: *IC awareness guidance no 8*, p 7, question 8.

M. Alteration of Records

Destruction

The DCA's *procedural guidance*, ch 2 states that the right of access to information under the Act applies to information held by a public authority at the time the request is received. If it appears that the requested information has been deleted or amended, it is important to establish whether this happened before or after the request was received. **5.179**

Instructing a computer to delete a particular item may not result in the item being destroyed immediately. At least for a period, the information might still be retrievable, albeit with a substantial cost and disruption to the system. However, where it is the intention that data should be permanently deleted, and this is not achieved only because the technology will not permit it, authorities may regard such data as having been permanently deleted. This information is no longer considered to be *held* by the authority and does not have to be retrieved or provided in response to a request.

This approach is not justified where the information has been only temporarily deleted and is stored in such a way that it could easily be recovered, for example from the deleted items folder in Outlook. This information is still considered to be held by the authority and may have to be provided if a request is received.

If requested information is deleted from any computer, hard copy records management system, or electronic filing system, in line with the authority's standard records management practices, after a request is received, the information is not considered to be held by the public authority. This will only apply if it can be shown that the person who made the deletion had no knowledge of the request and that he or she was following standard records management practice and timetables when the information was deleted: see DCA's *procedural guidance*, ch 2.

6

EXEMPT INFORMATION

A. Introduction

The following new paragraphs come at the beginning of section A of the Main Work:

6.00A The Department of Constitutional Affairs ('the DCA') and the Information Commissioner have both issued extensive guidance on the application of the

Freedom of Information Act 2000 ('the Act'). The DCA guidance is primarily aimed at officials in government departments.

The DCA's guidance is in four parts: (i) *an introduction to exemptions*; (ii) *procedural guidance*; (iii) *summaries of exemptions*, which summarizes sections 21–44; and (iv) *full exemptions guidance*, which contains an introduction to the general use of the exemptions and detailed advice on the individual exemptions contained in sections 21–44. The guidance is published on the DCA's website and can be downloaded. For the references, see Supplement para 5.00B. **6.00B**

The Information Commissioner has published a series of 28 guidance notes on his website, entitled *awareness guidance*. The notes are in two groups: (i) *procedural guidance*; and (ii) *exemptions guidance*. The notes can be downloaded. For the references, see Supplement para 5.00C. The Commissioner has also published notes entitled *casework guidance* on audit exemptions, court records, and the economy. **6.00C**

In this Supplement under ch 6 the significant points of the DCA's *full exemptions guidance* and the *exemption awareness guidance* issued by the Information Commissioner are noted and analyzed. **6.00D**

The guidance will be updated and officials must be sure to refer to the most recent version of the guidance available. Officials are advised that if a request appears to have precedent-setting implications, or to raise Whitehall-wide implications, or to refer to sensitive issues with a potentially high profile, it should be referred, via the official's departmental FOI specialists, to the DCA Central Clearing House: see the DCA's *introduction to exemptions*, ch 1. It obviously makes sense to have a central point in the government machine to co-ordinate practice under the Act, but it is to be hoped that centralization is not carried too far. It is reassuring that the DCA's *full exemptions guidance* makes clear that in difficult cases advice should be sought both from the DCA and from departmental lawyers: see the introduction, ch 1, para 1.12. **6.00E**

B. The General Operation of Section 2

The effect of exemptions

In applying the public interest test the DCA's guidance states that if the arguments are evenly balanced, then the outcome should be disclosure; there is no general interest in non-disclosure: see DCA's *full exemptions guidance*, introduction, ch 3, paras 3.17–3.18. **6.05**

C. Absolute Exemption

Section 21: information accessible to an applicant by other means

6.13 The Information Commissioner has issued a decision notice in the case of *Hertfordshire County Council*, case reference FS50063907 (25 August 2005), involving section 21. For further discussion of this case, see Supplement para 7.77U.

6.15 The Information Commissioner's *awareness guidance no 6*, p 2 confirms that cost could render information not *reasonably* accessible by the alternative means. The Commissioner gives the example of information contained in the authority's annual report; it may not be reasonable to require the applicant to purchase a copy of the report if the request is only for a small amount of the information contained in it. The Information Commissioner's view (p 5) is that section 21 is unlikely to give rise to many practical difficulties.

6.16 The DCA's *full exemptions guidance on section 21*, ch 2, para 2.4 makes the point that if the public authority is obliged by statute to communicate information to members of the public on request, that information is automatically *reasonably accessible* to the applicant. If, on the other hand, the statutory obligation is only to make the information available for inspection, section 21(2)(b) will not apply (although the section 21 exemption may still be available, depending on all the circumstances). See for example section 3 of the Commons Registration Act 1965, which requires registers of commons and greens to be kept and provides that 'any register maintained under this Act shall be open to inspection by the public at all reasonable times'. Although section 3 does not preclude copies being provided, the obligation is only to allow inspection. Section 33(1) of the Births and Deaths Registration Act 1953, in contrast, provides that 'any person shall on payment of a fee...and on furnishing the prescribed particulars, be entitled to obtain from the registrar a short certificate of the birth of any person'. Any information contained in a short certificate will therefore be exempt from the Act under section 21.

The test for the application of section 21 is whether information is reasonably accessible to the particular applicant who has requested it. This personalization of the test is unusual under the Freedom of Information Act: see DCA's *full exemptions guidance on section 21*, ch 2, para 2.14. The guidance suggests that a difficult question may arise in a case of information which would be *reasonably accessible* to the public in general but might not be reasonably accessible to a particular applicant because of his special disadvantage. The case will then have to be looked at on its merits, the public authority being under a duty to advise the applicant how he can obtain the information. The answer may well be to give it to him.

The Information Commissioner points out that many public authorities already have policies in place regarding access to information for those with physical disabilities and also as to the provision of information to non-English speakers. It is important that staff with responsibility for responding to FOI requests are fully aware of these policies and are able to follow them, see the Information Commissioner's *awareness guidance no 6*, p 5.

Section 23: information supplied by, or relating to, bodies dealing with security matters

The following new paragraphs come after paragraph 6.27 of the Main Work:

Section 23: the DCA's guidance

Although the identification of information supplied by or relating to security bodies may be straightforward in the majority of cases, this may become less clear where the authority has used the information to produce its own reports or documents. Where there is any doubt the originator of the original document should be consulted: DCA's *guidance on section 23*, chs 2 and 3, paras 2.1 and 3.4. **6.27A**

Officials should bear in mind that acknowledging that no information supplied by or relating to any of the security bodies is held may itself constitute information about one of the security bodies, and that it may therefore be appropriate to apply the 'neither confirm nor deny' provisions under section 23(5). This is a major theme of the guidance on section 23. It suggests that the following factors must always be taken into account: **6.27B**

(a) whether the information requested could reasonably have come from or be related to a security body;
(b) whether the information is about the kind of matter in which the department would be reasonably expected to have an interest;
(c) whether, at the time of the request, the subject matter is of such sensitivity that the department would not want to reveal either information or lack of information on the matter. For example, an access request is made to the Foreign and Commonwealth Office (FCO) asking for information on terrorist threats to a particular United Kingdom interest overseas. No information from the security bodies is held by the FCO relating specifically to that United Kingdom interest as there is no threat at present. Confirmation that no information is held might assist terrorist groups in their activities. The guidance says that claiming the section 23(5) exemption is likely to be justified: DCA's *guidance on section 23*, ch 4, para 4.5.

The guidance also deals with Ministerial certificates and says that a certificate will strengthen the position of the department in any legal proceedings. The guidance **6.27C** states that section 23 only allows Ministerial certificates to be signed in relation to specific information. The certificate cannot be general and prospective; in other words it cannot be prepared and signed in expectation of a request for information. The guidance goes on somewhat inconsistently to suggest that consideration should be given to drawing up a specific certificate template; departments may wish to ask their lawyers to prepare a draft which can be adapted for use when needed: DCA's *guidance on section 23* ch 4, paras 4.9–4.15. This is advice which should not be followed.

Section 32: court records, etc

6.28 The Information Commissioner's *awareness guidance no 9*, p 2 deals with information contained in court records. The Commissioner says that the thinking behind the exemption appears to be that it would be undesirable to interfere with the existing rules regarding access to/publication of information contained in court records or held for the purposes of inquiries or arbitration. These rules have developed to ensure the right to a fair trial including the presumption of innocence.

In *Bridgnorth District Council*, case reference FAC0065282 (17 May 2005), a decision of the Information Commissioner, the complainant requested a copy of the transcript of the case *R v Tompkinson & others* heard in Wolverhampton Crown Court, which involved former Council employees. The transcript had been obtained from the Court and paid for by the Council. Section 32(1)(c) provides that information is exempt if it is held by the authority only by virtue of being contained in any document created by (i) a court, or (ii) a member of the administrative staff of a court, for the purposes of proceedings in a particular case or matter. The complainant argued that as the document was not created by a member of the administrative staff of the Court, the exemption did not apply. The Commissioner rejected this argument, holding that the transcript was taken from the court tapes which were created by the Court. Bridgnorth District Council was at fault only because it did not give details of its complaints procedure in its refusal notice.

The DCA's *full exemptions guidance on section 32*, ch 3 paras 3.10–3.12 gives examples of the documents likely to fall under the categories set out in subsections (a), (b), and (c) of section 32(1).

6.31 The DCA's *full exemptions guidance on section 32*, ch 3, para 3.18 gives specific examples of inquiries set up under an enactment:

(a) the Bloody Sunday Inquiry (Tribunals of Inquiry (Evidence) Act 1921);
(b) the Marchioness Inquiry (Merchant Shipping Act 1995, section 268);
(c) the Joint Inquiry into Train Protection Systems (Health and Safety at Work Act 1974, section 14(2)(b));

(d) the Victoria Climbié Inquiry (Children Act 1989, section 81; National Health Service Act 1977, section 84; and Police Act 1996, section 49);
(e) a planning inquiry (Tribunals and Inquiries Act 1972).

The exemption in section 32 does not apply to the documents of inquiries which do not owe their existence to statute, including those set up under the royal prerogative, even if a judge heads the inquiry. The DCA's *guidance*, para 3.19 gives examples of such inquiries:

(a) Lord Butler's review of the intelligence on weapons of mass destruction;
(b) Sir Michael Bichard's inquiry arising from the Soham murders;
(c) Lord Penrose's inquiry into Equitable Life; and
(d) Lord Phillips' inquiry into BSE.

The exemptions under sections 39 (environmental information), 41 (confidential information), and 42 (legal professional privilege) may apply to such inquiries.

Section 34: Parliamentary privilege

The right to control publication of its proceedings. Much information which is privileged is now routinely published by Parliament itself. Both Houses, like all bodies covered by the Act, have publication schemes under section 19. The information now published by Parliament extends well beyond the record of proceedings to internal administrative documents and even individual members' expenditure against Parliamentary allowances. Both the DCA's *full exemptions guidance on section 34* at ch 2, para 2.4, and the Information Commissioner's *awareness guidance no 28 on Parliamentary Privilege*, p 1, make clear that the fact that Parliament has chosen to publish the information does not mean that it has ceased to be privileged. Within the context of the Act, however, it does mean that disclosure of published information cannot be taken as an infringement of privilege. **6.46**

The Information Commissioner has advised that as a matter of good practice, on all occasions where a public authority is considering relying on section 34, it should contact the Freedom of Information Officer at the appropriate House of Parliament to discuss the details of the request. Individuals whose application is refused should make their request for a review of the decision to the public authority and not to either House of Parliament: Information Commissioner's *awareness guidance on section 34*, p 3. **6.50**

Both the Information Commissioner's guidance and the DCA's *full exemptions guidance on section 34*, ch 2, para 2.7 identify, in similar terms, the range of information to which the exemption will apply. The Information Commissioner's list is as follows: **6.50–51**

(a) committee reports and drafts not otherwise published;
(b) memos (and drafts) to committees of Parliament;

(c) internal papers prepared by the officers of either House directly relating to House or committee proceedings;
(d) correspondence between Members, Officers, Ministers, and Government officials directly relating to House proceedings;
(e) papers concerning investigations by the Parliamentary Commissioner for Standards;
(f) Bills, amendments and motions, including those in draft, where they originate from Parliament or a Member rather than from Parliamentary Counsel or a government department;
(g) papers (including drafts) prepared by external special advisers and academics appointed for their special expertise in a given area;
(h) papers prepared by the Libraries of either House at the request of an MP if the subject matter was concerned with a forthcoming debate or parliamentary committee: Information Commissioner's *awareness guidance no 28*, p 3.

It is important to recognize that there is much information arising from or related to Parliament's wide range of activities that will not be considered privileged in that it does not relate to proceedings in Parliament. It is likely that this information will in the main be held by non-Parliamentary government departments and other public authorities. The Information Commissioner's *awareness guidance no 28* p 3 gives the following examples of information where Parliamentary privilege will not apply:

(a) Members' correspondence and other communications not specifically related to proceedings of either House or a formally constituted committee;
(b) any of the unpublished working papers of a select committee of either House, including factual briefings or briefings of suggested questions prepared by the committee staff for the use of the committee chairman and/or members, and draft reports. These are most likely to be in the possession of a department as a result of a Minister being, or having been, a member of such a committee;
(c) any legal advice submitted in confidence by the Law Officer or by the legal branch of any other department to the Speaker, a committee chairman or a committee, or any official of either House;
(d) drafts of motions, Bills or amendments which have not otherwise been published or laid on the Table of either House;
(f) any unpublished correspondence between Ministers, departmental officials or any of the Members of either House, relating specifically to proceedings on any Question, draft Bill, motion or amendment, either in the relevant House, or in a committee;
(g) any correspondence with or relating to the proceedings of the Parliamentary Commissioner for Standards or the Registrar of Members' interests in the House of Commons.

The DCA's *full exemptions guidance on section 34*, ch 2, para 2.8 has a similar list of categories of information not regarded as being *proceedings in Parliament.*

Where a conclusive certificate has been issued the Information Commissioner's *awareness guidance no 28*, p 4 makes it clear that his role is limited to verification of the certificate's existence and authenticity. Where a certificate is not issued the Information Commissioner will be able to consider the details of the complaint and the information requested. It will be most likely that he will wish to discuss and review these details with the appropriate House authorities. **6.54**

Section 40: personal information

The Information Commissioner has issued decision notices in the cases of the *Standards Board for England*, case reference FS50064699 (1 August 2005), and *Corby Borough Council*, case reference FS50062124 (25 August 2005), involving section 40. These cases are discussed further at Supplement paras 7.77I and 7.77R. **6.57**

The following new heading and paragraphs come after paragraph 6.62 of the Main Work:

Section 40: the DCA's guidance

Background to section 40

The DCA's *full exemptions guidance on section 40*, ch 1, para 1.1 explains the background to the section. It has its origins in a few relatively simple policy propositions, namely that: **6.62A**

(a) if an applicant has a right of access to information by virtue of the 1998 Act—that is, he is asking for his own personal data—the request should be considered under data protection rules, not under freedom of information rules;
(b) if someone could not get access to his own personal data under the 1998 Act, no-one else should be able to get access to it under the 2000 Act;
(c) in other cases, if general data protection rules about handling personal data would prevent disclosure, an applicant will not be able to have access to it;
(d) but otherwise, personal information is accessible under the 2000 Act.

Personal data

Section 40 applies only to *personal data* within the meaning of the 1998 Act definition, but in the case of information held by a public authority, the definition is particularly wide. In summary, the guidance at ch 2, para 2.1 says that *personal data* is information which relates to a living individual. That cannot be given an artificially narrow meaning, but on the other hand it is not the case, for example, that **6.62B** all information generated in the course of an enquiry in response to a complaint will amount to the personal data of the original complainant—that material may relate to his complaint, but it does not necessarily relate to him.

6.62C Although the guidance does not specifically refer to *Durant v Financial Services Authority* [2004] FSR 28, 573 it is consistent with the decision of the Court of Appeal in that case that to be *personal data* information had both to 'relate to' the individual (ie the individual must be the *focus* of the data) and to be information that affected that individual's privacy, whether in his personal or family life, business or professional capacity. For a full discussion of the *Durant* case, see Supplement para 10.08.

Deceased persons

6.62D The DCA's *full exemptions guidance on section 40* says that the definition of *personal data* is restricted to information relating to living individuals. Information which relates solely to a deceased person is not covered by this exemption and section 40 will only apply if the information relating to the deceased person is also the personal data of a living individual.

The identity of the applicant

6.62E Unusually for the 2000 Act, the DCA's *full exemptions guidance on section 40*, ch 2, para 2.3, points out that the application of this exemption depends to some degree on whether the applicants are seeking their own personal data or the personal data of a third person. If responding to a request will involve the disclosure of personal data, the first question to ask is, who is seeking the disclosure of the data? Is the information: (i) personal data of the applicant; or (ii) personal data of another person?

6.62F In summary, section 40 then applies as follows:

(a) if the information is personal data of the applicant, it is exempt from the 2000 Act and falls to be dealt with exclusively under the Data Protection Act 'subject access' regime;

(b) if the information is the personal data of someone else, it may be exempt from the 2000 Act in the following circumstances:
  - (i) if disclosing it would breach any of the data protection principles;
  - (ii) if disclosure would contravene a notice received under section 10 of the Data Protection Act (the right to prevent processing likely to cause damage or distress); or
  - (iii) if the person who is the subject of the data would not be entitled to access it under the Data Protection Act regime because one of the Data Protection Act subject access exemptions would apply.

Basic guidelines

The DCA's *full exemptions guidance on section 40* says that the basic guidelines for government departments for applying section 40 are as follows: **6.62G**

(a) if a request involves the personal data of the applicant, those personal data are exempt, and it must be considered as a subject access request under the Data Protection Act;
(b) if another exemption under the 2000 Act would apply to the personal information which has been requested, departments should usually cite that exemption rather than section 40;
(c) if personal information is not otherwise exempt under the 2000 Act, the application of section 40 should be considered;
(d) in respect of most requests for personal data which are received by non-statutory government departments, exemption under section 40 will stand or fall on whether disclosure of the information to a member of the public would be *unfair*, taking into account all the circumstances involved, in particular:
    (i) how the information was obtained;
    (ii) the likely expectations of the data subject regarding the disclosure of the information;
    (iii) the effect which disclosure would have on the data subject; and
    (iv) the public interest in disclosure of the information.

Section 40: the Information Commissioner's guidance

The Information Commissioner's *awareness guidance no 1* deals with personal information. The guidance says at p 1 that section 40 sets out what appears at first sight to be a complicated exemption from the right to know where the information requested consists of personal data. Fortunately, the exemption is not as difficult as it first appears. It can be summarized as follows: **6.62H**

(a) if the personal data is about the person requesting the information, then there is no right to know under the 2000 Act. There, is in other words, an absolute exemption. However, any such requests automatically become subject access requests under the 1998 Act and must be treated as such. This means that despite the exemption under the 2000 Act, the applicant has a right to his or her information under the Data Protection Act;
(b) if the personal data is about someone other than the applicant, there is an exemption if disclosure would breach any of the data protection principles.

The first principle requires personal data to be processed fairly and lawfully. In practice this will be the key issue when considering an application for third party data, *awareness guidance no 1*, p 4. **6.62I**

6.62J On p 2 of *awareness guidance no 1* the Commissioner says:

> Under the FOI Act, an applicant must simply state his or her name, provide an address for correspondence and describe the information requested. Only in exceptional circumstances will you be justified in seeking to verify an applicant's identity—for instance if you suspect that a request is a vexatious one, submitted under an assumed name. Under the Data Protection Act, by contrast, you must avoid making disclosure of personal information which would breach the Act. In sensitive cases or where you suspect that the applicant is not who they claim to be, you may therefore need to check signatures or ask for proof of identity.

On the same page, the Commissioner adds:

> If you calculate that you will be unable to respond within the 20 working day period provided by the FOI Act and that you need the full 40 calendar day period allowed for under the Data Protection Act, you should let the applicant know.

6.62K The Information Commissioner's *awareness guidance no 1*, p 5 identifies as an issue that will often arise the question of whether the 1998 Act prevents disclosure of information identifying members of staff; indeed the Commissioner has been asked to identify members of his own staff. The guidance is that if the information requested consists of the names of officials, their grades, job functions, or decisions which they have made in their official capacities, then disclosure would normally be made. On the other hand, information such as home addresses or internal disciplinary matters would normally not be disclosed. While it would be wrong to disclose bank account details of staff, it would be unlikely to be unfair to publish details of expenses incurred in the course of official business, information about pay bands, or, particularly in the case of senior staff, details of salaries. [Information about this in respect of government departments has for many years been published in *Whitaker's Almanack*.] While this information clearly does relate to staff personally, there is a strong public interest in provision of information about how a public authority has spent public money.

6.62L The guidance makes clear that these are not hard and fast rules. While names of officials should normally be provided on request, if there is some reason to think that the disclosure of even that information would put someone at risk—for instance confirming the work address of a member of staff who has been physically threatened—then it may be right not to give out that information. The guidance is too tentative here; it *will* be right not to give out the information.

6.62M The Data Protection Act contains a number of exemptions from the right of subject access. These are explained in the *Data Protection Act 1998 Legal Guidance*, published by the Commissioner. The Commissioner has also published a large amount of information about subject access rights which is available from the data protection section of his website or may be requested from the information line (01625 545745).

Section 41: information provided in confidence

The following new paragraphs come after paragraph 6.81 of the Main Work:

Section 41: the Information Commissioner's guidance

The Information Commissioner's *awareness guidance no 2* is about information provided in confidence. The Commissioner says that in trying to determine whether an obligation of confidence has arisen in a particular case, it is likely to be necessary to think first about the circumstances under which information was provided to the authority and second about the nature of that information. He says that there are essentially two sets of circumstances under which information can be provided in confidence: **6.81A**

(i) when explicit conditions are attached by the provider of the information as to its subsequent use or disclosure. This may take the form of a contractual term, or may be stated, for instance in a letter.
(ii) when conditions are not explicitly stated but are obvious or implied from the circumstances. For instance a patient does not need to tell a doctor not to pass on his or her information to a journalist; it is simply understood that those are the rules.

As to the nature of the information, there are two key elements: **6.81B**

(i) the information need not be highly sensitive, nor can it be trivial. The preservation of confidences is recognized by the courts to be an important matter and one in which there is a strong public interest. This notion is undermined if it is argued that even trivial matters are covered.
(ii) the information must not be readily available by other means. On the other hand, it is not necessary that the information be completely secret.

The Commissioner says that there are three broad circumstances under which confidential information may be disclosed: **6.81C**

(i) with consent;
(ii) where the law requires disclosure;
(iii) where there is an overriding public interest in disclosure.

There are no hard and fast rules here. The important thing to note, however, is that the courts have generally taken the view that the grounds for breaching confidentiality must be strong ones. Confidentiality is recognized as an important thing in itself. In balancing confidentiality against the public interest, the task is not to weigh the impact upon the individual against the good of society, but rather the good of society against the importance of preserving confidences. Examples of cases where the courts have required disclosure in the public interest include those where the information concerns misconduct, illegality or gross immorality.

6.81D The Commissioner lists some concerns. First, central government departments make use of protective markings (eg 'restricted', 'confidential', 'secret', 'top secret'). While these markings may provide a useful preliminary indication, it would be a mistake to rely upon them to make final decisions. A document may have been marked 'confidential' because it was sensitive at the time of creation but it may no longer be so. Documents may have been generated by the authority itself, and so not be capable of containing information falling within the exemption. If protective markings are to be of assistance, it may be necessary to record the period of time for which the markings are anticipated to be relevant together with any other information that might assist an FOI decision-maker. The DCA's *full exemptions guidance*, introduction, ch 4, paras 4.1–4.4 is to the same effect.

6.81E Second, similar considerations will apply to information which has been provided to a public authority marked 'confidential' or 'commercial in confidence' and so on. Very often such markings do not provide a good indication of whether the information has the necessary *quality of confidence*. As with internal markings, what was confidential at the time of writing may no longer be so at the time of a request for disclosure. It is also quite likely that some information will have been provided to an authority in the expectation that it would not be disclosed, even though no explicit restriction was placed upon it. In all these cases, if in doubt, it would be sensible to check the position with the provider of the information and any third parties who are involved, bearing in mind that it is the authority and not a third party which must decide whether the exemption is relevant.

6.81F Given the scope for misunderstanding, for instance over the extent of the obligation of confidence in respect of employees, it may be sensible to set out formally the circumstances under which the authority will regard information as confidential. This will alert anyone who wishes to place restrictions upon the use of information to the need to do so explicitly.

6.81G The Commissioner then refers to the fact that the first edition of the section 45 Code contains the following passage about contract terms with commercial organizations:

> When entering into contracts public authorities should refuse to include contractual terms which purport to restrict the disclosure of information held by the authority and relating to the contract beyond the restrictions permitted by the Act. Public authorities cannot 'contract out' of their obligations under the Act. Unless an exemption provided for under the Act is applicable in relation to any particular information, a public authority will be obliged to disclose that information in response to a request, regardless of the terms of any contract.

The Lord Chancellor has had second thoughts about this advice. The second edition of the Code (November 2004) expresses the advice in more tentative terms. The Lord Chancellor was required to consult the Information Commissioner before laying the second edition of the Code before Parliament. It is not known what was the reaction of the Information Commissioner, because he has not, as yet, revised his guidance. It is, however, instructive to compare the two sets of advice. The second edition says:

> When entering into contracts with non-public authority contractors, public authorities may be asked to accept confidentiality clauses, for example to the effect that information relating to the terms of the contract, its value and performance will not be disclosed. Public authorities should carefully consider the compatibility of such terms with their obligations under the Act. It is important that both the public authority and their contractor are aware of the limits placed by the Act on the enforceability of such confidentiality clauses.

The Campaign for Freedom of Information has criticized what it sees as a retreat by Ministers. However, despite the change of language it remains the law that public authorities cannot contract out of the Act. They will be prudent, therefore, to refuse to include contractual terms which purport to restrict the disclosure of information held by the authority beyond the restrictions permitted by the Act.

Section 41: the DCA's guidance

The DCA's *full exemptions guidance*, which was issued a month before the second edition of the section 45 Code, uses the same robust language on section 41 as the first edition of the Code. The guidance has not yet been recast in the light of the changes in the second edition of the Code. Authorities should check the DCA's website at http://www.foi.gov.uk/guidance/exguide/section 41/chap03/htm for the latest position. **6.81H**

Para 3.3.8 of the current guidance refers with approval to para 47 of the first edition of the section 45 Code as dealing satisfactorily with the circumstances in which a public authority should accept information in confidence: **6.81I**

(a) public authorities should only accept information from third parties in confidence if it is necessary to obtain that information in connection with the exercise of any of the authority's functions and it would not otherwise be provided;
(b) public authorities should not agree to hold information received from third parties in confidence if it is not confidential in nature;
(c) acceptance of any confidentiality provisions must be capable of justification to the Commissioner.

These three points have been removed from the Code. Points (b) and (c) remain valid and, as to point (a), authorities should be slow to accept information in confidence, if it is not needed for the exercise of any of their functions, or they could obtain it without the information being treated as confidential.

6.81J The DCA's guidance says that when considering whether to agree to hold information subject to a duty of confidentiality, the following factors may be relevant:

(a) the nature of the interest which is to be protected and whether it is necessary to hold the information in confidence in order to protect that interest;
(b) whether it is possible to agree a limit on confidentiality, for example by clearly stating the circumstances in which a public authority would disclose information;
(c) whether the information will only be provided on condition that it is kept confidential and, if so, how important the information is in relation to the functions of the authority;
(d) the nature of the person from whom the information is obtained and whether that person is also a public authority to which the Act applies. (Where the person supplying the information is also a public authority, departments must be particularly cautious in agreeing to keep the information confidential.)

6.81K If it is necessary and justifiable for a public authority to agree to keep the information confidential, that public authority should take practical steps to respect the confidential nature of the information:

(a) restricting circulation to those who need to see the information;
(b) indicating clearly on the file cover the confidential nature of the contents;
(c) ensuring that hard copies are physically secure in locked cabinets or drawers;
(d) ensuring that electronically held records are adequately protected;
(e) considering whether, and at what intervals, it will be necessary to review the confidentiality of the information to ensure that only information whose disclosure would still be exempt under section 41 is protectively marked: the need to keep information confidential is likely to decrease over time.

See DCA's *full exemptions guidance to section 41*, ch 3, paras 3.3.9 and 10, and Appendix B.

6.81L The circumstances in which information was obtained may impose an implied duty of confidence in relation to information which is not obviously of a confidential nature. For example, if a public authority has statutory powers of compulsion under section 20(2)(j) and (k) of the Health and Safety at Work Act 1974 or section 2(1) of the Criminal Justice Act 1987, that is to say if it can legally oblige people to provide information for certain purposes, a duty of confidentiality will often arise in relation to that information and the public authority may be prohibited from disclosing the information in other contexts. This may also apply where information is acquired under threat of compulsion: see para 3.3.13 of the guidance.

6.81M Other factors which may be relevant to ascertaining whether information is held subject to an implied duty of confidence could include:

(a) whether there is a long-standing, consistent and well-known practice on the part of the public authority of protecting similar information against disclosure and the supplier could reasonably have expected this to continue;
(b) whether the information is provided gratuitously or for consideration (in the latter case it is less likely that an obligation of confidence would arise). See para 3.3.14 of the guidance.

The public interest test

The courts have recognized that disclosure will not constitute an actionable breach of confidence if there is a public interest in disclosure which outweighs the public interest in keeping the information confidential. The following principles must be applied, according to the DCA's *full exemptions guidance to section 41*, ch 3, para 3.4.3, when conducting this balancing test: **6.81N**

(a) where a duty of confidence exists, there is a general public interest in favour of keeping that confidence;
(b) there is no general public interest in the disclosure of confidential information in breach of a duty of confidence. If the public interest in keeping the confidence is to be outweighed it will be necessary to identify a specific interest in favour of disclosure;
(c) there is a public interest in ensuring public scrutiny of the activities of public authorities. If disclosure would enhance the scrutiny of the activities of public authorities then this will be a factor in the balancing exercise. However, where the interests of a private person (whether an individual or an organization) are protected by a duty of confidence, the general interest in public scrutiny of information held by a public authority is unlikely by itself to override the public interest in keeping the confidence;
(d) the Act itself has no influence on the weight which attaches to the public interest in the disclosure of information for the purposes of section 41. This is emphasized by the words *otherwise than under this Act*: the fact that the Act would require disclosure were it not for section 41 is irrelevant;
(e) the public authority's own interests in non-disclosure are not relevant to the application of this exemption;
(f) no regard may be had to the identity of the person who is requesting the information or to the purpose to which the information will be put.

The DCA's *full exemptions guidance on section 41* gives in para 3.4.5 examples of where there may be a public interest in the disclosure of confidential information. They are: **6.81O**

(a) information revealing misconduct/mismanagement of public funds;
(b) information which shows that a particular public contract is bad value for money;

(c) where the information would correct untrue statements or misleading acts on the part of public authorities or high-profile individuals;
(d) where a substantial length of time has passed since the information was obtained and the harm which would have been caused by disclosure at the time the information was obtained has depleted.

6.81P Examples given in para 3.4.5 of where the public interest is unlikely to favour the disclosure of information are:

(a) where disclosure would engender some risk to public or personal safety;
(b) where disclosure would be damaging to effective public administration;
(c) where there are contractual obligations in favour of maintaining confidence;
(d) where the duty of confidence arises out of a professional relationship;
(e) where disclosure would affect the continued supply of important information (for example, information provided by whistle-blowers).

Section 44: prohibitions on disclosure

6.82 The Information Commissioner has issued a decision notice in the case of the *Standards Board for England*, case reference FS50064699 (1 August 2005), involving section 44. For further discussion of this case, see Supplement para 7.77I.

The power to repeal or amend existing statutory bars to disclosure

6.106 The DCA's Review of Statutory Prohibitions on Disclosure was published on 16 June 2005 on the DCA website: http://www.foi.gov.uk/understand.htm. The review identified 210 statutory provisions which prohibit the disclosure of information under section 1 of the Act. Of these, 27 cannot be amended using the power in section 75, 20 because they implement international confidentiality obligations and 7 because they were passed after the Act, that is after 30 November 2000.

Of the remaining 183 provisions which fall within the scope of the Freedom of Information Act power to remove or relax prohibitions on disclosure, 13 were amended or repealed by order in November 2004 (SI 2004/3363); 40 will be amended or repealed under the Act; 19 will be time limited under the Act and 111 will be retained for other reasons or are still under review. These are listed in chapter 4 of the Review.

The Government believes that some prohibitions are not suitable for repeal or amendment, even though they fall within the scope of the section 75 power. It is the Government's view that provisions meeting any of the following four criteria may be retained:

(a) the provision protects information obtained under compulsion;
(b) the provision applies to organizations which are not subject to Freedom of Information legislation, and it would not be practical or appropriate to have differing rules applying to disclosure;

(c) the provision implements an obligation on the United Kingdom stemming from international law; or
(d) the provision applies to a limited class of information, or in a limited range of circumstances, and a partial access regime (eg disclosure in summary form) exists.

Not all provisions which meet one of these criteria will necessarily be retained.

The review identified 238 provisions which had been considered as potentially operating as bars to disclosure, but which on examination were found not to do so. Of the 238, 122 do not operate as bars to disclosure while the remaining 116 have been repealed or amended by other legislation during the course of the review and are no longer bars to disclosure.

Chapter 1 of the Review sets out those prohibitions which have already been removed or relaxed using an order under section 75 of the Act. Chapter 2 gives details of prohibitions which the Government will remove or relax using this power. Chapter 3 details those prohibitions on disclosure into which the Government will put time limits so that they do not apply to information over the specified age.

Many of the provisions listed in previous reports form part of procedural rules for courts or tribunals. Because of the need to maintain consistency between rules passed before and after November 2000, it will be more appropriate to make any amendments to all such rules simultaneously by means other than an order under section 75 of the Act. A list of these provisions can be found at Annex A of the Review.

Finally, the Enterprise Act 2002 repealed or amended a large number of statutory prohibitions on disclosure, and replaced them with a single coherent access regime for consumer information. A list of these provisions can be found at Annex B of the review.

The following new headings and paragraphs come after paragraph 6.110 at the end of section C of the Main Work.

Section 44: the Information Commissioner's guidance

The Information Commissioner's *awareness guidance no 27* deals with prohibitions on disclosure. **6.110A**

Environmental information

The guidance at pp 2–3 is in these terms: **6.110B**

> Section 44(1)(a) applies to all information except that which is covered by the Environmental Information Regulations (EIR) at section 39 of the Act. Regulation 5(6) of the EIR provides that any enactment or rule of law that would otherwise

prevent the disclosure of information under the EIR does not apply. This means that if the information being requested is environmental information as defined by the EIR, the absolute exemption under section 44 is not available. The information may be exempt from disclosure under the exceptions at regulation 12 of the EIR, all of which are subject to the public interest test. It is, therefore, crucial to distinguish between environmental information and any other type of information that is the subject of a request for disclosure.

In practice, however, when dealing with requests for environmental information subject to a prohibition on its disclosure under other legislation, public authorities should be aware that the existence of a statutory reason not to disclose will form a very strong public interest argument for withholding the information. Therefore, even though regulation 5(6) of the EIR disapplies statutory prohibitions on environmental information the disclosure of which will, in most cases, be subject to the public interest test under the EIR, the existence of a statutory prohibition will be a significant factor in balancing the public interest in disclosing or withholding the information.

Community obligations

6.110C The Information Commissioner's *awareness guidance no 27* helpfully summarizes what the term *community obligation* in section 44(1)(b) includes:

(a) *EU regulation*—this is of general application and is binding in its entirety and directly applicable in all Member States. Regulations usually do not require any further enactment in United Kingdom law in order to be given legal effect;

(b) *EU Treaty*—articles of EU treaties and the protocols to those treaties may have direct effect where those provisions are designed to give individuals rights;

(c) *Directive*—this is binding, as to the result to be achieved, upon each Member State to which it is addressed but leaves to the national authorities the choice of form and method of implementing it. This may have direct effect against the public authority even where it has not been enacted in United Kingdom law;

(d) *Decision*—this is binding in its entirety upon those to whom it is addressed.

Recommendations and *opinions* have no binding force and would not be a *community obligation.*

Section 44: the DCA's guidance

The Human Rights Act 1998

6.110D The DCA's *full exemptions guidance on section 44* ch 2, para 2.4 says:

It is important to bear in mind that while some enactments impose very limited or specific prohibitions on disclosure, others impose prohibitions of much wider or more general application. The most important of these is the Human Rights Act 1998. Section 6 of the Human Rights Act makes it unlawful for public authorities, including government departments, to act in a way that is incompatible with a Convention right. Disclosures that are so incompatible are therefore included within the scope of subsection (1)(a) of this exemption. Disclosures which would breach a Convention right are very likely to be the subject of other exemptions—but section 44 reinforces an absolute bar on such disclosures. The most relevant Articles of the Convention which may need to be considered in this context are:

Article 6, the right to a fair trial. This would be relevant if the public disclosure of information could prejudice a fair trial.

Article 8, the right to respect for private and family life. One area, for example, in which section 44 has potential to prohibit disclosure is that of personal information which relates to deceased persons. Personal information relating solely to deceased persons will not be exempt under section 40 because 'personal data' includes only information relating to living persons. But it is possible in some circumstances for disclosure of information relating to the dead to interfere with Article 8 rights of others—for example family members, or victims of the deceased's crimes. Whether a disclosure would be barred as a consequence would depend very much on the precise circumstances of the case, of course.

D. Conditional Exemption

The effect of conditional exemption

In applying the public interest test the DCA's guidance states that if the arguments are evenly balanced, then the outcome should be disclosure; there is no general interest in non-disclosure. See the DCA's *full exemptions guidance*, introduction, ch 3, paras 3.17–3.18. **6.113**

Section 22: information intended for future publication

The following new headings and paragraphs come after paragraph 6.136 of the Main Work:

Section 22: the DCA's guidance

Section 22 recognizes that the happenstance of individual requests for information should not determine the publication timetables of public authorities, for example by forcing them into premature publication. This is a view which is very important to Whitehall and it is therefore reassuring that the DCA's *full exemptions guidance on section 22*, ch 1, para 1.5 stresses that section 22 is subject to two important qualifications. The guidance says: **6.136A**

- it must be reasonable in all the circumstances to withhold the information until the date of publication; and
- the public interest test must be satisfied.

These conditions recognize that in some circumstances, there will be a genuine public interest in the public knowing the information prior to the intended publication date; and public authorities should not be able to avoid putting information in the public domain by adopting unreasonable publication timetables or an 'intention' to publish where there is little prospect of that intention being realized within the reasonable future.

6.136B The guidance is that the precise interaction between the two qualifications is not clear. In practice departments may find it convenient to consider all the relevant circumstances of the situation and determine whether the public interest in immediate disclosure of the information outweighs the public interest in delaying until general publication, paying particular attention to the reasonableness of the date of publication.

6.136C Para 2.15 of the guidance gives the following examples of the sort of consideration which may be relevant:

(a) *The nature of the proposed publication timetable itself*—as a general guideline, the more distant, contingent or undetermined the prospective publication date, the less heavily it is likely to weigh in the balance, and the less reasonable delay is likely to be.

(b) *Possible prejudicial effect of prematurity or delay*—what are the practical disadvantages of delay? Are any interests likely to be prejudiced? What are the practical disadvantages of immediate disclosure? If, for example, a third party's private interests would be harmed, or unnecessary public concern be caused, by premature disclosure, then there may be a stronger public interest in favour of withholding information.

(c) *Simultaneity or universality as a consideration in itself*—would the giving of a privilege to an applicant result in unfairness to others who might be affected by the announcement? Is it important for the information to be disclosed to everyone at the same time?

(d) *Pre-publication procedures*—on the other hand, would immediate disclosure undermine any relevant pre-publication procedures, such as consultation with or pre-disclosure to particular bodies or individuals? For example in the case of a complaint it would normally be good practice first to disclose the information to the complainant or the subject of the complaint before publication.

(e) *Publication procedures*—it can be important in some instances to ensure publication of material takes place in accordance with certain procedures. For example, the reports of public inquiries are often published under the protection of the Parliamentary Papers to avoid a defamation or other civil action.

(f) *Previous undertakings as to nature of publication*—it may be that Ministers have promised to provide Parliament first with the information sought. Similarly, there may be have been an undertaking to inform the family first of the result of an inquiry into a death in custody. It is unlikely in circumstances such as these that the public interest will favour disclosure to the applicant.

Section 22: the Information Commissioner's guidance

The Information Commissioner's *awareness guidance no 7* is on information intended for future publication. Page 2 of the guidance states that two key questions to ask in all cases are: (i) is there in fact an intention to publish the information requested?; and (ii) is the information which is intended for publication in fact the information which the applicant has requested? For instance, if an applicant asks for the reasons why a planning authority turned down an application, it may not be sufficient to inform the applicant that a policy document setting out the basis of planning decisions is due to be published when, in fact, the applicant wants to know how a particular application was decided. **6.136D**

The section does not apply to drafts in general, although it may cover drafts of documents intended for publication. The section is not designed to protect information held for research purposes in general. In some instances, however, research may be carried out with a settled intention to publish. For instance, a government department may commission annual research into public attitudes to its services. If it is intended when commissioning the research to publish the findings, then it may be reasonable to claim the exemption. By contrast, another department is carrying out research into an area of social policy. Having conducted its research and identified a number of policy options, it decides to issue a consultation paper. While drafts of the consultation paper may be covered by the exemption, the information generated by the research programme which preceded it is unlikely to be covered since there was no clear intention to publish that material. **6.136E**

Awareness guidance no 7 at p 4 says that given that there is already an intention to publish, the critical issue in deciding whether to respond to a request for information is one of timing. The Commissioner recognizes a number of reasons why an authority might want to adhere to its original publication schedule: **6.136F**

(a) The release of information to the applicant may result in unfairness to others. For instance, the information may consist of an offer to subscribe for a particular service. To be fair to all, the service may be offered on a 'first come, first served' basis which would be undermined by premature disclosure. In the case of press releases, it will usually be fair to release information to all the media simultaneously.
(b) The public authority may be under a duty to present a report in the first instance to a particular individual, say in the case of a complaint, or to make

an announcement to a particular forum, say a report to Parliament or its staff, before making it generally available.

(c) An announcement may be designed to prompt enquiries from the public and may be expected to result in an increase in workloads, for instance a press release or leaflet advertising a new service. An authority may reasonably wish to ensure that it has made its own administrative arrangements before the information is released to the public.

Section 24: national security

The following new headings and paragraphs come after paragraph 6.143 of the Main Work:

Section 24: the DCA's guidance

6.143A The DCA's *full exemptions guidance on section 24*, ch 2, points out that the term 'national security' has never been defined in United Kingdom legislation and both domestic and European courts have considered that the assessment of the threat to national security is essentially a matter for the executive. In addition, when considering safeguarding national security the courts have accepted that it is proper to take a precautionary approach. That is, it is necessary not only to consider circumstances where actual harm has occurred or will occur to national security, but also to consider preventing harm occurring and avoiding the risk of harm occurring. (See: *Secretary of State for the Home Department v Rehman* [2003] 1 AC 153.)

6.143B The guidance suggests in para 2.3 that:

(a) the security of the nation includes its well-being and the protection of its defence and foreign policy interests, as well as its survival;
(b) the nation does not refer only to the territory of the United Kingdom, but includes its citizens, wherever they may be, or its assets wherever they may be, as well as the United Kingdom's system of government; and
(c) there are a number of matters which United Kingdom law expressly recognizes as constituting potential threats to, or otherwise being relevant to, the safety or well-being of the nation, including terrorism, espionage, subversion, the pursuit of the Government's defence and foreign policies, and the economic well-being of the United Kingdom. But these matters are not exhaustive; the Government would regard a wide range of other matters as being capable of constituting a threat to the safety or well-being of the nation. Examples include the proliferation of weapons of mass destruction and the protection of the Critical National infrastructure, such as the water supply or national grid, from actions intended to cause catastrophic damage.

6.143C The guidance balances these very wide statements by recognizing that national security is not the same as the interest of the government of the day and that the test for reliance on this exemption is that non-disclosure should be *required* for the purpose of safeguarding national security; see DCA's *full exemptions guidance on section 24*, ch 2 paras 2.4 and 2.5.

When applying the exemption, officials must clearly record the justification for the decision: DCA's *full exemptions guidance on section 24*, ch 3, para 3.4. **6.143D**

The public interest. If non-disclosure is required to safeguard national security it is likely to be only in exceptional circumstances that consideration of other public interest factors will result in disclosure: see DCA's *full exemptions guidance on section 24*, ch 3, para 3.7. This is fair comment, but the public interest will have to be considered and it may sometimes prevail. In the light of the London bombings in July 2005, the editorial in the *Observer* on 23 July 2005 said: **6.143E**

> Placing a full account of the events of July 2005 in the public domain is the best way of helping all of us—government, intelligence and emergency services and citizens—achieve the correct balance between preserving traditional freedoms and accepting heightened security.
>
> Fear and terror spread in the gaps where there is ignorance. Give us the full picture and let us judge for ourselves how and when to go about business as usual.

These are wise words and there will be times when the public interest will require the disclosure of even sensitive information.

Ministerial certificates. Where a department holds particular categories of information, the disclosure of which is always likely to be against the interests of national security, it may be appropriate to hold a prospective certificate, already signed by the Minister, relating to that particular category of information. However, each decision to deploy a certificate should be taken on its own merits in the light of the prevailing circumstances: DCA's *full exemptions guidance on section 24*, ch 4, para 4.12. **6.143F**

Annex A to the DCA's *full exemptions guidance on section 24* gives general guidance about appeals where a Ministerial certificate has been served, Annex B gives general guidance about applications to the Commissioner where no Ministerial certificate has been served, and Annex C gives general guidance about the need for and use of the 'neither confirm nor deny' exemptions. These annexes cover sections 23 and 24. **6.143G**

Section 26: defence

The following new headings and paragraphs come after paragraph 6.146 of the Main Work:

Section 26: the Information Commissioner's guidance

The term 'prejudice' is not defined in the Act. In simple terms, however, information will be covered by the exemption if its disclosure would assist or be likely to assist an enemy or a potential enemy: *IC awareness guidance no 10*, p 1. **6.146A**

The public interest test

6.146B The Commissioner has suggested that among the factors that would weigh in favour of disclosure are:

(a) furthering the understanding of and participation in public debate on issues of the day.

Decisions as to whether to deploy troops or go to war are clearly among the most difficult and sensitive faced by governments and Parliament. There is a strong public interest in facilitating an informed debate about the merit of such decisions. A more informed debate should lead to improved decision-making and, therefore, an increase in public confidence in and support for military operations. Before decisions have been taken there are, however, likely to be strong arguments against the disclosure of operational information.

(b) promoting accountability and transparency by public authorities for decisions taken by them.

In principle, the public has the right to know that military operations have been conducted properly and effectively, and that there has been an attempt to minimize any casualties and so forth. While it may occasionally be argued that disclosures may adversely affect morale, there is a stronger counter-argument that members of the armed forces have even more right than the general public to reliable information.

(c) bringing to light information affecting public health and public safety.

Almost inevitably, where military operations lead to loss of life there is debate about the safety of equipment and the direction of those operations. Factors in favour of disclosure might include enhanced accountability, improvements to equipment and planning, and allowing individuals to challenge the basis of decisions affecting them personally.

Section 26: the DCA's guidance

6.146C The DCA's *full exemptions guidance on section 26*, ch 1 clarifies the meaning of some of the key terms used in the exemption: defence; the British Islands; colony; capability; effectiveness; security and relevant forces.

6.146D Chapter 2 of the DCA's *full exemptions guidance on section 26* gives examples of the type of information covered by the exemption:

(a) defence policy and strategy, military planning, and defence intelligence;
(b) the size, shape, organization, logistics, order of battle, state of readiness, and training of the armed forces of the Crown;
(c) the actual or prospective deployment of those forces in the United Kingdom or overseas, including their operational orders, tactics, and rules of engagement;

(d) the weapons, stores, transport, or other equipment of those forces and the invention, development, production, technical specification, and performance of such equipment and research relating to it;
(e) plans and measures for the maintenance of essential supplies and services that are or would be needed in time of conflict;
(f) plans for future military capabilities;
(g) plans or options for the defence or reinforcement of a colony or another country;
(h) analysis of the capability, state of readiness, performance of individual or combined units, their equipment or support structures; and
(i) arrangements for co-operation, collaboration, consultation, or integration with the armed forces of other countries, whether on a bilateral basis or as part of a defence alliance or other international force.

This is a list of examples; the guidance does not suggest that it is exhaustive, nor is it suggested that information on the topics listed will necessarily be exempt.

Chapter 3 of the DCA's *full exemptions guidance on section 26* gives examples of disclosures likely to prejudice defence. They are: **6.146E**

(a) where disclosure of the information would be likely to lead to a reduction or withdrawal of willingness to provide overseas bases or other support and co-operation;
(b) where disclosure of the information could reveal sensitive assessments of the capabilities, facilities or defence posture of other countries;
(c) where to reveal information could result in a loss of tactical advantage in terms of defence or capability or effectiveness of the relevant forces;
(d) where to do so would enable commercial concerns to exploit information in order to influence defence planning or defence procurement processes;
(e) where disclosure of the information could undermine the safety of relevant forces by confirming involvement in a sensitive operation or the counter-measures which may be used in the situation;
(f) where disclosing the information would provide knowledge or know-how liable to assist potential adversaries (including a terrorist group).

Public interest test

The DCA's *full exemptions guidance on section 26*, ch 3, paras 3.7–3.8 states that there is widespread interest in defence policy and the activities of the armed forces, and it is appropriate for the public to understand how and why key decisions are taken in these areas. The public interest will therefore be strong in relation to the disclosure of information that will inform debate and improve public understanding. Examples given include the disclosure of information relating to concerns on matters such as: **6.146F**

(a) the safety of military personnel or loss of life;
(b) risks to the safety of civilians;
(c) the use of land or environmental impact of military activity (section 39 may also be relevant here);
(d) the factual and analytical basis used to develop defence policies;
(e) the use of public funds.

On the other hand, the public interest is likely to weigh against the disclosure of defence information if this could undermine the conduct of a specific military operation or have an adverse impact on security or safety. In addition, the disclosure of information in the face of an objection from an allied country, or in breach of a clear undertaking to preserve confidentiality, may well prejudice the United Kingdom's defence relations by restricting exchanges of information or by jeopardizing military co-operation.

6.146G It will generally be good practice to consult MoD officials about the impact of any disclosure to which section 26 has potential application: DCA's *full exemptions guidance on section 26*, ch 3, para 3.11.

6.146H Section 26 applies to all recorded information, including that in records over 30 years old: DCA's *full exemptions guidance on section 26*, ch 3, para 3.13.

Section 27: international relations

The following new paragraphs and headings come after paragraph 6.153 of the Main Work:

Section 27: the Information Commissioner's guidance

6.153A The Information Commissioner's *awareness guidance no 14* deals with international relations. Section 27 contains two closely related provisions: an exemption for information disclosure of which would be likely to harm United Kingdom interests, dealt with in section 27(1), and an exemption for information obtained in confidence from another state or international organization or court, dealt with in sections 27(2) and (3). The Commissioner says at p 1 that the important point to note under section 27(1) is that the prejudice must be to the interests of the United Kingdom itself rather than simply to the public authority which holds the information. Sections 27(2) and (3) relate primarily not to the subject of the information, or the harm resulting from the disclosure, but to the circumstances under which it was obtained and the conditions placed on it by its supplier. Although there is no explicit test of prejudice attached to this provision the guidance is that it is difficult to envisage cases where information was in fact confidential but where its disclosure would not result in any harm.

There is no requirement that an actionable breach of confidence must occur (as is the case in the exemption at section 41 relating to information provided in confidence) for this part of the exemption to apply. **6.153B**

The interests of the United Kingdom abroad which are the focus of this exemption span a broad spectrum. The Information Commissioner gives examples. This is the Information Commissioner's list: **6.153C**

(a) communications between public authorities in the United Kingdom and other states, international organizations or organs of other states;
(b) the exchange of political views between states;
(c) United Kingdom policy and strategic positioning in relation to other states or international organizations;
(d) diplomatic matters between states;
(e) international trade partnerships;
(f) consular matters in relation to United Kingdom citizens abroad or visitors to the United Kingdom;
(g) procedures of overseas offices;
(h) state visits by overseas officials and Ministers;
(i) international funding matters;
(j) cases before international courts or cases pending;
(k) controversial visitors to the United Kingdom;
(l) international events, for example the Olympic Games;
(m) the international relations and strategic alliances of universities for research and attracting funding;
(n) local authorities in relation to town twinning;
(o) district or county councils or regional development agencies in relation to their applications for EU funding.

Section 27: the DCA's guidance

The DCA's *full exemptions guidance on section 27* covers much the same ground. **6.153D** The guidance says that the exemption under section 27 exists to protect the United Kingdom's international relations, its interests abroad and the United Kingdom's ability to protect and promote those interests. The United Kingdom's interests abroad and thus the subject matter of its international relations cover a wide and changing range of matters, including for example trade, defence, the environment, human rights and the fight against terrorism and international crime. Furthermore, the ways in which the United Kingdom's interests are protected and promoted and its international relations are conducted also take a wide variety of forms, ranging from diplomatic exchanges to informal conversations. If in doubt, the guidance says, as to whether a disclosure of information would prejudice any of the matters mentioned in section 27(2), consult the government department concerned, usually the Foreign and Commonwealth Office.

The public interest test

6.153E Chapter 3, para 3.7 of the guidance suggests that the public interest in maintaining the international relations exemption is likely to be strong when the disclosure of information would, for instance, significantly weaken the United Kingdom's bargaining position in international negotiations, inhibit other governments' willingness to share sensitive information with the United Kingdom or inhibit frankness and candour in diplomatic reporting.

6.153F When considering the balance of the public interest in respect of confidential information covered by section 27(2) the guidance gives examples of matters which might be taken into account:

(a) whether disclosure would be contrary to international law (for example where disclosure would be a breach of a treaty obligation);
(b) whether disclosure would undermine the United Kingdom's reputation for honouring its international commitments and obligations;
(c) whether disclosure would be likely to undermine the willingness of the state, international organization or court which supplied the information to supply other confidential information in the future (or whether it would be likely to have such an effect on the willingness of states, international organizations or courts in general to do so);
(d) whether disclosure would be likely to provoke a negative reaction from the state, international organization or court which supplied the information that would damage the United Kingdom's relations with them and/or its ability to protect and promote United Kingdom interests;
(f) whether disclosure would be likely to result in another state, international organization or court disclosing confidential information supplied by the United Kingdom, contrary to the United Kingdom's interests;
(g) whether the state, international organization or court which supplied the confidential information has objected to its disclosure and good relations with them would be likely to suffer if the objection were ignored.

Section 28: relations within the United Kingdom

The following new headings and paragraphs come after paragraph 6.156 of the Main Work:

Section 28: the DCA's guidance

Northern Ireland

The DCA's *full exemptions guidance on section 28*, ch 2, para 2.4 states that the Northern Ireland Assembly is currently suspended. The offices of the First Minister and Deputy First Minister of Northern Ireland, and of Northern Ireland Ministers and junior Ministers continue to exist, but remain vacant during the suspension. Therefore there is currently no Executive Committee of the Northern Ireland Assembly. Information may fall within the section 28 exemption on the basis that its disclosure would damage relationships between the currently functioning government of Northern Ireland (that is, the government of the United Kingdom in the form of the Northern Ireland Office or a Northern Ireland Department acting under the direction and control of the Secretary of State), and the Scottish Executive or the National Assembly of Wales. **6.156A**

Memorandum of understanding

Details of the relationships between the four administrations in the United Kingdom and their respective responsibilities are set out in the Memorandum of Understanding Command Paper 5240 (MoU). Under the MoU administrations will: **6.156B**

(a) state what restrictions (if any) there should be on information they share;
(b) treat information received in accordance with restrictions placed on its usage;
(c) disclose information in accordance with the Act (but in doing so have regard to the safeguards in (a) and (b) and in difficult cases refer back to the originator of the information);
(d) accept that some information is subject to statutory or other restrictions and there will be a common approach to the classification and handling of sensitive material.

Prejudice

The exemption is subject to both a prejudice test and a public interest test. The guidance at ch 3, paras 3 and 4 gives examples of where there might be prejudice: **6.156C**

(a) sensitive information held by United Kingdom government departments on devolved matters which pre-date devolution but which concern the devolved administrations;
(b) information held by devolved administrations relating to reserved or excepted matters;
(c) briefing or comments on another administration's plans or policies;
(d) an options analysis in an area of reserved policy which also includes an assessment of the operation of policy in a devolved area;
(e) information about another administration that has come direct from a third party.

The public interest test

6.156D The guidance gives examples of where the public interest might favour withholding information and disclosing it, respectively. To take withholding information first:

(a) confidential briefing for United Kingdom Ministers provided for Ministerial meetings;
(b) policy plans received from devolved administrations on a confidential basis which have not yet been announced;
(c) details of meetings between the four administrations the disclosure of which could affect the effectiveness of such meetings;
(d) details of sensitive United Kingdom negotiating positions in the EU which affect devolved matters;
(e) United Kingdom assessments of politics and policies in the devolved administrations.

6.156E The examples of circumstances favouring disclosure are:

(a) information which helps public understanding of the devolution settlement;
(b) information which would explain how decisions were taken (after an announcement has been made);
(c) details of negotiations which are no longer sensitive because of the passage of time; and
(d) cases where the administration which provided the information would have disclosed the information (even if a case can be made for non-disclosure).

6.156F Annex A of the *full exemptions guidance on section 28* contains a helpful statement of the devolution settlement, explaining what powers are devolved to each administration.

Section 28: the Information Commissioner's guidance

6.156G The Information Commissioner's *awareness guidance no 13* deals with relations within the United Kingdom. It covers much the same ground as the DCA guidance. On p 7 the Commissioner says:

> It is unlikely that information which originates with a body other than a central government department or a devolved administration will be exempt under s.28. From time to time, however, it may be that another public authority is given information by one of those bodies and that disclosure would engage the exemption.
>
> Where information carries a sensitivity marking or where it dates from a time before such markings were widely used, it is likely to be sensible to consult with the administrations whose interests may be damaged by disclosure (this will typically be the administration from which the information was received). Given that response to requests must be given within 20 working days, it may be sensible to establish a regular channel of communication if it is expected that the s.28 exemption will be widely used by the authority.

Section 29: the economy

The following new paragraphs and headings come after paragraph 6.161 of the Main Work:

Section 29: the DCA's guidance

The DCA's *full exemptions guidance on section 29* begins by explaining the terms *economic interests* and *financial interests* used in the section: **6.161A**

> *economic interests*: A central aim of government is economic and financial management which supports the maintenance of a stable macroeconomic framework, maintains sound public finances and promotes United Kingdom economic prospects and productivity. Associated with these are the oversight of a competitive financial services market and efficient tax and benefits systems. The economy exemption exists in recognition of the instability and economic damage to the wider economy that could be caused by the disclosure of some information.
>
> *financial interests*: Governments seek to conduct their financial dealings efficiently and so reduce costs to taxpayers. Public accountability necessitates that sufficient information is available to assess the probity and cost-effective nature of such dealings. This needs to be balanced against the damage to an administration's financial interests that could arise if too much information is disclosed about its financial dealings or if information is disclosed after too short a time period. The financial interests exemption exists in recognition of the long-term cost to the taxpayer that could be caused by the very disclosure of some information and the premature disclosure of other information.

The guidance lists examples of potentially prejudicial disclosures. The list is not exhaustive: **6.161B**

(a) information contained in Standing Committee and financial stability papers (of HM Treasury, Bank of England, Financial Services Authority);
(b) vulnerability assessments;
(c) gilt auctions;
(d) budget information;
(e) government cash flows and borrowing requirements;
(f) terrorism reinsurance.

The public interest test

Chapter 2, para 2.10 lists particular factors that will tend to point towards the public interest being served by disclosing the information. They include: **6.161C**

(a) the need to hold public authorities to account for their stewardship of public resources; and
(b) the objective of building public trust and establishing transparency in the operation of the economy so as to increase the credibility of economic policy

decision-makers and enhance the United Kingdom's reputation as a fair and honest business environment.

6.161D Chapter 2, para 2.11 lists factors that will tend towards the public interest being served by withholding information relating to the economy. They include:

(a) where disclosure could result in financial instability of institutions or countries, either in the United Kingdom or abroad;
(b) where disclosure could pre-empt announcements on taxation, national insurance or benefits;
(c) where selective disclosure of the information could affect financial markets. Financial regulation and government policy requires the transparent release of market-sensitive data simultaneously to the whole market. This reinforces confidence in market integrity by investors and liquidity providers, thereby reducing the cost of capital in financial markets. Selective or premature release of information undermines confidence in dealing in United Kingdom markets;
(d) where information has been obtained from confidential sources (eg overseas governments or regulators) who would be damaged by the disclosure and who will not provide information in the future; and
(e) where the information consists of assessments of (an institution's/economy's) viability.

Section 29: the Information Commissioner's guidance

6.161E The Information Commissioner's *awareness guidance no 15* deals with the economy. It adds little to the DCA's guidance. On p 2 the guidance addresses the term *prejudice* in the section. The advice is that the term *prejudice* is generally taken to mean harm or damage. The term *would be likely to* does not imply that the probability of the harm occurring has to be greater than the probability of no harm being caused; however, there does have to be a significant and realistic prospect of the damage being incurred.

Section 30: investigations and proceedings conducted by public authorities

The following new headings and paragraphs come after paragraph 6.175 of the Main Work:

Section 30: the Information Commissioner's guidance

6.175A The Information Commissioner's *awareness guidance no 16* deals with investigations. In broad terms, section 30 creates an exemption for information which is or has been held for the purposes of an investigation or proceedings conducted by a public authority or which was obtained or recorded for the purpose of various investigative functions.

Section 30(1) covers particular criminal investigations and proceedings conducted by public authorities. The purpose of this part of the section is to protect particular investigations and proceedings. The second part of the exemption is broader and provides protection to investigative processes both criminal and civil and to information obtained through confidential sources. In many cases it may be impossible to draw a clear line between the information covered by the two parts of the exemption. **6.175B**

Superficially, there is a similar overlap between sections 30 and 31. Section 30 covers investigations and proceedings; meanwhile, section 31 covers law enforcement more generally. Under section 31 for instance, information is exempt if its disclosure might prejudice the prosecution of offenders. Such information might easily also fall under section 30. However, the Act is clear that section 30 takes precedence. A public authority can only rely upon the section 31 exemption if section 30 does not apply. **6.175C**

The public interest test

Awareness guidance no 16 at p 4 says that, as to the public interest test, a critical issue is likely to be the timing of disclosure. As a general rule, the Commissioner recognizes that the public interest in disclosure of information is likely to be weaker whilst an investigation is being carried out. However, once an investigation is completed the public interest in understanding why an investigation reached a particular conclusion or in seeing that the investigation had been properly carried out is more likely to outweigh the public interest in maintaining the exemption. **6.175D**

By the same token, there is likely to be a weaker public interest in disclosure of information about investigations which have been suspended but which may be reopened, than about those which have been concluded or abandoned. **6.175E**

The guidance is that there is a strong public interest in access to justice and in ensuring that justice is done. There will be occasions when this factor favours disclosure, for instance where there is a well-founded suspicion that justice was not done either to the accused or to a victim. In some cases this may shift the balance of public interest in favour of disclosure of information about completed cases or those which have been abandoned with no prospect of them being reopened. There will be other cases, however, where disclosure would be likely to prejudice the right to a fair trial. **6.175F**

Finally, the guidance notes that the presumption that information relating to ongoing investigations will not be released is not invariable. Much will depend upon the effect of disclosure, with a stronger case for maintaining the exemption **6.175G** where the confidentiality of the information is critical to the success of the investigation. In rare cases where a prosecution has collapsed for reasons of procedural failure or dishonesty on the part of the investigating authority, there may be a strong public interest argument in favour of disclosure of information about other, similar investigations.

Who is likely to use the exemption

6.175H Some public authorities have the duty or power to investigate complaints, some to bring prosecutions. Some combine both roles. It is not possible to provide a definitive list; however, they include:

(a) the police;
(b) the Environment Agency;
(c) the Crown Prosecution Service;
(d) the Serious Fraud Office;
(e) the General Medical Council;
(f) the Department of Trade and Industry;
(g) local authorities (eg in respect of trading standards and environmental health).

Section 30: the DCA's guidance

6.175I The DCA's *full exemptions guidance on section 30* at ch 2, para 2.4.2 adds to the list of those who are likely to use the exemption:

(h) the Inland Revenue;
(i) HM Customs and Excise;
(j) the Department of the Environment;
(k) the Food Standards Agency;
(l) the Health and Safety Executive;
(m) the Financial Services Authority;
(n) the Office of Fair Trading.

Confidential sources

6.175J The DCA's guidance at ch 2, para 2.5 says that section 30(2) concerns information which has two sets of components. The first set relates to the purposes for which it was acquired, but it is the second set which essentially characterizes section 30(2)—the information must relate to 'the obtaining of information from confidential sources'.

6.175K Information may relate to the obtaining of information from confidential sources in many ways. It may identify those sources, describe the processes of obtaining the information, or indeed itself constitute information obtained from confidential sources.

Confidential sources are providers of information operating in a context which is to some degree necessarily covert; they are also characterized by a relationship of confidence, or protection, with the authority (or indeed other body or individual) to which they provide information. *Confidential sources* certainly includes informers—that is to say external individuals who covertly provide information under conditions of confidentiality, particularly as to their own identification. But it is not clear that the expression includes agents or officers of the authority itself working under cover, as such; information about this sort of information gathering does not obviously relate to confidential, as opposed to covert, sources, nor is it clearly about gathering information from sources rather than by means of an authority's own activities. Still less is this provision likely to be considered applicable to information gathered by means of covert technology. The obtaining of information from confidential sources should be regarded as essentially limited to arrangements for acquiring information from third parties who have an expectation of confidentiality from the authority to which they gave the information. However, the information in question need not itself be confidential; it is the relationship with the source which must be confidential. **6.175L**

The guidance says that it is important to note that to the extent that the information in question relates to a living, identifiable, individual, it is likely to constitute personal information within the terms of section 40. Disclosure of personal information always needs to be considered in that context, whether or not section 30(2) also applies. It is also important to note that to the extent that the information is itself obtained from a confidential source, then section 41 is likely to be relevant. Both section 40 and section 41 need to be considered prior to section 30, because disclosure of information to which either of those sections applies is capable of exposing authorities to legal proceedings. Section 30(2) is therefore most likely to be relevant to information which does not identify individuals and the disclosure of which would not be an actionable breach of confidence (for example, it might not be actionable because it was obtained by one government department from another). Examples might include: **6.175M**

(a) a diary which recorded appointments to meet an unnamed informer;
(b) details of any surveillance and investigative techniques associated with the management of external confidential sources;
(c) an indication that certain information had been obtained from an unnamed confidential source.

Section 31: law enforcement

The Information Commissioner has issued decision notices in the cases of *Chief Police Officer for Hampshire Constabulary*, case reference FS50068017 (2 August 2005); *Chief Police Officer for Hampshire Constabulary*, case reference FS50067279 (2 August 2005); and *Chief Police Officer Essex Constabulary*, case **6.176** reference FS50068601 (3 August 2005), involving section 31. These cases are discussed further at Supplement para 7.77J.

The following new headings and paragraphs come after paragraph 6.182 of the Main Work:

Section 31: the DCA's guidance

The structure of the section

6.182A The DCA's *full exemptions guidance on section 31* deals with the structure of section 31 in ch 1, para 1.5:

(a) *section 31(1)(a)–(f)*—these provisions stand by themselves. The exemption works by indicating a list of law enforcement interests which may be prejudiced by disclosure. These are broad, and potentially overlapping areas—the administration of justice in general, crime, tax, immigration and prisons. The guidance deals with each topic by considering the application of the exemption (ie what aspect of the topic could be prejudiced by the disclosure of information) and the public interest test;
(b) *section 31(1)(g)–(i) and section 31(2)*—these provisions need to be read together.

Section 31(2) contains a list of law enforcement purposes. Some of these are quite general, some focused on very specific sectors of law enforcement. The exemption does not work by applying the prejudice test directly to these purposes. The test is applied indirectly through section 31(g),(h), or (i). That means that one or more of the purposes has to be engaged by one or more of those provisions before a disclosure falls within the terms of this exemption.

Section 31(1)(g) is engaged where a disclosure would be likely to prejudice the exercise of a public authority's function for a relevant purpose.

Section 31(1)(h) is engaged where a disclosure would be likely to prejudice an authority's civil litigation arising out of certain investigations for a relevant purpose.

Section 31(1)(i) is engaged where a disclosure would be likely to prejudice certain fatal accident inquiries held under Scottish legislation for a relevant purpose.

The guidance considers each of these provisions in a separate chapter.

The prevention or detection of crime and the apprehension or prosecution of offenders—31(1)(a) and (b)

6.182B Examples of circumstances in which prejudice is most likely to be relevant are: (i) information relating to planned police operations; and (ii) information relating to the identity and role of police informers.

Maintaining confidence in law enforcement is crucial to the public interest. 6.182C

Law enforcement—31(1)(c)

Examples of aspects of the administration of justice that could be prejudiced by disclosures are: (i) the operation of the judicial appointments system; and (ii) the maintenance of an independent and effective legal profession. 6.182D

The public interest in the administration of justice is very high. It is moreover a public interest which is expressly recognized by the courts as fundamental to their work. 6.182E

Tax—31(1)(d)

Examples of disclosures with a high potential for prejudicing the assessment and collection of tax include (i) details of plans to close tax loopholes; and (ii) details of strategies, investigative practices or even negotiating tactics used to assist in the collection of taxes or duties. 6.182F

There is a strong public interest in having stable and secure public finances. 6.182G

Operation of immigration controls—31(1)(e)

Examples of circumstances where disclosure might prejudice the operation of immigration controls include disclosure of information which would reveal an incidence of suspected illegal working which was to be investigated by the immigration service. In this case the disclosure of the information about the proposed investigation might prejudice the operation of the immigration controls because it could alert the employers and the illegal workers in advance and enable them to escape investigation. 6.182H

In the immigration context there are a number of public interest considerations which may favour disclosure. There is a public interest in ensuring that there is public confidence in the operation of our immigration controls and one way to do this is to keep the public informed of policies, developments, and proposals for the future, together with explanations of them. Linked in with this there is a public interest in ensuring that the public have access to correct information—because immigration is an emotive issue set in a complex framework, it is inevitable that there may be inaccurate information about immigration circulating in the public domain which ought to be corrected. 6.182I

The maintenance of security and good order in prisons—31(1)(f)

Disclosure of information might prejudice the maintenance of security and good order in prisons in two ways: (i) by in some way causing security to be compromised or good order to break down; and (ii) by impairing an institution's ability to restore security or good order or to prevent them breaking down in the first place. 6.182J

6.182K There is a public interest in ensuring that there is public confidence in the operation of the prison system, and one way of ensuring this is to keep the public informed. The public interest is not served by releasing information which might aid an unlawful escape or put anyone within the institution at real risk of harm.

The purpose linked parts of section 31(1)

6.182L As indicated above, the exemptions in sections 31(1)(g)–(i) all work as follows. A request for information will be refused where disclosure would prejudice one of the processes described in (1)(g),(h), or (i), if, but only if, and to the extent that that process is for one of the purposes set out in subsection (2) and the balance of the public interest in disclosing and withholding the information comes down in favour of withholding it.

The structure of the Act means that the prejudice must be to the process and not the purpose. The public interest on the other hand must be considered in the round. In each case, (i) the nature, degree and likelihood of the prejudice; (ii) the public interest in the avoidance of prejudice to the particular process; and (iii) the public interest in the furtherance of the relevant purpose are all likely to be very relevant.

6.182M Chapters 7–16 of the DCA's *full exemptions guidance* consider:

(a) the nature of the processes in subsections (1)(g)–(i) and how disclosure of information might prejudice those processes; and
(b) the nature of the purposes in subsection (2).

In each case, an indication of the most relevant public interest considerations is also suggested.

Section 31: the Information Commissioner's guidance

6.182N The Information Commissioner's *awareness guidance no 17* which deals with law enforcement does not add anything to the DCA's guidance.

Section 33: audit functions

6.186 Other bodies to fall within the scope of the section include Wales Audit Office, the Commission for Healthcare Audit and Inspection, HM Inspectorate of Constabulary, HM Inspectorate of Prisons, Ofsted, and the Commission for Social Care Inspection.

Note that by no means all the bodies which carry out public audit are public authorities. For instance, auditors who are appointed by the Audit Commission and exercise functions under the Audit Commission Act 1998 are not caught by the definition of *public authority* contained in the Act and will not therefore be covered by the Act unless it is decided in the future to define them by order as public authorities.

The following new headings and paragraphs come after paragraph 6.187 of the Main Work:

Section 33: the Information Commissioner's guidance

The Information Commissioner's *awareness guidance no 18* deals with public audit and makes the point that public authorities who are subject to audit and who may therefore hold information which relates to public audit, for instance correspondence with auditors, draft reports and comments upon them, cannot claim the exemption. **6.187A**

What information is covered by the exemption

Examples of the types of information covered by the exemption include draft reports, audit methodologies, correspondence between auditors and bodies subject to audit and information provided to auditors by whistle-blowers or other informants. **6.187B**

The Environmental Information Regulations do not contain an equivalent to the public audit exemption. **6.187C**

Prejudice

The Commissioner says on p 4 of *awareness guidance no 18*: **6.187D**

> Two broad types of prejudice may arise through the release of information by an auditor. Firstly there may be prejudice to a particular audit or other process (such as the appointment of auditors). The key issue here is likely to be one of timing: the release of information about an ongoing exercise may well be likely to cause prejudice, for instance where a draft report may contain inaccuracies or provisional recommendations. By contrast, where an exercise has been completed and a final audit report has been published, it would be difficult to see how there would be prejudice to that particular exercise.
>
> Secondly, however, there may be more general prejudice to the function of audit. For instance if the release of information supplied in confidence or on a voluntary basis to an auditor were to discourage cooperation with the auditor in future, it may be reasonable to argue prejudice. Similarly, while there would be unlikely to be prejudice in the release of information about standard audit methodologies, the release of information about other techniques might cause prejudice if it were to reduce the likely effectiveness of those techniques in the future.

The public interest

The Information Commissioner gives particular guidance about the public interest test on p 5 of *awareness guidance no 18*. There are public interest arguments **6.187E** against disclosure which may be summarized as ensuring that the Act does not prevent auditors from carrying out their duties, both by giving protection to individual audits and by safeguarding the general integrity of the audit process. The Commissioner continues:

> The Commissioner recognises the public interest in maintaining the exemption in many cases, not least because the purposes of public audit, namely providing assurances to Parliament and the public that public bodies are able to account for the public funds allocated to them and that they deliver value for money, are so similar to the factors favouring the disclosure of information listed above [the Commissioner's list of general factors weighing in favour of disclosure].
>
> Nevertheless the Commissioner believes that in particular cases, the public interest may be better served by disclosure. There is a general public interest in understanding the nature of public audit and the processes by which reports are compiled and other statutory functions are discharged. This may be an interest on the part of the wider public or an interest on the part of bodies subject to audit. There may also be cases where an auditor's report is controversial or where it deals with an issue of national importance, and where there are strong public interest arguments in favour of disclosure of other material not included in the report. For instance, a report may have been prompted as a result of a complaint by a whistleblower or a series of press reports on a particular issue. Although in many cases the auditor may wish to argue that this other material is subject to a duty of confidence and that disclosure would discourage future cooperation, there may be cases where it is more important to provide assurances that the report has been properly compiled by releasing some of the background material.

Section 33: the DCA's guidance

Explanation of general terms

6.187F The DCA's *full exemptions guidance on section 33* contains some useful explanations of general terms used in the section.

Functions includes both powers and duties; they may therefore be in the nature of formal statutory duties, or less formal supervisory activity. For example, Ministers may charge a department with examining the efficiency of another department or departments generally across government. An example would be the *Lyons Review*, which was established within the Cabinet Office to look at whether efficiencies could be achieved by moving parts of departments out of central London; or one public authority may be asked to carry out a peer review of another public authority. When government departments are charged with such tasks it is their function to carry them out. For this reason no list of functions is ever going to be exhaustive.

Economy, efficiency and effectiveness in section 1(b) refers, in this context, to value-for-money audits. While no agreed definition of economy, efficiency and effectiveness exists the following are intended to be useful guidelines. In terms of *economy* such audits are concerned with whether the public body secured resources for the lowest possible cost, subject to maintenance of an adequate standard of quality. *Efficiency* involves the auditor in an assessment of performance, in terms of a comparison between the output in respect of results achieved and input in respect of resources consumed. And *effectiveness* is concerned with the extent to which a body, project or programme achieves its stated objectives. Any department or agency which has responsibility for examining the performance of another public authority, including a consideration of how that public authority employs its resources in carrying out its functions, will fall within the scope of this section.

On questions of prejudice and public interest the DCA's guidance does not add anything to the Information Commissioner's guidance. **6.187G**

Section 35: formulation of government policy, etc

The following new paragraphs and headings come after paragraph 6.195 of the Main Work:

Section 35: the Information Commissioner's guidance

The Information Commissioner's *awareness guidance no 24* deals with policy formulation, Ministerial communications, law officers' advice and the operation of Ministerial private offices. Section 35 is only available for government departments and the Welsh Assembly. **6.195A**

Statistical information

The guidance is that once policy decisions are made, statistical information is not exempt and must be disclosed. Statistical information incorporates analyses, projections and meta-data, as well as the statistics themselves: numerical data, which may simply be a sum total or take the form of a table or graph. Statistics must be derived from a recorded or repeatable methodology. Commentary on this methodology is also statistical information. **6.195B**

Formulation or development of government policy

Awareness guidance no 24 p 2 says: **6.195C**

> Policy is not a precise term and what is regarded as policy depends on context. However there is a general consensus that policy is about the development of options and priorities and the determination of which option should be translated into political action and when. The *Modernising Government* white paper defines policy as the process by which governments translate their political vision into programmes and actions to deliver outcomes or desired changes in the real world.
>
> Policy can be sourced and generated in a variety of ways. For example it may come from ministers' ideas and suggestions, manifesto commitments, significant incidents such as a major outbreak of foot and mouth disease, European Union policies or

public concern expressed through letters, petitions and the like. Proposals and evidence for policies may come from external expert advisers, stakeholder consultation, or external researchers, as well as civil servants. Policy is unlikely to include decisions about individuals or to be about purely administrative matters. Whilst departmental policy will frequently be derived from and be identical to government policy, where a departmental policy applies only to the internal workings of the department it would not be caught.

6.195D *Awareness guidance no 24*, p 3 says:

> Formulation suggests the output from the early stages of the policy process where options are generated and sorted, risks are identified, consultation occurs and recommendations/submissions are put to a minister. Though the two terms are often used interchangeably, development may go beyond formulation. It may refer to the processes involved in improving on or altering existing policy such as piloting, monitoring, reviewing, analysing, or recording the effects of existing policy. At the very least, 'formulation or development' suggests something dynamic—that is, something must be happening to the policy. The exemption cannot apply to a 'finished product policy' or a policy which is agreed to, in operation, or already implemented.
>
> The thinking behind this exemption is that it is intended to maintain the government's 'private thinking space'.

Public interest test in relation to policy

6.195E Arguments to consider in favour of disclosure will be arguments related to public participation in and accountability of government decisions. Participation refers to the ability of people to input into policy prior to a final decision being taken, whereas accountability refers to the need for government to explain why something has happened, or show that it has been rigorous in taking into account all relevant considerations.

Ministerial communications: public interest test

6.195F The Information Commissioner says at p 4 that he will expect the public interest test to be applied robustly. In the absence of good reason to believe that the disclosure of Ministerial communications will, on balance, be harmful to the public interest, it will be difficult to justify a decision to withhold. He continues:

> Public interest arguments in favour of disclosure would challenge the assumption that the public are not already aware that there are differences of opinion between ministers. As such, disclosure would in fact promote accountability and transparency by showing that decisions have been made after a variety of views has been expressed and a robust debate has occurred. On the other hand, collective responsibility protects high level government decisions from becoming personalised and also enables ministers to be totally frank and candid in their discussions.
>
> Finally, a public authority may, in applying the public interest test, try to justify withholding information because of embarrassment likely to be caused to an individual minister. It is important to understand that there is no such exemption and any consideration of likely ministerial embarrassment cannot be justified.

Public interest test in relation to the Law Officers' advice

A preliminary point: it is not the case that the advice of the Law Officers is wholly protected by section 42 relating to legal professional privilege. The Attorney-General is not just the legal adviser to the Government; he is a departmental Minister and the guardian of the public interest. Section 35(1)(c) covers a broader range of advice than is covered by the legal professional privilege exemption. **6.195G**

Awareness guidance no 24 says on p 5 in addressing the public interest that although the exemption gives statutory recognition to an existing convention, it is important that this does not result in a reduced level of disclosure of advice. Whilst the Commissioner recognizes the strong public interest arguments for maintaining the convention, it is not impossible for advice to be disclosed, and the guidance makes it clear that the public interest test must be considered carefully in each case. The Commissioner says: **6.195H**

> The matter of convention is a fact, but not a deciding consideration in assessment of the public interest, although the reasons for the existence of the convention may turn out to be the same as those offered to justify upholding the exemption.

The public interest test in relation to the operation of Ministerial private offices

In applying the public interest test, the exact nature of the information requested in relation to the operation of the Ministerial private office is likely to have a significant bearing on the decision to disclose. The Information Commissioner says at p 6 that he will expect government departments to apply the public interest test in a robust manner to ensure that the maximum information is made available. **6.195I**

It is likely, the guidance continues, that a distinction will be made when deciding the balance of public interest between requests for information concerning, respectively, a Minister's private affairs and his official business. Authorities will be likely to take the view that details of a Minister's private arrangements should be withheld. In the current climate, concern regarding security issues may also be given as a public interest justification for refusal of information regarding details of those working arrangements, etc. In considering requests for information regarding the details of those working within the private office, section 40 may also apply. **6.195J**

Section 35: the DCA's guidance

The DCA's *full exemptions guidance on section 35*, ch 1, para 1.1 states that this section of the Act is especially important for government departments; it is specifically aimed at them, and its proper use is essential to protecting the policy-making process and ensuring that this process remains able to deliver effective government. It is sensible to remember that the DCA's guidance represents the government's point of view, and it does not necessarily represent the view which **6.195K** will prevail with the Information Commissioner, the Information Tribunal and the courts, who between them will have the final say.

6.195L Chapter 1, para 1.2 helpfully discusses the relationship between sections 35 and 36. Section 36 applies only to information that is not exempt information by virtue of section 35. The sections can, however, be cited in the alternative. Section 36 is designed explicitly to protect information whose disclosure:

(a) would, or would be likely to, prejudice–
  (i) the maintenance of the convention of the collective responsibility of Ministers, or
  (ii) the work of the Executive Committee of the Northern Ireland Assembly, or
  (iii) the work of the Executive Committee of the National Assembly for Wales;
(b) would, or would be likely to, inhibit–
  (i) the free and frank provision of advice, or
  (ii) the frank exchange of views for the purposes of deliberation, or
(c) would otherwise prejudice, or would be likely otherwise to prejudice, the effective conduct of public affairs.

6.195M The protection of the collective responsibility of Ministers, and the free and frank provision of advice and exchange of views are not explicitly mentioned in section 35. Section 35 does, however, deal with the formulation of policy, Ministerial communications and the need to protect cabinet documents, all of which are likely to involve the provision of advice, exchange of views and collective decision-making. If section 35 appears to apply, the *full exemptions guidance on section 35* says, it should be asserted. Using section 36 instead effectively means asserting that section 35 does not apply.

The public interest test

6.195N The DCA's guidance lists general considerations in favour of disclosure. They are:

(a) there is a general public interest in disclosure;
(b) greater transparency makes government more accountable to the electorate and increases trust;
(c) as knowledge of the way government works increases, the public contribution to the policy-making process could become more effective and broadly based;
(d) the public interest in being able to assess the quality of advice being given to Ministers and subsequent decision-making;
(e) the greater the impact on the country or on public spending, the greater the public interest may be in the decision-making process being transparent.

6.195O The DCA's guidance also lists general considerations in favour of non-disclosure. They are:

(a) good government depends on good decision-making and this needs to be based on the best advice available and a full consideration of the options;

(b) advice should be broad-based and there may be a deterrent effect on external experts or stakeholders who might be reluctant to provide advice because it might be disclosed;
(c) the impartiality of the Civil Service might be undermined if advice was routinely made public as there is a risk that officials could come under political pressure not to challenge ideas in the formulation of policy, thus leading to poorer decision-making [this view underestimates the quality and resilience of the Civil Service];
(d) Ministers and officials also need to be able to conduct rigorous and candid risk assessments of their policies and programmes, including considerations of the pros and cons without there being premature disclosure, which might close off better options;
(e) there needs to be a free space in which it is possible to think the unthinkable and use imagination, without the fear that policy proposals will be held up to ridicule;
(f) the factual information in the public domain, or disclosed after considering the provision in section 35(4) [which emphasizes the public interest in the disclosure of factual information] may be sufficient to demonstrate that appropriate factors are or have been taken into account;
(g) disclosure of interdepartmental consideration and communication between Ministers may undermine the collective responsibility of the government.

Papers of previous administrations

This is considered in ch 3 of the guidance at paras 3.16–3.19. There is an important long-standing convention that governments are not permitted to see Ministerial papers of a previous administration of a different political persuasion. The purpose of this convention is the same as that on collective responsibility: to give Ministers and their officials a secure space in which to develop and document their thinking on policy options. In this case, the particular danger which the convention guards against is the risk of exposing Ministers to improper political attacks by their opponents in the future. **6.195P**

Requests for papers of a previous administration (within the 30-year period) should therefore be considered on the same public interest principles as papers of the current administration. **6.195Q**

To ensure consistency the DCA guidance suggests the requests should be referred to the DCA. Those cases requiring Ministerial intervention will be handled by the Attorney-General. The relevant former Minister should be consulted before a decision is made. As a general principle, the harm to the public interest from disclosure of such documents will need to be weighed up with especial care. **6.195R**

Papers on working assumptions

6.195S Annexes B, C, D, and E to the DCA's *full exemptions guidance on section 35* consists of papers on working assumptions for civil servants in respect of:

(a) Cabinet and Cabinet Committee information;
(b) policy advice;
(c) requests for legal advice;
(d) legal advice.

Section 36: prejudice to effective conduct of public affairs

The following new headings and paragraphs come after paragraph 6.208 of the Main Work:

Section 36: the Information Commissioner's guidance

6.208A The Information Commissioner's *awareness guidance no 25* covers the effective conduct of public affairs. The guidance starts by asking what the Act says.

What does the Act say?

6.208B Section 36 of the Act sets out an exemption to the right to know if the disclosure of information, in the reasonable opinion of a qualified person, would prejudice the effective conduct of public affairs through:

(a) prejudice or likely prejudice to the maintenance of the convention of collective responsibility of Ministers of the Crown, the work of the Executive Committee of the Northern Ireland Assembly or the work of the Executive Committee of the National Assembly for Wales;
(b) inhibition or likely inhibition of the free and frank provision of advice or exchange of views;
(c) any other prejudice to the effective conduct of public affairs.

For information (other than statistical information) to be exempt by virtue of section 36, it must in the 'reasonable opinion of a qualified person' be capable of either prejudicing or inhibiting the matters listed above.

Who is the qualified person?

6.208C The Act defines the qualified person for a number of specified public authorities listed in sections 36(5)(a)–(n). The qualified person for government departments is a Minister. The qualified person in relation to the public authorities not listed is either a Minister or the public authority itself if authorized by the Minister, or an individual officer or employee of the authority if similarly authorized. The DCA is responsible for the authorization of a qualified person within a public authority. The Information Commissioner has no role in this process [this is one of the defects of the Act]. All authorized qualified persons will be senior individuals in the public authority. Within local authorities, for example, the Monitoring Officer under the Act has been authorized in all cases as the qualified person. Authorities, the Commissioner says, should be aware of who has been authorized within their organization. The Commissioner expects that, as the qualified person is a senior person, the responsibility under this section will be treated as a significant one, and that the opinion will not be expressed lightly.

What is a 'reasonable opinion'?

The Information Commissioner considers a reasonable opinion to be one which lies within the bounds of reasonableness or range of reasonable opinions and can be verified by evidence. Any opinion which is not outrageous, or manifestly absurd or made with no evidence, or made on the basis of irrelevant factors or without consideration of all relevant factors, will satisfy such a test. **6.208D**

Collective responsibility

In cases where the prejudice to collective responsibility is insignificant because of the age of the information in question, the Commissioner would usually expect the information to be disclosed. **6.208E**

Likely to inhibit the free and frank provision of advice or exchange of views

'Inhibit' is not defined in the Act. The Information Commissioner's view is that in the context of section 36 it means to restrain, decrease, or suppress the freedom with which opinions or options are expressed. **6.208F**

The Information Commissioner's view is that there must be some clear, specific and credible evidence that the substance or quality of deliberations or advice would be materially altered for the worse, by the threat of disclosure under the Act. **6.208G**

Otherwise prejudice the effective conduct of public affairs

The Act does not define 'effective conduct' or 'public affairs'. Arguably, everything that a public authority does could be labelled 'public affairs'. Although section 36(2)(c) has been described as a 'catch all' exemption, the Information Commissioner says this is misleading. During the Parliamentary debates on the Freedom of Information Bill, the Government had indicated that the intention of the section was to cover those rare situations which could not be foreseen and which cannot be covered by another exemption, where it would be necessary to withhold information in the interests of good government, rather than catching anything and everything which is not otherwise going to be exempt. **6.208H**

The Commissioner considers that section 36(2)(c) would only be available in cases where the disclosure would prejudice the public authority's ability to offer an effective public service, or to meet its wider objectives or purpose (rather than to **6.208I** simply function) due to the disruption caused by the disclosure and the diversion of resources in managing the impact of disclosure.

Internal reviews

6.208J The Information Commissioner expects public authorities to offer an internal review to applicants who are dissatisfied with a decision to exempt information which they have requested. Where it is not credible to offer an internal review under section 36 because of the seniority of the qualified person, it may be reasonable for public authorities to direct a dissatisfied applicant to the Information Commissioner without first conducting an internal review. Further advice on when to offer an internal review is given in the second edition of the section 45 Code at paras 36–46.

Section 36: the DCA's guidance

6.208K The DCA's *full exemptions guidance on section 36*, ch 1, para 1.1 says that section 36 is central, along with section 35, to protecting the delivery of effective central government. Whilst there is an important public interest in disclosure of information about, for example, the advisory and deliberative processes of central government, there is also a powerful public interest in ensuring that there is a space within which ministers and officials are able to discuss policy options and delivery, freely and frankly. It is as well to remember that the DCA is in the business of the delivery of effective central government and that their guidance is written from that point of view. They are not the people who have the final say about what should be disclosed.

6.208L The DCA's guidance makes the point that section 36 is closely related to section 35. There are a number of key points to note about the similarities and differences between sections 35 and 36. These are discussed at Supplement paras 6.195L and 6.195M.

Collective responsibility

6.208M The maintenance of this convention, the DCA guidance says at ch 2, para 2.2, is fundamental to the continued effectiveness of Cabinet government, and the public interest in maintaining it is recognized by its inclusion not only in this exemption but also in the special provision made in section 35 for the protection of information relating to Cabinet proceedings.

The public interest test

6.208N Considerations which the DCA's *full exemptions guidance* says may weigh in favour of disclosure are these:

(a) open policy-making may lead to increased trust and engagement between citizens and government;

(b) it is desirable that citizens are confident that decisions are taken on the basis of the best available information;
(c) knowledge that the arguments relating to a debate will be disclosable will in fact improve the quality of those arguments. Far from inhibiting the frank provision of advice, there might be circumstances where the prospect of disclosure would enhance the quality of advice;
(d) the response to new policy initiatives may improve, and government become better;
(e) more open policy-making can result in better policy formulation. A wider range of views and opinions, including expert knowledge, is canvassed;
(f) as knowledge of the way government works increases, public contribution to the policy-making process could become more effective and broadly based, rather than being limited to a possibly unrepresentative minority who know their way around;
(g) the public interest in knowing that Ministers are adhering to the Code which regulates their conduct would be satisfied;
(h) the information would expose wrongdoing on the part of the government;
(i) the information would demonstrate that wrongdoing had been effectively dealt with;
(j) the substance of the information may relate closely to a matter of public importance, debate about which could be informed by its disclosure.

Considerations which the DCA's guidance says may weigh in favour of withholding information are these: **6.208O**

(a) Ministers and their officials need space in which to develop their thinking and explore options in communications and discussions with other Ministers;
(b) there needs to be a free space in which it is possible to think the unthinkable and use imagination, without the fear that policy proposals will be held up to ridicule;
(c) Ministers and their officials need to be able to think through all the implications of particular options. In particular, they need to be able to undertake rigorous and candid assessments of the risks to particular programmes and projects;
(d) premature disclosure of preliminary thinking may end up closing off better options because of adverse public reaction;
(e) disclosure of the process of interdepartmental consideration may undermine the collective responsibility of the government;
(f) the decision-making process may not be properly recorded to avoid creating information which is disclosable;
(g) appropriate expert advice is not sought because of the reluctance of those who might supply it to engage in a debate where their contribution might be disclosable.

Papers on working assumptions

6.208P Annexes A, B, and C to the DCA's *full exemptions guidance on section 36* consist of papers on working assumptions for civil servants in respect of (A) oral Parliamentary Questions, (B) written Parliamentary Questions and (C) press releases and handling strategies.

Section 37: communications with Her Majesty, etc and honours

The following new headings and paragraphs come after paragraph 6.211 of the Main Work:

Section 37: the Information Commissioner's guidance

6.211A The Information Commissioner's *awareness guidance no 26* deals with communications with Her Majesty and the awarding of honours. It is worth noting that the provisions of the Act do not apply directly to the Royal Family or the Royal Household. The exemption is about information which is in the hands of public authorities who have been in communication with Her Majesty, other members of the Royal Family, or the Royal Household.

Communications with Her Majesty

6.211B The Act does not define the Royal Family or the Royal Household. The Commissioner's guidance is that the Royal Family will include all those individuals who hold or are entitled to hold the title of 'Majesty' or 'Royal Highness' and their spouses. [This definition presumably does not include the late Diana, Princess of Wales.] The Royal Households comprise the permanent members of the relevant private office and those who from time to time assist members of the Royal Family with their public or private lives. Contractors supplying goods and services to the Royal Household, including by Royal warrant are not included. The Royal website is at www.royal.gov.uk.

6.211C The guidance says that when considering whether to disclose information, account should be taken of the overlap between the Queen's public and private roles and functions. There is considerable media and public interest in both. Where requests for information relate to her private role section 40 of the Act will apply. Personal information is not exempt, however, under section 40 where it relates to a deceased individual. This may be particularly relevant when considering requests for information concerning the late Diana, Princess of Wales.

6.211D In circumstances where information is withheld because of its sensitivity, the Information Commissioner has advised that this will diminish over time, with the effect that information will be disclosed. Given the Queen's constitutional position, however, and that as Sovereign she remains in office for life, it is more likely that any views on policy or individuals expressed by her will remain sensitive after the policy has been implemented or an individual has ceased to have any direct contact. It is also likely to be the case that information relating to the individual communications of other members of the Royal Family will remain sensitive for similar reasons.

Perhaps this part of the guidance needs reconsideration. Other members of the Royal Family are not in the same constitutional position as the Queen. **6.211E**

Honours and dignities conferred by the Crown

The guidance suggests that the range of information sought which is most likely to come within the section 37 exemption will be information relating to individual candidates for or the recipients of awards; information about the process itself, including, for example, details of the assessment committees, etc; and information about the policy behind the awarding of honours and dignities, including, for example, qualifying conditions and proposals for new awards. **6.211F**

Awareness guidance no 26 p 5 states: **6.211G**

> The Information Commissioner encourages public authorities when applying the public interest test to recognise the considerable need for public confidence in the integrity of the honours system. Specially, if the system and the individual honours and dignities themselves are valued and respected, the public will wish to know that the process for awarding them is objective, accountable and transparent. In particular therefore where the requests for information concern the process of and policy behind the awards of honours and dignities authorities are encouraged to take a positive approach in their application of the public interest test and disclose the maximum information possible.

Section 37: the DCA's guidance

Communications with Her Majesty

The DCA's *full exemptions guidance on section 37*, ch 2, para 2.1 sets out the sort of information on departmental files which will need to be considered: **6.211H**

(a) direct communications between the Sovereign or other members of the Royal Family and government Ministers;
(b) correspondence between the Royal Households and either Ministers or officials;
(c) notes, records, or agendas of ministerial audiences (that is private meetings between a member of the Royal Family and one or more Ministers, although the term 'audience' may not appear on the record itself);
(d) material detailing possible contents of correspondence or discussion with the Sovereign, other members of the Royal Family, or their households;
(e) material which has been, or will be shown to Her Majesty;
(f) material concerning the drafting of broadcast statements, speeches and messages sent by or on behalf of the Sovereign or other members of the Royal Family.

Awarding of honours

6.211I The section does not apply to judicial appointments or the appointment of Queen's Counsel.

6.211J Senior Church of England appointments are unique due to the nature of the Church of England as the established Church, the DCA's *full exemptions guidance on section 37* says at para 3.6. The appointments all involve correspondence between the Crown Appointments Office in No 10, the Prime Minister and the Queen and information regarding preferred and other candidates will often be extremely sensitive, as will material issued in the appointment process and the nature of the discussions regarding the appointments. Disclosure of sensitive information about appointments would subject those involved in the process to considerable pressure from or on behalf of individuals or from pressure groups within and outside the Church. Archbishops and three senior diocesan bishops have a right to sit in the House of Lords on their appointment and 21 of the remaining diocesan bishops have a seat in the House of Lords at any one time, according to their seniority and length of service. The pressures which would arise in relation to these appointments are therefore likely to be particularly great. The effect might be to constrain the appointment process, which would not be in the public interest. It could be detrimental to the relationship between the Church and the state as a whole in that it could undermine the balance that has been struck between them. The public interest against disclosure of such information is therefore particularly strong.

Section 38: health and safety

6.212 The Information Commissioner has issued decision notices in the cases of *Chief Police Officer for Hampshire Constabulary*, case reference FS50068017 (2 August 2005); *Chief Police Officer for Hampshire Constabulary*, case reference FS50067279 (2 August 2005); and *Chief Police Officer Essex Constabulary*, case reference FS50068601 (3 August 2005), involving section 38. These cases are discussed further at Supplement para 7.77J.

The following new headings and paragraphs come after paragraph 6.217 of the Main Work:

Section 38: the Information Commissioner's guidance

6.217A The Information Commissioner's *awareness guidance no 19* deals with health and safety.

What information is covered?

6.217B Insofar as the information under request involves living individuals it will also be covered by section 40 relating to personal information. The focus of section 38 will be on other information the disclosure of which might pose a risk. This may include:

(a) information about sites of controversial scientific research which may be targets for sabotage. There may be well-founded fears that if the location of such sites were disclosed to individuals or groups opposed to research there would be risks to the physical safety of staff;
(b) information relating to the dead (not, therefore, covered by the personal information exemption) disclosure of which might endanger the mental health of surviving relatives;
(c) information disclosure of which might have an adverse effect on public health.

The prejudice test

The word 'endanger' is used in section 38 instead of the word 'prejudice' which is used in many of the exemptions. The word 'endanger' is perhaps used because it has more meaning in the context of the individual than 'prejudice'. The guidance is that the Commissioner does not consider that the use of the term 'endanger' represents a departure from the test of prejudice to which section 38 is subject. **6.217C**

The public interest test

The guidance gives a helpful example of how the test might be applied. A health authority is asked to disclose details of research which it has commissioned into the safety of a particular medication. Disclosure might endanger public safety if the disclosure caused people to discontinue the medication. Nevertheless, there may be a stronger overall public interest in disclosing the information to enable wider public debate about how health authorities ensure the safety of medicines that are prescribed to the public. **6.217D**

Assessing the risk to the mental health of any person

Awareness guidance no 19 says at p 4 that it would be wrong to equate endangerment of mental health with the causing of distress. There are some obvious difficulties for FOI officers and other officials who have no medical training or any particular knowledge of the individual whose health might be endangered by a disclosure in judging whether it is legitimate to rely upon this part of the exemption. The difficulty is not insuperable. The Commissioner advises that, if a public authority wishes to withhold information because it poses a risk to mental health, it should consider obtaining an expert opinion confirming that the disclosure of the information would be likely to endanger the mental health of the applicant or any other individual. **6.217E**

Section 38: the DCA's guidance

6.217F The DCA's *full exemptions guidance on section 38* gives some elucidation of the terms used in the section:

(a) *likely to endanger*—in this context can be interpreted as meaning 'likely to put someone's health or safety at risk, or at greater risk'. It connotes risk of harm rather than harm itself; *likely to* suggests a result which could reasonably be expected, but which does not have to be specifically foreseeable.

(b) *physical or mental health*—may and should be given a natural, general meaning to include bodily or psychological integrity and well-being. There are signs (particularly in Commonwealth cases) that courts take a broad approach to these kinds of definitions where the protection of these sorts of interest are concerned and they may include such matters as physical or mental impairment, injury, illness or disease (including the recurrence, aggravation, acceleration, exacerbation, or deterioration of any pre-existing impairment, injury, illness, or disease). Mental health in particular may in an appropriate case include emotional and psychological well-being, and should not necessarily be artificially limited to mental consequences identifiable by some particular medical or psychiatric pathology, nor to what is often called shock or trauma.

(c) *safety*—should be given its ordinary (OED) dictionary meaning of 'the state of being protected from or guarded against any hurt or injury; freedom from danger'. As in the present context the term concerns the safety of individuals, a broad approach is again likely to be right.

The public interest test

6.217G There is a public interest in disclosing information in order to reduce potential danger to people and to increase their personal freedom by making them aware of risks and enabling them to take appropriate action. If the recommendations and information supplied by the departments with specific responsibilities to inform the public of health and safety issues are to be trusted and acted upon, that relies on a level of trust which may in turn be enhanced by a high level of disclosure. While it could be argued, for example, that it is in the public interest to withhold speculative or incomplete information about the efficacy and safety of a particular drug on the grounds that it could dissuade people who need to take it from taking it (thereby endangering their health), this will need to be carefully balanced against the importance of giving the fullest possible information to individuals about matters relating to their own health, and the risk that withholding the information is likely to give the impression that there is something to hide that could undermine public trust, and consequently the Government's ability to persuade people to follow its recommendations. This is an area in which the public interest in disclosure may be particularly strong.

Section 39: environmental information

The Environmental Information Regulations 2004, SI 2004 No 3391, were made on 21 December 2004 and came into force on 1 January 2005. The regulations are discussed in Supplement ch 16 and the text of the regulations ('the EIR') is in Supplement Appendix G2. **6.219**

The following new heading and paragraphs come after paragraph 6.221 of the Main Work:

Section 39: the DCA's guidance

The DCA's *full exemptions guidance on section 39*, ch 2, para 2.1 says that the effect of this section is to ensure that requests for 'environmental information' within the meaning of the EIR are dealt with under the separate access regime set out by those regulations. **6.221A**

Under the EIR, 'environmental information' has the same meaning as in Article 2(1) of the Council Directive 2003/4/EC. The definition is discussed at Supplement para 16.73A. At Supplement para 16.73B DEFRA's guidance on the definition is discussed. There is no geographical restriction on the definition. So for example, information on the estates of embassies or an overseas aid programme for schemes which impact upon the environment are included within the definition of environmental information for the purpose of these regulations. **6.221B**

Experience from the implementation of the environmental information regime has established that environmental information is interpreted very broadly. The Government has treated all information relating to GM crop trials, to pesticide testing, to diseased cattle and to land-use planning (including the reasons for decisions to approve as well as decisions to refuse planning permission) as environmental information. **6.221C**

Section 42: legal professional privilege

The Information Commissioner has issued a decision notice in the case of *Standards Board for England*, case reference FS50064699 (1 August 2005), involving section 42. This case is discussed further at Supplement para 7.77I. **6.223**

The following new headings and paragraphs come after paragraph 6.228 of the Main Work:

Section 42: the Information Commissioner's guidance

The Information Commissioner's *awareness guidance no 4* deals with legal professional privilege. Legal professional privilege is based on the need to protect a client's confidence that any communication with his or her professional legal adviser will be treated in confidence and not revealed without consent. This is to **6.228A** ensure the greatest chance that justice is administered to the client. Legal professional privilege protects communications between a professional legal adviser and client from being disclosed, even to a court of law.

6.228B Professional legal advisers include qualified solicitors, barristers, and licensed conveyancers. The Information Commissioner accepts that for the purposes of the Act legal executives who hold a professional qualification from the Institute of Legal Executives are to be treated in the same manner as solicitors.

6.228C The privilege attaches to the information itself and belongs to the client. Although there are circumstances in which a professional legal adviser ceases to be bound by privilege, an adviser cannot waive the privilege without instructions from his client.

Cases where privilege ceases to exist

6.228D Privilege exists in order to advance justice. The guidance is that it does not apply to information that conceals fraud, crime or the innocence of an individual. Loss of it occurs even where the professional legal adviser is unaware of the wrongdoing. Advice warning a client about the dangers of a prosecution would normally attract privilege since the fraud or crime has yet to be committed, but once a professional legal adviser becomes aware of the wrongdoing the associated information ceases to be privileged. Furthermore, a distinction must be drawn between the legal advice given after a wrongdoing has been committed, which would normally attract privilege, and advice given with the intention of furthering a criminal purpose before a wrongdoing, which does not.

The purpose test

6.228E For legal professional privilege to apply, information must have been created or brought together for the dominant purpose of litigation or the seeking or provision of legal advice.

6.228F The Information Commissioner's *awareness guidance no 4*, p 5 says that the issue of 'dominant purpose' of communications was considered by the Court of Appeal in *Three Rivers District Council v Governor and Company of the Bank of England.* The Court of Appeal confirmed that the purpose and scope of advice privilege is to enable legal advice to be sought and given in confidence about legal rights and obligations because this is the subject-matter that may form the basis of litigation. The emphasis of this case was on the distinction between advice regarding presentational issues, and thus (according to the Court of Appeal) not privileged, and advice concerning the substantive rights and obligations of the Bank, which was privileged. However, that decision has now been reversed by the House of Lords: [2005] 1 AC 610. See Supplement paras 18.46E–18.46J. The guidance has to be read with that in mind.

'The likelihood test'

For information to attract litigation privilege it must have been created or brought together for the purposes of litigation or anticipated litigation. The courts have ruled that there must be a 'reasonable prospect of litigation' at the time the information was created or brought together. **6.228G**

The public interest test

Legal departments and professional legal advisers are becoming increasingly involved in policy development. The disclosure of such communications would allow individuals to understand the reasons for decisions made by the relevant authority. Since *awareness guidance no 4* was written the House of Lords in *Three Rivers District Council v Bank of England (No 6)* [2005] 1 AC 610 has decided that 'legal advice' extended to advice as to what should prudently and sensibly be done in a 'a relevant legal context'. See Supplement paras 18.46E–18.46J. The Information Commissioner's guidance that policy advice from professional legal advisers not being about the substantive rights and obligations of an authority should not be considered privileged will need to be reconsidered in the light of this decision. **6.228H**

The next point the Commissioner makes, at p 8 of *awareness guidance no 4*, remains a good one. One of the themes of the Act is to make public 'reasons for decisions' made by an authority and the Information Commissioner says he would expect public authorities to consider the position in the light of this, the new environment of openness. In making its decision the authority will have to weigh up the significance of its decision, including the number of people affected, and the public interest in promoting public debate and increasing accountability, against the importance of maintaining the privilege. **6.228I**

Legal professional privilege is one of the guarantees of a fair trial and as such there are powerful public interest arguments in support of its not being waived in many cases. The Commissioner would not expect privilege to be waived in cases where disclosure might prejudice the right either of the authority itself or of any third party to obtain access to justice. **6.228J**

Section 42: the DCA's guidance

The DCA's *full exemptions guidance on section 42*, ch 2, para 2.2 says that legal professional privilege has been established by the courts in recognition of the fact that there is an important public interest in a person being able to consult his lawyer in confidence. As Lord Taylor of Gosforth CJ said in *R v Derby Magistrates' Court ex parte B* [1996] 1 AC 487 at 507: **6.228K**

> The client must be sure that what he tells his lawyer in confidence will never be revealed without his consent. Legal professional privilege is thus much more than an

ordinary rule of evidence, limited in its application to the facts of a particular case. It is a fundamental condition on which the administration of justice as a whole rests.

6.228L Section 42 of the Act applies to information in respect of which a claim to legal professional privilege could be maintained in legal proceedings. It does not require that any legal proceedings are in fact afoot, although it will certainly be of potential relevance where that is the case. The exemption focuses instead on the kind of information which would be protected if legal proceedings were afoot. It applies the legal professional privilege test in the separate context of the Freedom of Information Act.

6.228M The guidance says at ch 2, para 2.7 that the operation of this exemption is complex and in some cases potentially uncertain. Legal professional privilege is a principle of common law. The precise details of the principle are still evolving in developing case law. It is important that legal advice is taken where it appears that information which is the subject of a request might fall under section 42.

Scotland

6.228N Section 42 refers to the Scottish rule of confidentiality of communications. Appendix B to the DCA's *full exemptions guidance on section 42* contains a summary of the rule of confidentiality of communications in Scotland.

Section 43: commercial interests

6.229 In *National Maritime Museum*, case reference FS500634478 (20 June 2005), a decision of the Information Commissioner, the complainant sought the documents and correspondence relating to any payments made to Conrad Shawcross for his exhibition 'Continuum' which was staged at Queen's House at the Museum. The Museum refused to disclose the information, relying on section 43(2) and deciding that disclosure would prejudice the commercial interests of both the Museum and Mr Shawcross. The Commissioner agreed that the commercial interests exemption applied and there was potential prejudice to both the Museum and Mr Shawcross. He then considered, in the case of each of the Museum and Mr Shawcross, whether the public interest came down on the side of disclosure.

The Museum

The Commissioner recognized the public interest in financial transparency and accountability where public authorities commission new works of art, particularly where that is not their core activity. The commissioning of new works of art is not the Museum's core activity. He also recognized that the disclosure of the requested information might inform the debate about museum funding and charges since it relates to the choice the Museum has made to attract greater numbers and generate revenue in competition with other venues.

However, the Commissioner understood that at the time of the request in January 2005 the Museum was involved in active negotiations with another artist for its New Visions programme. The Commissioner recognized that the premature release of the financial arrangement between the Museum and Mr Shawcross would be likely to prejudice the Museum's bargaining position to such an extent that the public interest in maintaining the exemption outweighed the public interest in releasing the information. The Commissioner gave particular weight to the fact that the Museum was dealing with public funds and needed to ensure value for money. The Commissioner also considered that the likelihood of prejudice would diminish with time and that with the conclusion of active negotiations with the new artist, any prejudice to the Museum's commercial interests would no longer outweigh the public interest in releasing the information which the complainant requested.

Mr Shawcross

The Commissioner recognized the potential prejudice to Mr Shawcross's commercial interests by the release of the requested information. The Commissioner also acknowledged the public interest in encouraging new artists and entrepreneurs to flourish and the role that public authorities can play in bringing them to wider attention. By withholding this information until Mr Shawcross had negotiated his next sale or commission, arguably the public authority would be affording Mr Shawcross an important degree of commercial protection at a crucial stage of his career. However, the Commissioner was of the view that those who engage in commercial activity with the public sector must expect that there may be a greater degree of openness about the details of those activities than had previously been the case prior to the Act coming into force. The Commissioner was not persuaded that the potential prejudice to Mr Shawcross's commercial interests was, of itself, sufficient reason to maintain the exemption.

This is an important decision because it gives some insight into the way the Commissioner will judge the public interest. It is also interesting because it shows that both the authority (the Museum) and the Commissioner were required, under section 43(2), to consider the position of Mr Shawcross, though he was not the person to whom the request was made.

Section 43 does not apply beyond 30 years, the point at which information becomes a historical record, see section 63 of the Act and Main Work para 8.19.

The following new paragraphs come at the end of section D of the Main Work:

Section 43: the Information Commissioner's guidance

The Information Commissioner's *awareness guidance no 5* is about commercial **6.239A**
interests. He makes the general point that in one respect the Act treats 'trade

secrets' differently from other information, disclosure of which might harm a commercial interest in that whether or not it is decided to disclose, the public authority must always confirm or deny that it holds the information.

Trade secrets

6.239B In attempting to decide whether information is in fact a trade secret, it may be helpful to ask a number of questions, including:

(a) Is the information used for the purposes of a trade? Information may be commercially sensitive without being the sort of secret which gives a company a 'competitive edge' over its rivals. For instance a public authority may hold information about the state of repair of a manufacturer's equipment. While information about the design of the equipment may constitute a trade secret, information about its state of repair would not (even though it may be commercially sensitive) since it is not information which is used to help generate profits.
(b) Is it obvious from the nature of the information or, if not, has the owner made it clear that he or she considers that releasing the information would cause them harm or be advantageous to their rivals?
(c) Is the information already known?
(d) How easy would it be for competitors to discover or reproduce the information for themselves?

See *IC awareness guidance no 5*, pp 3 and 4.

Commercial interests

6.239C Trade secrets are one example of commercial interests. The Commissioner says the concept is, however, far wider. A commercial interest relates to a person's ability to participate successfully in a commercial activity, for example the purchase and sale of goods. The Commissioner goes on to point out that there is an important distinction between commercial interests and financial interests. While there may be many cases where prejudice to the financial interests of a public authority may affect its commercial interests, this is not necessarily the case: see *IC awareness guidance no 5*, p 4.

6.239D The guidance (at p 5) lists a number of reasons why a public authority may possess commercial information:

(a) procurement—public authorities are major purchasers of goods and services and will hold a wide range of information relating to the procurement process. This could be procurement plans, information provided during a tendering process, including information contained in unsuccessful bids, right through to the details of the contract with the successful company. There may also be details of how a contractor has performed under a contract;

(b) regulation—public authorities may be supplied with information in order to perform their functions, eg issuing licences. Alternatively, they may obtain commercial information whilst investigating potential breaches of regulations for which they are responsible;
(c) the public authority's own commercial activities;
(d) policy development;
(e) policy implementation;
(f) private finance initiatives;
(g) public–private partnerships.

In each case it is necessary to consider whether the release of such information would prejudice someone's commercial interests, ie it is necessary to apply the test of prejudice. It will then be necessary to apply the public interest test.

The test of prejudice. The Commissioner suggests that the approach to this should be to consider the questions that need to be asked in order to determine the impact of releasing the information: **6.239E**

(a) does the information relate to, or could it impact on a commercial activity?
(b) is that commercial activity conducted in a competitive environment?
(c) would there be damage to reputation or business confidence? (Note that there is no exemption for embarrassment.)
(d) whose commercial interests are affected?
(e) is the information commercially sensitive? Companies compete by offering something different from their rivals. That difference will often be the price at which the goods or services can be delivered but that difference may also relate to quality or specification. Information which identifies how a company has developed that unique element is more likely to be commercially sensitive. For example, where a company competes on price, it may be that the final price charged is readily available; however, information disclosing how the company is able to offer the product at that price may not be. Any information revealing profit margins is likely to be commercially sensitive.
(f) what is the likelihood of prejudice being caused?

The Commissioner adds that as to likelihood, while prejudice need not be certain, there must be a significant risk rather than a remote possibility of prejudice: see *IC awareness guidance no 5*, p 7.

The public interest test

The guidance is that in practice this is likely to involve weighing the prejudice caused by possible disclosure against the likely benefit to the applicant and the wider public. Factors to be taken into account include: **6.239F**

(a) accountability for the spending of public money. Where a public authority is purchasing goods or services there is a public interest in ensuring they get value for money. This is particularly true at a time when there is a public debate around the increasing role private companies have in delivering public services;

(b) protection of the public. There would be strong public interest arguments for allowing access to information which would help to protect the public from unsafe products or unscrupulous practices, even though this might involve revealing a trade secret or other information whose disclosure might harm the commercial interest of a company;

(c) the circumstances under which the public authority obtained the information. Where the information was obtained using statutory powers the disclosure of that information may not prejudice the obtaining of similar information in the future;

(d) competition issues. There is a public interest in ensuring that firms are able to compete fairly. Public authorities should be wary of accepting arguments that the potential for commercial information to be released would reduce the number of companies willing to do business with the public sector, leading to reduced competition and increased costs. In practice, many companies may be prepared to accept greater public access to information about their business as a cost of doing business with the public sector. Increasing information about the tendering process may in fact encourage more potential suppliers to enter the market. A better understanding of the process, the award criteria, knowledge of how successful bids have been put together, could also lead to improved bids in the future. This will lead to more competition and tend to decrease the costs to the authority. Indeed, where a contract comes up for renewal limiting this kind of information is likely to favour the current contractor and so may be anti-competitive.

See *IC's awareness guidance no 5*, pp 7–9.

Timing

6.239G Very often, in a commercial environment, the timing of the disclosure will be of critical importance. Take the example of information submitted during the tendering process, which is more likely to be commercially sensitive whilst the tendering process is ongoing than after the contract has been awarded. Simply because a request was refused at one point in time does not mean that the information can be permanently withheld. Market conditions will change and information relating to costs may very quickly become out of date: *IC's awareness guidance no 5*, p 9.

This guidance is well illustrated by the *National Maritime Museum* case, reference FS500634478 (20 June 2005): see Supplement para 6.229.

Consultation

6.239H Time for consultation will be limited once a request for information has been received. The guidance therefore is for public authorities to have discussions, now, with major suppliers and contractors: to ask them what disclosure might harm their businesses. The guidance goes on to say that it might be helpful to agree with suppliers and contractors what consultation should take place in the future when requests for information are made.

During the procurement process public authorities may be asked by contractors to accept confidentiality clauses which attempt to prevent the disclosure of information. In many cases such a clause may be perfectly proper and serve to make clear that information which the supplier considers should not be made public, and that which can be freely disclosed. Clauses may also be helpful in providing a framework for redress in the event of an unauthorized disclosure. **6.239I**

There is, however, a risk that contractors and suppliers will propose blanket clauses which would prevent the disclosure of any information. The Information Commissioner warns that unless clauses are necessary or reasonable he will order disclosure. On the other hand, if the issue is properly addressed as contracts are negotiated, confidentiality clauses may prove of real assistance in identifying prejudice to a third party's commercial interests: see *IC's awareness guidance no 5*, pp 10–11. **6.239J**

Public sector contracts

The annex to *IC's awareness guidance no 5* deals with public sector contracts. **6.239K**

At the start of a procurement exercise there will be a number of opportunities for public authorities to inform contractors about their responsibilities under the Act. One approach would be to identify clearly what information held in connection with the tendering process or the subsequent performance of a contract, or contained in the contract, is commercially sensitive and over what period that information is likely to remain sensitive. Once identified the information could be listed in a schedule or appendix to the contract. This would have the advantage of providing the contractor with a degree of certainty as to what information is likely to be withheld in response to a request (subject to the public interest test). It would also assist the public authority in determining whether an exemption applies within the time limit allowed. **6.239L**

Alternatively, a public authority may wish to provide a more general assurance to the contractor that commercially sensitive information will be protected (subject to the public interest test). **6.239M**

The Commissioner recognizes that there is a place for confidentiality clauses where they serve to identify information that may be exempt. However, a confidentiality clause which provides a false sense of security that information can be withheld when it is in fact not covered by an exemption in the Act will only damage commercial relationships. Public authorities will, therefore need to be very careful when negotiating such clauses. By agreeing to wide definitions of what constitutes 'confidential information' or information which may prejudice **6.239N** commercial interests, the public authority may unwittingly place itself in a future dilemma when faced with a request for information covered by such a clause: to breach its statutory obligation or to breach a contract.

6.239O As to existing contracts, a public authority may consider it wise to review high-value contracts or other contracts that are likely to attract requests, for example those implementing or relating to controversial policies. When reviewing such contracts public authorities should aim to advise contractors as to the circumstances in which information may be released under the Act and to establish consultation procedures.

Section 43: the DCA's guidance

6.239P There is considerable overlap between the guidance offered by the Information Commissioner and that offered by the Department. On the definition of trade secrets and commercial interests the DCA adds nothing. On the question of *prejudice* the DCA gives helpful examples of information the disclosure of which may have a particular potential to damage commercial interests:

(a) research and plans relating to a potential new product;
(b) product manufacturing costs information;
(c) strategic business plans, including for example, plans to enter, develop or withdraw from a product or geographical market sector;
(d) marketing plans, to promote a new or existing product;
(e) information relating to the preparation of a competitive bid;
(f) information about the financial and business viability of a company; and
(g) information provided to a public authority in respect of an application for a licence or as a requirement of a licence condition or under a regulatory regime: see DCA's *full exemptions guidance on section 43*, ch 3, para 3.5.

Prejudice to a third party's commercial interests

6.239Q Prejudice to third-party interests has to be assessed objectively and by the authority. However, the third party's perspective as to the likely effects of disclosure (established at the outset of a transaction and when contemplating disclosure) must be taken into account in that process: see DCA's *full exemptions guidance on section 43*, ch 3, para 3.9.

The public interest test

6.239R The DCA's approach to the public interest is similar to that of the Information Commissioner. The guidance is that there is generally speaking a public interest in the disclosure of commercial information in order to ensure that:

(a) there is transparency in the accountability of public funds;
(b) there is proper scrutiny of government actions in carrying out licensing functions in accordance with published policy;

(c) public money is being used effectively, and departments are getting value for money when purchasing goods and services;
(d) departments' commercial activities, including the procurement process are conducted in an open and honest way; and
(e) business can respond better to government opportunities.

Factors that weigh in favour of the public interest in withholding information in this area are: **6.239S**

(a) where disclosure would make it less likely that companies, or individuals, would provide the department with commercially sensitive information in the future and thus undermine the ability of the department/agency to fulfil its role;
(b) where disclosure would be likely to prejudice the commercial interests of the department by affecting adversely its bargaining position during contractual negotiations, which would result in the less effective use of public money;
(c) where disclosure would make it more difficult for individuals to be able to conduct commercial transactions or have other dealings with public bodies which are not a typical commercial transaction—for example where an organization obtains a grant or financial assistance from a public authority—without fear of suffering commercially as a result. It would not, for example, be in the public interest to disclose information about a particular commercial body if that information was not common knowledge and would be likely to be used by competitors in a particular market to gain a competitive advantage: see DCA's *full exemptions guidance on section 43*, ch 3, para 3.23.

Procurement

Annex A to the DCA's guidance on section 43 deals with procurement-related information and lists a number of examples where the application of section 43 should be considered: **6.239T**

(a) information relating to general/preliminary procurement activities, eg market sounding information; information relating to programme project procurement strategies; and contextual information about the authority, its business objectives and plans;
(b) information relating to supplier selection, eg qualification information for potential bidders; information about requirements including specifications; details of the qualification process; and details of qualified bidders;
(c) information relating to contract negotiation and award, eg bids; papers about capabilities of bidders, evaluations of bids, negotiating briefs and recommendations; the contract; information about successful bid and bidder, and information about other bids and bidders: and
(d) information relating to contract performance and post-contract activities, eg information about implementation; information about performance;

information about contract amendments with supporting papers; and any information which may be provided and reviewed by third parties (eg consultants/auditors).

6.239U Annex A further points out that authorities will need to take the public procurement regime into account when considering disclosure of information. The guidance draws attention to the EC Public Procurement Directives, implemented in the Public Works Contracts Regulations 1991, the Public Service Contracts Regulations 1993, and the Public Supply Contracts Regulations 1995, which recognize that the interest of suppliers in sensitive information supplied by them in a procurement must be respected and that both the interests of suppliers and the public interest may mean that certain information relating to a contract award is withheld from publication. The new Public Procurement Directive (2004/18EC), expected to be implemented in the United Kingdom from 1 January 2006, continues to recognize these interests and prohibits the disclosure of information which suppliers have designated as confidential in a procurement, except as provided by the Directive and national law.

6.239V Annex A concludes by drawing some lessons from overseas:

> Experience of the enforcement of access to information legislation in Ireland is instructive here, although care should be taken not simply to read across from the Irish experience, as the FOI regime is similar but not identical. The picture in Ireland tends to support the view that the public interest in the disclosure of procurement related information is not sufficiently strong to override the harm that may be done to commercial interests before the award of the contract. However, the public interest in making available information after the award of the contract—such as the total tender price and the evaluation details of the successful tenderer, along with information about the fee rates and other details necessary to understand the nature of the services contracted—was found to be much stronger.

The Irish authority referred to seems to be *Henry Ford & Sons Limited, Nissan Ireland and Motor Distributors Ltd v Office of Public Works* [1999] IEIC 12 (31 March 1999), but see also *McDonnell Douglas Corp v US Department of the Air Force* 375 F 3d 1182 (DC Cir 2004) and the other US cases considered at Supplement paras 17.63A–17.63B. The guidance concludes by saying it is vital that where a decision is taken to withhold information there are clear reasons for refusing to disclose information which are capable of standing up to scrutiny by the Information Commissioner and ultimately the courts: see DCA's *full exemptions advice on section 43*, annex A.

Gateway reviews

6.239W Annex B to the DCA's guidance on section 43 deals with Gateway Reviews. It explains that, in simple terms, a Gateway Review is a review of an acquisition programme or procurement project carried out at a key decision point by a team of experienced people independent of the project team. The review is carried out on a confidential basis. The guidance says this:

> The clear message that is emerging from departments is that the OGC Gateway Process has produced substantial benefits and is, increasingly, adding significant value to those who are trying to implement successful programmes and projects. Moreover, it has been argued that the process is one of the most useful tools for achieving the delivery agenda. In view of this, it is essential that the value added by the review process is not impaired; the review process relies on an open and honest approach and provision of a report for the sole use of the Senior Responsible Owner for the programme or project under review.
>
> Departments will therefore need to consider any requests for the disclosure of Gateway information very carefully if the considerable benefits the OGC Gateway process has delivered to date, are not to be jeopardised.

This remarkable piece of prose seems calculated to ensure that departments do not disclose information about Gateway reviews notwithstanding that it is followed by the somewhat perfunctory statement that 'This is not to imply that the presumption in the Act in favour of disclosure of information does not apply to Gateway information'. Departments will have to make up their own minds on where the public interest lies in each individual case which they have to consider on its own facts and it is questionable whether advice couched in such partisan terms is helpful.

The Information Commissioner and the Government have entered into a **6.239X** Memorandum of Understanding which sets out the way in which they hope to operate the Act. For the text of the Memorandum, see Supplement Appendix L.

7

ENFORCEMENT

D. Enforcement

Complaints procedure

Chapter 9 of the Department of Constitutional Affairs' *Procedural guidance* deals with internal reviews. It provides that if a department receives a complaint from a dissatisfied applicant the department's FOI specialist must be contacted and it may be a trigger for the involvement of senior officials, Ministers, or the Clearing House. (For information on the Clearing House, see Supplement paras 5.67A–5.67D.) **7.63**

The DCA's guidance states that the internal review *may* be conducted by a person who was not party to the original decision and each department should give active consideration to training and maintaining a list of staff of suitable seniority who can be called upon to conduct internal reviews. This gives a regrettably different emphasis from the second edition of the section 45 Code which says at para 41 that, where practicable, the complaints procedure should be handled by a person who was not party to the original decision. The guidance states that, as a minimum, all internal reviews must consider the information released against the information requested and make a full review of the papers associated with the original application. It is also best practice that the internal reviewer discuss the decisions made with the staff member, or members, who dealt with the original application in order to build a full picture of how the decisions were made. After concluding the internal review, the reviewer should discuss his conclusions with the departmental FOI specialist in order to ensure that any internal processes which may need to be altered are fully reviewed.

Internal reviews have to be completed in a reasonable timescale. As a matter of best practice, the DCA guidance recommends that departments should aim to deal with (i) simple cases within two to three weeks of receiving the complaint; and (ii) complex reviews, in particular where it is necessary to reconsider the public interest test, within six weeks. Irrespective of the outcome, the guidance says that departments must ensure that the final outcome of the review is recorded.

Application for decision by the Information Commissioner

The following new heading and paragraphs come after paragraph 7.77 of the Main Work:

The Information Commissioner's first decisions

The Information Commissioner's decisions are available on his website at http://www.information commissioner.gov.uk.

Enforcement notice—adverse effect on amenity

7.77A In the *Bridgnorth District Council* case, case reference FS50062329 (12 July 2005) the complainant requested the right to inspect information contained in an enforcement file relating to a piece of land he owned. The Council, following a complaint from a member of the public about the condition of the land, had carried out an investigation under the Town and Country Planning Act 1990, section 215, to decide whether or not to serve an enforcement notice. The Council treated the request as one made under the Freedom of Information Act and refused to give the information, relying on section 32 (2)(c) (law enforcement).

7.77B The Information Commissioner advised that the request should be dealt with under the Environmental Information Regulations (the 'EIR'). He did so because the information in the file related to the exercise of a statutory power in circumstances where it was alleged that the condition of land was having an adverse effect on the amenity of the area.

The Council then relied on regulation 12(5)(f) of the EIR, on the ground that the disclosure would adversely affect the interests of someone who had supplied the information on a voluntary basis; and on regulation 12(5)(b), on the ground that the disclosure would adversely affect a criminal investigation. The Commissioner held that the case under regulation 12(5)(b) was not made out because an enforcement notice is a civil remedy. **7.77C**

As to regulation 12(5)(f), the third party had advised the Council that it was concerned that releasing its identity would have an undesirable impact on its relationship with the complainant, so that the exception was engaged. **7.77D**

The Commissioner therefore considered the public interest test. He recognized that there is a very real public interest in safeguarding the free flow of information to the local planning authority, on which it relies in order to carry out its regulatory functions under planning legislation. The Commissioner was satisfied that people would be deterred from volunteering such information if they were concerned that their identities could be revealed and that this would hinder the ability of the local planning authority to deal with such planning issues. **7.77E**

In the light of this, the Commissioner was satisfied that the public interest in maintaining the exception in relation to the identity of the third party outweighed the public interest in disclosing that information. The decision notice required the Council to provide access to all the information in the enforcement file apart from that which revealed the identity of the third party. **7.77F**

Inquiry about allotments—fees

In the case of *Ferryhill Town Council*, case reference FS50075378 (14 July 2005) the complainant requested detailed information in relation to the Council's allotments. The information he wanted to know included the vacancies which existed on each of the Council's allotment sites, the number of people who had applied for allotments over the past two years, information about the proposed sale of the Store House site, information about the lease of another site, details of a meeting on 12 May, and full details of the income and expenditure relating to all of the Council's recreation services, with each service shown separately. **7.77G**

The complainant said that he was dissatisfied with the fees notice issued by the Council in response to his request. The Council said that the cost of complying with the request would exceed the appropriate limit as identified in the Fees Regulations, but it agreed to supply the information on receipt of the full costs. The Commissioner, after investigation, was satisfied that the Council had estimated the costs in accordance with the regulations. However, it had not given the complainant the opportunity to refine his request, or offered to supply him with the information which could be supplied within the appropriate limit. **7.77H**

The decision notice therefore stipulated that the Council must offer appropriate advice and assistance to the complainant.

Complaint about conduct—personal information—legal professional privilege

7.77I In the case of *Standards Board for England*, case reference FS50064699 (1 August 2005), the complainant requested information relating to the investigation of a complaint about him. The Standards Board refused this request, on the grounds that the information consisted of personal data and that the exemption in section 40 applied, some of the information relating to the complainant and some to third parties, and that in either case disclosure would breach the Data Protection Act. Having conducted an internal review, the Board also cited additional exemptions, namely those covering information subject to legal professional privilege (section 42) and information whose disclosure is prohibited by law (section 44) because disclosure would contravene section 63 of the Local Government Act 2000. The Commissioner considered that the public authority had handled the request correctly and that it was entitled to rely on the exemptions cited. The complainant has lodged an appeal.

Speed traps

7.77J The Information Commissioner issued three decision notices in respect of requests for information from police authorities about speed cameras in August 2005. The three cases are:

(a) *The Chief Police Officer for Hampshire Constabulary*, case reference FS50068017 (2 August 2005);
(b) *The Chief Police Officer for Hampshire Constabulary*, case reference FS50067279 (2 August 2005);
(c) *The Chief Officer of Police Essex Constabulary*, case reference FS50068601 (3 August 2005).

The statements of reasons in the three cases cover much the same ground.

7.77K In case no 017 the following information was requested: data on the number of speeding tickets issued (and monetary revenue raised) per camera site across Portsmouth, Gosport, Havant and Fareham in 2004–05.

7.77L In case no 279 the complainant requested the following information about two fixed speed cameras located on Mountbatten Way (A35) in Southampton:

(1) the number of offences detected by each camera at this site for the period covered by the 2003–04 annual review;
(2) the revenue generated by each camera at this site for the period covered by the 2003–04 annual review.

In case no 601 the request was for the identity of the 20 fixed camera locations in Essex that catch the most drivers speeding; how many drivers per month or year are caught at each of those locations; and how much money was raised from each location per month or year. 7.77M

In each of the three cases the police refused to disclose the information and relied on the exemptions in section 31 (law enforcement) and section 38 (health and safety). In each of the three cases the Information Commissioner decided that both of these exemptions applied, and in each of the three cases he decided that the public interest came down on the side of maintaining the exemptions. 7.77N

In the statement of reasons in case no 017, the Information Commissioner said: 7.77O

> With regard to the exemption under section 31 the Commissioner recognises the concern raised by HC [the Hampshire Constabulary], that the requested information contains working practices which, if known, would have an impact on operating policing. Camera housings are located at sites that have a history of significant casualties caused by speeding. Currently, the effectiveness of the system relies on the perception that all cameras are active whereas some two thirds of housings contain dummy cameras. This perception allows the police to keep traffic speeds lower by carrying out minimal real enforcement. Site specific information such as that requested by NE would indicate the differing levels of speed enforcement that appertained throughout the area. With such information, drivers could ascertain those locations where apprehension for speeding was less likely. This could seriously affect the level of compliance owing to the likely increase in the level of speeding.
>
> With regard to the exemption under section 38 the Commissioner acknowledges the correlation between the amount of visible enforcement, increases in speed and increases in accidents. HC's evidence in support of withholding the information includes studies such as the three year analysis completed by University College London in 2004. This clearly shows that the presence of cameras significantly reduces injury accidents and deaths. HC's evidence from the UK Transport Research Laboratory shows that speed is the biggest single contributor to casualties on our roads. Their evidence from other UK traffic studies strongly indicates that higher speeds and increases in casualties result when the public becomes aware of sites that are never or seldom enforced. Consequently the Commissioner is of the opinion that the release of this information would jeopardise the safety of the road users due to the risk of increases in speeding and therefore agrees that the exemption under section 38 to withhold the requested information on safety grounds is appropriate.

Turning to the public interest test, the Commissioner was not persuaded that the public interest in disclosing site specific information outweighed the public interest in maintaining the exemptions. He believed that there was a stronger public interest in avoiding both the increased risk to the safety of individuals and the likely increase in non-compliance with road traffic laws. The Commissioner was also persuaded that the release of the requested information would require the public authority to take countermeasures to negate the increased risks that had been identified and that such countermeasures would entail an increase in public expenditure. 7.77P

7.77Q The statements of reasons in cases 279 and 601 were to the same effect.

Payments to a finance officer

7.77R In the case of *Corby Borough Council*, case reference FS50062124 (25 August 2005) the complainant asked Corby Borough Council for the total amount paid to the former Temporary Finance Officer, Gary Moss, by the former Chief Executive, Nigel Rudd.

7.77S In his statement of reasons, the Commissioner said that he was aware from the information in the public domain of the circumstances surrounding Mr Moss's employment. The Audit Commission had made critical comments about the way in which Mr Moss's appointment and continued employment had been handled by the Council's former Chief Executive. The daily rate agreed at the time of the appointment reflected the temporary nature of the position and the fact that it did not attract holiday pay or sickness benefits. However, the Chief Executive subsequently agreed to include holiday and pension contributions in the contract, without any reduction in the daily rate. In view of this, not only was the amount of money paid to Mr Moss significantly higher than the average rate paid to a full-time employee but it was above the range of rates agreed for this type of temporary placement.

7.77T The Council refused to supply the information sought, claiming that the exemption in section 40(2) of the Act (personal data) applied. It was common ground that the total monies paid to Mr Moss constituted his personal data. The Council argued that the disclosure of the information would breach the first data protection principle because it was unable to satisfy any of the conditions for processing stated in Schedule 2 to the Data Protection Act 1998. The Commissioner was satisfied that the Council could satisfy the sixth condition for processing listed in Schedule 2 to the 1998 Act, because there was a legitimate interest in making the public aware of the amount of money spent in employing senior staff. Further, in view of the circumstances of the case, the Commissioner was satisfied that disclosing the information would not be unwarranted by reason of prejudice to the rights, freedom, or legitimate interests of Mr Moss. In addition, it had been recognized for some time that individuals occupying senior posts within public authorities are likely to be subject to greater levels of scrutiny than those in more junior roles. This helps to ensure accountability of those individuals for their actions. The Commissioner was satisfied that Mr Moss could not reasonably have expected that the requested information would remain confidential. The Commissioner said that disclosure of the requested information should inform the ongoing debate on this issue and help to ensure that processes are implemented by the Council to avoid similar problems in the future. In the light of this, the Commissioner was satisfied that disclosing the information would not be unfair or unlawful.

Information already provided about care for the elderly

In the case of *Hertfordshire County Council*, case reference FS50063907 (25 August 2005) the complainant requested information relating to the care of his late mother by the Council's Social Services Department. The Council issued a refusal notice in which it stated that it required an extension to the usual 20-working-day period allowed for response, in order to consider the public interest in confirming or denying that it held the information requested. As a result of the Commissioner's intervention, the Council belatedly issued a second refusal notice in which it stated that the information was exempt by virtue of section 21 of the Act (information accessible to applicant by other means) because it had previously been provided to the complainant and was thus reasonably available to the applicant by other means. **7.77U**

The Commissioner found that the first refusal notice was inadequate. However, the Commissioner considered that the second refusal notice, albeit issued after a considerable delay, met the requirements of the Act. He also upheld the Council's reliance on section 21, after being provided with copies of significant documents which had previously been supplied to the complainant. **7.77V**

F. The Ministerial Veto

The DCA's guidance states that the Government has decided that the Ministerial veto should be used by the Cabinet in the first instance, ie a collective decision of the Cabinet. The guidance states that it may become appropriate to delegate this function to a Cabinet Committee, for example MISC 28: see the DCA's *full exemptions guidance*, introduction, ch 5, para 5.19. **7.103**

8

HISTORICAL RECORDS

A. The Public Records Act 1958: Transfer to the Public Record Office

On 1 April 2003, the Public Record Office and the Historical Manuscripts Commission came together to form The National Archives, which is both a government department in its own right, reporting directly to the Lord Chancellor, and an Executive Agency of the Department of Constitutional Affairs. However, the two bodies remain separate legal entities. Each is a public authority for the purposes of the Freedom of Information Act, with its own publication scheme. The Public Record Office's publication scheme is available on the National Archives website: http://www.nationalarchives.gov.uk/foi/pubscheme/pubscheme_printable.asp (8 September 2005). **8.03**

n10 A consultation paper entitled *Proposed National Records and Archives Legislation* was issued in August 2003. An analysis of the (generally positive) responses received was published in March 2004. Ongoing consideration is being given to legislative reform at both national and local levels, including in particular the introduction of specific provision for the management and preservation of digital records, and legal merger of the Public Record Office and the Historical Manuscripts Commission.

B. Access to Records in the Public Record Office

Statutory rights to access—the end to the 30-year rule

8.16–8.17 The amendment to section 5 of the Public Records Act 1958 came into force on 1 January 2005: SI 2004/3122.

'Open information'

The following new paragraphs come after paragraph 8.50 of the Main Work:

8.50A In December 2004 the National Archives published detailed guidance on the review of public records which have been selected for transfer to places of deposit (Part 1) and on the handling of access requests in respect of transferred public records (Part 2). The document, *Procedures and guidance relating to public records transferred to and held by places of deposit*, is available on the National Archives website at http://www.nationalarchives.gov.uk/policy/foi/pdf/foi_guide.pdf (8 September 2005).

8.50B Key points identified in Part 1 of the guidance are as follows.

- Managing the transfer of records is an essential part of the FOI process: section 1.2.
- There should be framework agreements between transferring authorities and places of deposit governing such issues as the timing and frequency of transfers, preparation of records for transfer, methods of transfer, and communication arrangements: para 1.2.2.
- To enable places of deposit to respond to access requests under the 2000 Act, they must be informed at the time of transfer what records are being transferred, what access conditions are recommended, and whom to contact at the creating authority if help is required: para 1.2.6. This information should be supplied by way of an inventory and a transfer form: section 1.5.
- Details of exemptions which creating authorities would like to be applied must be communicated by them at the point of transfer; all records will be considered as open to the public on transfer unless an exemption in the 2000 Act is identified and reasons for its application are given: para 1.4.4. (This follows the provisions of the Code of Practice on record management discussed in the Main Work paras 8.40–8.41.)
- Redaction of records may be carried out as part of the review process before transfer, so that a redacted version (ie one in which sensitive information has been blanked out) can accompany the complete record: para 1.4.9.
- It would be helpful for the creating authority to draw attention to any transferred information to which it is likely that the Environmental Information Regulations 2004 apply, rather than the 2000 Act: para 1.5.5.

Part 2 of the guidance draws extensively on the section 45 Code of Practice and on the National Archives' own proposed practices for dealing with access requests. It includes guidance on the following issues of particular relevance to transferred public records: **8.50C**

- The Information Commissioner's Office has confirmed that the section 21 exemption (for information which is reasonably accessible to the applicant otherwise than under section 1 of the 2000 Act) can, as a general rule, be claimed in respect of transferred public records which are catalogued and open to inspection, and which are included in the publication scheme of the place of deposit: section 2.8.
- There is scope for claiming the section 22 exemption (for information held with a view to publication) in respect of uncatalogued records which are in a programme of cataloguing, or records which are currently too fragile to be handled but are included in a programme of conservation: section 2.8. A place of deposit hoping to rely on section 22 will need to be able to demonstrate that organized, structured efforts are being made to deal with any backlogs.
- Section 2.10 contains detailed guidance on the procedures for consultation and decision-making regarding access requests for transferred public records which are not yet open.
- Paragraph 2.12.5 advises that if, on examination of a requested record, it is discovered to contain no exempt information, it should be made open to the public generally, subject to consulting the creating authority.

9

A COMPARISON WITH FREEDOM OF INFORMATION ELSEWHERE

B. Access to Official Information as of Right

Who enjoys the right and what use has been made of it?

9.10 There has been a significant decrease in the level of requests since the coming into force of the Irish Freedom of Information (Amendment) Act 2003. Among the changes it effected to the original statutory scheme was the introduction, by means of an amendment to section 47 of the 1997 Act (see Main Work para 25.147), of 'up-front fees'. A fee of such amount as may be prescribed is now automatically payable on the making of an access request under section 7, an application for an internal review under section 14, or an application to the Information Commissioner under section 34, in all cases save where the records concerned contain personal information relating to the requester/applicant. In the event of non-payment, the request or application cannot be accepted and is deemed not to have been made. See new subsection 47(6A). In her annual report for 2004, the Irish Information Commissioner noted a decline in overall usage of the Act of over 50%, a fall of 75% in non-personal requests, and an 83% fall in the number of requests by journalists. She also expressed concern about the significant decline (50%) in appeals to her office relating to non-personal information, and said:

> I regard this as a very serious matter not just for the requesters who have almost certainly been deterred by the high cost of appealing to my office [Euro 150], but also for my role in relation to monitoring the work of the Act.
>
> I do not believe that the Oireachtas could have anticipated so great a decline in usage of the Act when amending the Act and approving the scale of fees to be charged. I believe that so great has the decline in usage been that a review of the scale and structure of the charges, particularly in relation to my office should be undertaken.

Information or records

9.14 In *Yeager v Canada (Correctional Service)* (2003) 223 DLR (4th) 234 the Federal Court of Appeal had for the first time to interpret section 4(3) of the Canadian Access to Information Act (see Main Work para 25.46) to determine whether computer software is 'a record' within the meaning of section 3 of the Act, and whether a government institution can be required to create and supply records that do not exist. As to the former question, it was held that software is not a record, but an item used to generate, view, or edit a record. As to the latter question, it was held that in enacting section 4(3) the legislature must necessarily have contemplated a new and distinct record being produced from an existing machine-readable record. The evidence before the Court showed that the Correctional Service had the ability to create a new record embodying the requested set of data from machine-readable records under its control. However, there were limitations on the obligation of government institutions to produce otherwise non-existent records. Regulation 3 of the Access to Information Regulations provides that they need not do so where this would unreasonably interfere with the operations of the institution; and on the evidence, the first instance judge had erred in finding that exemption not to apply.

C. Exemptions: The General Approach

Canada

The following new paragraph comes after paragraph 9.36 of the Main Work:

In *Sherman v Minister of National Revenue* (2003) 226 DLR (4th) 46 the Federal Court of Appeal allowed Mr Sherman's appeal against a decision to uphold the Minister's refusal to disclose statistical information regarding the extent to which the Canada Revenue Agency and the Internal Revenue Service of the United States had requested assistance from one another for tax collection purposes pursuant to the Canada–United States Tax Convention. It held that information about the numbers of requests made was not exempt from disclosure under section 13(1) of the Canadian Access to Information Act, not being information obtained in confidence from the US authorities, and remitted the matter to the Trial Division for detailed examination of the requested records. Mr Sherman was, in due course, successful: (2005) 245 DLR (4th) 758. The Minister's attempt to rely on the exemptions under section 16 (for information relating to, or the disclosure of which could reasonably be expected to be injurious to, lawful investigations) was rejected on the basis that collection action is not investigatory; the request was not for specific information about individuals; and disclosure of the statistics sought could not reasonably be expected to harm relations with the US or prejudice future co-operation under the Convention. In reaching its decision the Court of Appeal noted what Layden-Stevenson J called 'a number of factors of import' of general application. He set them out in his own judgment in the following terms: **9.36A**

- the burden of proof required to establish an exemption from disclosure rests on the party resisting disclosure;
- the entitlement to an exemption must be established on a balance of probabilities;
- the opinion of the Information Commissioner is a factor to consider when determining whether the information should be disclosed;
- the purpose of the Act is to provide a broad right of access to information in records under the control of a government institution;
- all exemptions must be limited and specific and in the case of ambiguity, the interpretation that least infringes on the public's right to access must be chosen.

D. Particular Exemptions

International relations

9.46 In *Secretary, Department of Foreign Affairs and Trade v Whittaker* (2005) 214 ALR 696 the Federal Court of Australia considered both limbs of section 33 of the Australian Freedom of Information Act in the context of a request for documents relating to the proposed appointment of a new Australian High Commissioner to Canada. The Administrative Appeals Tribunal had heard and accepted evidence from the department that the process of *agrément* (whereby the government of one country seeks the consent of another country's government for its nomination for the post of head of its diplomatic mission in that other country) was conducted on a strictly confidential basis as a matter of general international diplomatic practice. Strict procedures were in place within the department to protect the integrity of the process and prevent its becoming public knowledge. However, the Tribunal had concluded that disclosure could take place because the Canadian Government having accepted the particular nomination in question (although in the event the appointment did not proceed), the cloak of confidentiality which had covered the documents at the time of creation had been lifted. According to the Federal Court, that was a misconception because the condition for application of section 33(1)(b) was that the information had been communicated in confidence in the first place; whether it subsequently remained confidential was not to the point. In contrast, the relevant time for judging whether section 33(1)(a)(iii) applied and the disclosure would (or could reasonably be expected to) damage international relations was the date when access was sought, not when the documents came into being. The Tribunal had (correctly) recognized that sensitivity of documents could evaporate over time or in changed circumstances, such that a release of information which would once have damaged international relations might be harmless. However, it had arrived at the conclusion that this exemption did not apply without having made a specific finding to that effect in respect of these particular documents. On the contrary, it had accepted that the department had a legitimate concern that release of documents concerning an appointment could harm Australia's relations with other countries by casting doubt on its reliability in maintaining confidence.

Legal matters

9.50 The ambit of Exemption (c) was considered by the US Supreme Court in *National Archives and Records Administration v Favish* 541 US 157 (2004). The subject-matter of Mr Favish's request was a set of ten colour photographs taken by the Parks Police of the dead body of Vincent Foster, Jr, Deputy Counsel to President Clinton, where it was found in Fort Marcy Park. Despite the unanimous conclusion of five separate official investigations that Mr Foster had committed suicide, Mr Favish remained sceptical as to how he had met his end. The first issue was whether the personal privacy exemption could be invoked by anyone other than the individual in the photographs. It was held that the deceased's family did indeed have a protectable privacy interest in the pictures. The Court noted that the common law had long recognized the family's right to control the body and death images of a deceased family member. In its opinion, Congress must have intended to permit family members to assert their own privacy rights against public intrusion long deemed impermissible under the common law and as a matter of cultural tradition. It also took account of the undesirability of construing the section so narrowly that access to autopsy records of deceased victims would have to be given to their murderers if they asked for it (which, the Court was told, is not uncommon). That was not the end of the case, however, because the term 'unwarranted' required the family's privacy interest to be balanced against the public interest in disclosure. The Court pointed out that, as a general rule, citizens should not be asked to explain why they seek information under the Act.

> A person requesting the information needs no preconceived idea of the uses the data might serve. The information belongs to citizens to do with as they choose.

But to effect the balance between the competing interests in privacy and disclosure and give practical meaning to this particular exemption, that usual rule must be inapplicable.

> Exemption 7(c) requires the person requesting the information to establish a sufficient reason for the disclosure. First, the citizen must show that the public interest sought to be advanced is a significant one, an interest more specific than having the information for its own sake. Second, the citizen must show the information is likely to advance that interest.

The Court did not attempt a general definition of what reasons would suffice. However, it offered some guidance. In the case of photographic images and other data pertaining to an individual who died in mysterious circumstances, the justification most likely to satisfy the public interest requirement was that the information was necessary to show that the investigative agency or other responsible officials acted negligently or improperly in the performance of their duties. The Court of Appeals had erred in not insisting on credible evidence pointing to some actual misfeasance or impropriety. In such a case as this, the requester must establish more than a bare suspicion. He must produce evidence that would warrant a belief by a reasonable person that the alleged government impropriety might have occurred. This Mr Favish had not done, despite his stated conviction that the investigations into Mr Foster's death were 'grossly incomplete and untrustworthy'; and the balancing exercise was not even reached.

Bennett v Chief Executive Officer of the Australian Customs Service (2004) 210 ALR **9.51**
220 (a decision of the Federal Court of Australia) arose out of proceedings

brought by Mr Bennett against the Australian Customs Service (for which he worked) in relation to disciplinary action taken against him for making public comments on the conduct of customs matters. In September 1999, the Australian Government Solicitor (who was acting for the Customs Service) wrote to Mr Bennett's solicitors, making proposals for settlement of the litigation. It contained an outline of advice given by the Australian Government Solicitor to his client regarding Mr Bennett's claim. The principal issue for decision was the effect of that letter on the applicability to the documents sought by Mr Bennett of the exemption in section 42 of the Australian Freedom of Information Act for documents covered by legal professional privilege. The Court held that the voluntary disclosure of the gist or conclusion of the Government Solicitor's legal advice had amounted to waiver of legal professional privilege and exemption from production under section 42 in respect of the whole of the advice to which reference was made, including the reasons for the conclusions.

Constitutional conventions

9.58 The exemptions in sections 19 and 20 of the Irish Act have been broadened by the Freedom of Information (Amendment) Act 2003, sections 14–15. Among the changes were a doubling of the five-year period during which records relating to government decisions cannot be released, and the introduction of a mandatory exemption for records which have been certified by the Secretary General of a Department of State as containing matter relating to the deliberative processes of a Department of State: new subsection 20(1A).

9.59 *Re Richardson and Federal Commissioner of Taxation and Martinek* [2004] 55 ATR 1091 was a decision of the Australian Administrative Appeals Tribunal regarding a request by Mr Richardson for access to letters which Ms Martinek had written to the Taxation Office about him. He had been refused access by reference to various exemptions, including that in section 36 of the Australian Freedom of Information Act (disclosure of 'matter in the nature of, or relating to, opinion, advice or recommendation obtained, prepared or recorded, or consultation or deliberation that has taken place, in the course of, or for the purposes of, the deliberative process involved in the functions of an agency or Minister or Government of the Commonwealth…'). The Tribunal found that the contents of Ms Martinek's letters did not satisfy that description because her expressions of opinion, advice, and recommendations had been proffered gratuitously to the Taxation Office, without being explicitly or implicitly sought by it. One of the four letters was nonetheless held to be exempt from disclosure, under section 45 of the Act (disclosure would found an action for breach of confidence). The other three were not exempt because, while labelled 'without prejudice', they were not marked 'confidential'; they were copied to two other organizations; and they contained information which would seem to be widely known. However, those three letters were ordered to be disclosed in part only. That was because section 38 of the Act exempts documents disclosure of which is prohibited under certain statutory provisions except insofar as they contain personal information about the requester. One such provision prohibits release of information about a person's affairs 'disclosed or obtained under the provisions of' the Income Tax Assessment Act. The Tribunal held that Ms Martinek's letters were from her point of view directed towards assisting the Commissioner of Taxation in the exercise of his functions (whether or not useful to him), and so were exempt under section 38 save insofar as they contained personal information about Mr Richardson which was separable from personal information about others.

Blanchard J's approach was endorsed by the Federal Court of Appeal ((2003) 224 DLR (4th) 498), save to the extent that his order was modified to make it clear that a line-by-line analysis of memoranda was not called for. Disclosure would be required only if there existed within or appended to another document an organized body or *corpus* of words which, looked at on its own, satisfied the definition of *discussion paper* and which could reasonably be severed from the rest of the document. **9.61**

Personal information

The following new paragraphs come after paragraph 9.66 of the Main Work:

The question of when it is appropriate to release or to withhold details of agency staff in response to an access request arose in the Australian case *Re Kristoffersen and Centrelink* (2004) 80 ALD 452. Centrelink was defending the deletion of names and direct telephone numbers of officers from documents it produced, on the basis that there had been a history of threats and abuse by Mr Kristoffersen towards its staff. The particular exemptions on which it relied were those in sections 37(1)(c) (disclosure would endanger the life or physical safety of any person) and 40(1) (disclosure would have a substantial adverse effect on the proper and efficient conduct of its operations), not—as one might have expected—section 41 (unreasonable disclosure of personal information). The Administrative Appeals Tribunal upheld its application of the section 37 exemption, holding that the release of the information would impact on efficient conduct of its business and that there was no public interest in releasing such information to the applicant. **9.66A**

In contrast, in *Electronic Privacy Information Center v Department of Homeland Security*, a recent decision of the United States District Court for the District of Columbia, reliance was placed—successfully—on the exemption in the United States Act for 'personnel and medical files and similar files the disclosure of which would constitute a clearly unwarranted invasion of personal privacy' to withhold the names and other identifying details of government employees from otherwise disclosable documents. The factual background was as follows. **9.66B**

After 11 September 2001, the second defendant, the Transportation Security Administration ('TSA'), an agency within the Department for Homeland Security ('DHS'), began developing a new system, the Computer Assisted Passenger Prescreening System, to confirm passenger identities and identify terrorists or individuals with terrorist connections. It came to light that several airlines had supplied passenger data to companies competing for TSA contracts, to assist in developing the system. The plaintiff, a non-profit organization concerned with privacy and civil liberties issues, requested disclosure of documents relating to the Government's attempts to acquire passenger data from airlines. A number of exemptions were involved. The basis for contending that employees' identities should be withheld was that release would make them vulnerable to harassment and would not help the plaintiff understand the operations of the Government. The plaintiff argued that federal employees had only a 'negligible' privacy interest and the threatened invasion of their privacy was merely speculative.

9.66C In holding for the defendants on this issue, the Court noted that according to case law, the privacy interest of civilian federal employees included the right to control information related to themselves and to avoid disclosures that could conceivably subject them to annoyance or harassment in their official or private lives; 'harassment' did not require their lives or physical safety to be endangered; but to justify withholding their names, a real (not speculative) threat to their privacy must be shown. Here, the Court accepted the defendants' evidence that 'as advocates for security measures that may be unpopular' DHS and TSA employees were likely to experience annoyance or harassment following the disclosure of their involvement with the new passenger screening system, and that unfettered access to their identities could have substantial security implications. Once the documents were released, they would probably be published on the Internet and reporters and others would seek out the employees to question them: 'This contact is the very type of privacy invasion that Exemption 6 is designed to prevent.' On the other hand, the public interest in learning the names of lower-echelon employees was small; the plaintiff had not shown how such knowledge would shed light on the agencies' dealings with the airlines. However, the Court pointed out that it was not endorsing a blanket exemption for all federal employees involved in homeland security. It also emphasized that it did not base its conclusion on evidence about the employees' own concerns: 'An agency cannot establish that a threat to privacy exists based on an employee's subjective fears of harassment.'

Confidence

Australia

9.70 In *Jorgensen v Australian Securities and Investments Commission* (2004) 208 ALR 73 Weinberg J said that under section 45 of the Australian Freedom of Information

Act, the onus rested upon the agency resisting disclosure to establish the facts that would support a claim for breach of confidence. He found that the Commission had not discharged that onus and the Administrative Appeals Tribunal had erred in law in upholding its claim for exemption on the basis of that section.

Canada

The following new paragraph comes after paragraph 9.73 of the Main Work:

The vigilance exercised by the Canadian courts in respect of inappropriate claims to **9.73A** withhold information in reliance on section 20 was exemplified again in *Minister of Public Works and Government Services Canada v Hi-Rise Group Inc* (2004) 238 DLR (4th) 44. Hi-Rise Group Inc made a successful bid to provide leased office accommodation for various federal government departments in Hamilton, Ontario. It was awarded the contract in December 2000. In May 2001 a request was made of the Ministry under the Access to Information Act for records containing information on the bidding process. The company, relying on the exemption in section 20(1)(b) of the Act for 'confidential information supplied to a government institution by a third party and...treated consistently in a confidential manner by the third party', disputed the Ministry's decision to disclose certain documents which, the judge found would, if released, enable competitors to calculate with reasonable certainty the annual rents and the prices of options for renewal. The Federal Court of Appeal held that he had erred in finding that the company had a reasonable expectation of continuing confidentiality. The confidentiality attaching to the bidding process ceased once the process was complete. The company could not reasonably expect amounts paid or payable to it out of public funds pursuant to the ensuing contract to be kept secret. In the judgment of the Court:

> The public's right to know how government spends public funds as a means of holding government accountable for its expenditures is a fundamental notion of responsible government that is known to all.

E. Answering Requests

Timetables

In practice, it seems, the United States courts have recognized the difficulties of **9.80** processing all requests within 20 days, and have allowed the executive to process requests on a 'first-in, first-out' basis where expedited processing is not appropriate. However, there are limits to the courts' tolerance. In *American Civil Liberties Union et al v Department of Defense et al* 339 F Supp 2d 501 (2004), the United States District Court for the Southern District of New York severely criticized the defendant agencies for having failed, after 11 months, to produce or identify any documents or claim any exemptions in response to a request for information about the treatment of detainees since 11 September 2001. He ordered them to produce or identify all responsive documents within 30 days.

> It is the duty of the court to uphold FOIA by striking a proper balance between plaintiffs' right to receive information on government activity in a timely manner and the government's contention that national security concerns prevent timely disclosure or identification...Merely raising national security concerns cannot justify unlimited delay. The information plaintiffs have requested are matters of significant public interest. Yet, the glacial pace at which defendant agencies have been responding to plaintiffs' requests shows an indifference to the commands of FOIA, and fails to afford accountability of government that the act requires. If the documents are more of an embarrassment than a secret, the public should know of our government's treatment of individuals captured and held abroad...To permit further delays in disclosure or providing justification for not disclosing would subvert the intent of FOIA.

Fees

9.86 See Supplement para 9.10 on the introduction in Ireland of additional fees payable on the making of access requests and requests for internal and external reviews.

Rights of third parties

9.91 Section 27 of the Canadian Access to Information Act provides for written notice of intended disclosure of any records which might fall within one of the exemptions in section 20 (covering trade secrets, commercially confidential information and the like) to be given to the potentially affected third parties, who have a right to make representations and challenge an adverse decision in the Federal Court (see Main Work paras 25.63–25.67). In *HJ Heinz Co of Canada Ltd v Canada (Attorney-General)* (2004) 241 DLR (4th) 367, the Federal Court of Appeal rejected an argument that when making such a challenge the third party was restricted to reliance on the section 20 exemptions. HJ Heinz Co was entitled to invoke section 19 (personal information) as well—notwithstanding that had section 19 been the only potentially relevant exemption, it would not even have been entitled to notice.

G. Enforcement and Appeals

Australia

9.112 In *Jorgensen v Australian Securities and Investments Commission* (2004) 208 ALR 73, Weinberg J found himself faced with a practical problem which he summarized as follows:

> It is obviously difficult, in a case of this nature, to undertake the task of going through each document sought by the applicant, testing it against the particular

> exemption claimed, and considering whether or not the tribunal erred in law in arriving at the conclusion that it did. The sheer breadth of the applicant's request…led to some 768 documents totalling almost 3000 pages being regarded as potentially relevant. The applicant's request has been considered by ASIC, by the Ombudsman, and by the Tribunal. He now seeks to have this court embark upon a similar exercise.

Having regard to the restriction of the court's jurisdiction to questions of law, the solution he adopted was as follows. He did not engage in a detailed examination of every page of every document in dispute (which he said would have taken 'literally weeks'). Instead, he 'examined a representative sample of the documents in question, chosen essentially at random, in order to gauge whether the Tribunal's interpretation of the various provisions upon which it relied in upholding ASIC's claims for exemption revealed some legal error'.

Ireland

The following new paragraphs come after paragraph 9.116 of the Main Work:

Holland v Information Commissioner [2004] IEHC 176 explored the role of the Information Commissioner on an application for a review under section 34 of the Irish Act. The context in which the issue arose was a refusal of an access request by the Department of Justice Equality and Law Reform in reliance on section 10(1)(a), ie on the basis that the requested report did not exist within the Department. The Department said that it was held by the *Garda*, which is not a public body for the purposes of the Act, and the inquiries made internally and of the *Garda* indicated that no copy had been supplied to the Department. Mr Holland appealed against the Commissioner's decision in favour of the Department. He argued that its evidence should not have been accepted at face value, and challenged the statement in the Commissioner's decision that 'it is not the role of my office to carry out a search for the report in question' as being an unduly restrictive interpretation of that role. The Judge disagreed. Following the approach of Quirke J in the earlier case of *Ryan v Information Commissioner*, he held that in carrying out a review where the refusal was based on section 10(1)(a), the Commissioner's function was not to search for records, but rather to review the decision of the public body to refuse access. In so doing, he must have regard to the evidence which was available to the decision-maker and the reasoning used by the decision-maker in arriving at the decision. The Commissioner must decide whether the decision-maker had regard to all relevant evidence and was justified in coming to its decision. **9.116A**

What the then Information Commissioner's successor has described in her 2004 annual report as 'an important legal principle' was confirmed by the High Court of Ireland in *In re an application by CW Shipping Co Ltd and others* [2004] IEHC 1. The substantive matter under appeal was a decision of the Commissioner to grant **9.116B** access to a report in the records of the Department of Communications, Marine and Natural Resources notwithstanding the contention of the third party appellants that the information it contained was commercially sensitive and therefore exempt. The Commissioner, who had not been named as a respondent to the appeal, contended that she should have been. The Judge rejected the appellants' objection to her joinder, holding that she was not only entitled to be a party in order to answer the grounds of challenge to her decision, but was a necessary party to the proceedings.

9.116C The Freedom of Information (Amendment) Act 2003 repealed the provision in the principal 1997 Act that the decision of the High Court should be final and conclusive. Appeals can now proceed further to the Supreme Court. The first case under the legislation to come before the Supreme Court was *Sheedy v Information Commissioner* [2005] IESC 35. The decision turned principally on a question of interpretation of a provision in a different statute, the Education Act 1998, and whether that operated in the circumstances to prevent disclosure of the requested record (a school inspection report prepared for the Department of Education) by virtue of the exemption for records the disclosure of which is statutorily prohibited. A majority of the Court held that to be the case. However, some general comments were made about the interpretation and operation of the legislation. Fennelly J quoted with approval from the judgment of McKechnie J in *Deely v Information Commissioner* [2001] 3 IR 439:

> As can thus be seen the clear intention is that, subject to certain specific and defined exceptions, the rights so conferred on members of the public and their exercise should be as extensive as possible, this viewed, in the context of and in a way to positively further the aims, principles and policies underpinning this statute, subject and subject only to necessary restrictions.
>
> It is on any view, a piece of legislation independent in existence, forceful in its aim and liberal in outlook and philosophy.

He also endorsed McKechnie J's observations about the scope and limitations of an appeal to the High Court pursuant to section 42 of the Act:

> It was submitted...that findings made by the respondent [the Commissioner] on questions of primary fact should not be reviewed by this court as part of the appeal process under s.42 of the Act. There is no doubt but that when a court is considering only a point of law, whether by way of a restricted appeal or via a case stated, the distinction in my view being irrelevant, it is, in accordance with established principles, confined as to its remit, in the manner following:–
>
> (a) it cannot set aside findings of primary fact unless there is no evidence to support such findings;
> (b) it ought not to set aside inferences drawn from such facts unless such inferences were ones which no reasonable decision making body could draw;
> (c) it can however, reverse such inferences, if the same were based on the interpretation of documents and should do so if incorrect; and finally;

(d) if the conclusion reached by such bodies shows that they have taken an erroneous view of the law, then that also is a ground for setting aside the resulting decision…

Kearns J described McKechnie J's propositions (a)–(d) as 'a helpful resumé with which one would not disagree' but added that 'it would be obviously incorrect to apply exclusively judicial review principles to matters of statutory interpretation in the way that might be appropriate to issues of fact'.

10

DATA PROTECTION

A. Introduction

For a brief explanation of the difference between the Data Protection Act 1998, the Freedom of Information Act 2000, and the Environmental Information Regulations 2004, see the introduction to this Supplement. **10.01**

B. The Data Protection Acts—Origins and Purpose

The Data Protection Act implements the Data Protection Directive 95/46/EC. In *Campbell v MGN Ltd* [2003] 2 WLR 80, in the Court of Appeal, Lord Phillips **10.04** of Worth Matravers MR said:

> In interpreting the Act it is appropriate to look to the Directive for assistance. The Act should, if possible, be interpreted in a manner that is consistent with the Directive. Furthermore, because the Act has, in large measure, adopted the wording of the Directive, it is not appropriate to look for the precision in the use of language that is usually to be expected from the parliamentary draftsman. A purposive approach to making sense of the provisions is called for.

Although the House of Lords reversed the Court of Appeal in *Campbell v MGN Ltd* [2004] 2 AC 457, it did not consider the claim for compensation under the 1998 Act, and the observations of Lord Phillips have been adopted by the Court of Appeal in *Durant v Financial Services Authority* [2004] FSR 28, 573 ([3]) and by Munby J in *R (Lord) v Secretary of State for the Home Department* [2003] EWHC 2073 ([83]).

C. The Data Protection Act 1998

Data covered by the 1998 Act

The following new paragraphs come after paragraph 10.08 of the Main Work:

10.08A In *Criminal proceedings against Lindqvist* [2004] QB 1014 Mrs Lindqvist had been charged with a breach of the Swedish legislation on the protection of personal data, for publishing on her internet site personal data on a number of people working with her on a voluntary basis in a parish of the Swedish Protestant Church. The Court of Justice of the European Communities, on a reference to it, held that the term 'personal data' used in Article 3(1) of Directive 95/46/EC covered the name of a person in conjunction with his telephone details or information regarding his working conditions or hobbies. The Court also held that the operation of loading such personal data on an internet page must be considered to be 'processing' of such data within Articles 2(b) and 3(1) of the Directive.

10.08B The meaning of 'personal data' was considered further by the Court of Appeal in *Durant v Financial Services Authority* [2004] FSR 28 at 573. This is an unusual case in that the applicant was not seeking to protect his privacy but was seeking to use the 1998 Act as a means of obtaining information which he thought would assist him in litigation which he had been pursuing unsuccessfully. The Court held that the information he sought was not personal data.

10.08C The Court of Appeal found that it was not sufficient that the data in question recorded the applicant's name and his involvement in some matter or event in which he had no personal interest. To be 'personal', data had both to 'relate to' the individual (ie the individual must be the *focus* of the data) and to be 'information that affects [that individual's] privacy, whether in his personal or family life, business or professional capacity' (*per* Auld LJ at [28]).

This is a different approach to the problem from that adopted by the High Court of Ireland in *EH v Information Commissioner* [2001] IEHC 182, and has been thought by some commentators to be too narrow. Rosemary Jay, a partner in Pinsent Masons, in her paper *Data Protection and Freedom of Information Interface* for the Justice Conference on 16 December 2004, said that the decision has been criticized by the European Commission as failing to meet the requirements of Directive 95/46/EC. **10.08D**

Mr Durant sought disclosure of information which he claimed was personal data relating to him held by the Financial Services Authority ('the FSA'). Mr Durant had earlier brought proceedings against Barclays Bank of which he had been a customer. He lost the litigation in 1993, but since then had sought, without success, disclosure of various records in connection with the dispute giving rise to the litigation because he believed that the records might assist him to re-open his claims or to secure an investigation into the conduct of the bank. In September and October 2001 Mr Durant made two requests to the FSA in its role as the single regulator of the financial services sector, seeking disclosure of personal data held by it, both electronically and in manual files. The application was rejected by the judge and the Court of Appeal. Auld LJ said at [30]: **10.08E**

> Looking at the facts of this case, I do not consider that the information of which Mr Durant seeks further disclosure—whether about his complaint to the FSA about the conduct of Barclays Bank or about the FSA's own conduct in investigating that complaint—is 'personal data' within the meaning of the Act.

Auld LJ suggested at [28] two notions that would be of assistance in determining whether or not the data could be described as 'personal'. The first was whether the information was biographical in a significant sense, in that it went beyond simply recording the data subject's involvement in a matter or an event without any personal connotations or any breach of his privacy. The second notion he described as one of focus. In order to be personal, the data had to have the data subject as its focus rather than some other person with whom he might have been involved or some transaction or events in which he might have figured or have had an interest. An example of non-personal data would be the *Durant* case itself, where the applicant simply instigated an investigation into some third party's conduct and the data concerning that investigation. In short, it is information that affects the data subject's privacy, whether in his personal or family life, business or professional capacity. **10.08F**

The Court of Appeal also held that a narrow meaning of 'personal data' derives not only from its provenance and form of reproduction in section 1(1), but **10.08G** also from the way in which it is applied in section 7 of the 1998 Act. Auld LJ said:

> That section [section 7], picking up the definition of 'data subject' in s.1(1), sets out the basic entitlement of an individual to access to personal data 'of which...[he] is the data subject'. I agree with Mr Sales [counsel for the FSA] that the inclusion in s.1(1) of expressions of opinion and indications of intention in respect of him supports an otherwise narrow construction. If the terms had the broader construction for which Miss Houghton [counsel for Mr Durant] contended, such provision would have been otiose. A similar pointer to the focus of attention being on the data subject rather than on someone else with whom for some reason he is involved or had contact is in the special provision for 'sensitive personal data' in s.2 of, and schs 1, paragraph 1(b) and 3 to, the 1998 Act, giving effect in large part to Arts 6 to 8 of the Directive.

Buxton LJ said at [79]:

> The guiding principle is that the Act, following Directive 95/46, gives rights to data subjects in order to protect their privacy. That is made plain in recitals (2),(7) and (11) to the Directive, and in particular by recital (10), which tells us that:
>
> > the object of the national laws on the processing of personal data is to protect fundamental rights and freedoms, notably the right to privacy, which is recognised both in Art 8 of the European Convention for the Protection of Human Rights and Fundamental Freedoms and in the general principle of Community law.

10.08H Mr Durant lost the case because the Court of Appeal did not consider that the information he sought affected his privacy, whether in his personal or family life, business or professional capacity (see [28]). It is interesting to contrast the decision in *Durant* with *R (Robertson) v Wakefield Metropolitan District Council* [2002] QB 1052 where Maurice Kay J held that the sale of the name and address of an individual from a public electoral register could amount to a breach of Article 8 of the European Convention for the Protection of Human Rights. It was not disputed in the *Wakefield* case that the name and address were personal data. It is easy to see why this was so. Maurice Kay J had before him a detailed submission from the Data Protection Registrar which said that technological advances and developing business practices meant that the sale of the electoral register now impacted on the privacy of individuals to a significantly greater extent than was the case in the past. The Registrar said:

> Any consideration of the impact of the sale of the register should bear in mind not just the personal information that is actually published in the register but also other information that can be derived from it. The published information includes the dates of birth of 16-and 17-year olds as well as the full names and addresses of all those entitled to vote. By comparing the current register with the previous one it is possible to produce a list of 'new movers'. By going further back it is possible to establish how long someone has lived at their address and whether they have 'residential stability'. It is also possible to produce lists of men or women who appear to be living alone, or couples who have recently left home. It is even possible to estimate ages. For example, a 'David' living with an 'Ethel' is likely to be in a different age band to a 'David' living with a 'Kylie'.

The conclusion to be drawn from these two cases is that each case will turn very much on its own facts, but that *personal data* is linked to Article 8 of the European Convention and has to be information which affects the data subject's privacy, whether in his personal or family life, business or professional capacity.

The second issue raised in *Durant v Financial Services Authority* [2004] FSR 28 at 573 was what is meant by a 'relevant filing system' in the definition of 'data' in section 1(1) of the 1998 Act, so as to render personal information recorded in a manual filing system 'personal data' disclosable to its subject under section 7(1). The Court of Appeal held (at [50]) that a 'relevant filing system', for the purposes of the 1998 Act, is limited to a system: **10.09**

(1) in which the files forming part of it are structured or referenced in such a way as clearly to indicate at the outset of the search whether specific information capable of amounting to personal data of an individual requesting it under section 7 is held within the system and, if so, in which file or files it is held; and
(2) which has, as part of its own structure or referencing mechanism, a sufficiently sophisticated and detailed means of readily indicating whether and where in an individual file or files specific criteria or information about the applicant can be readily located.

n21 For discussion of the restrictions provided for by section 7 of the Freedom of Information Act 2000, see Main Work para 5.35. **10.12**

Rights of data subjects

In *Johnson v Medical Defence Union Ltd* [2005] 1 WLR 750 Laddie J held that a consultant orthopaedic surgeon could obtain an order for disclosure of documents in proceedings against Medical Defence Union Ltd for breaches of the 1998 Act, seeking, *inter alia*, damages under section 13, and rectification, blocking, or destruction of data under section 14, notwithstanding that he had previously sought access to the same data under section 7 and had had his request denied by the Court. The determination was solely concerned with whether requests for information pursuant to an access request under section 7 had been complied with properly and not with whether there had been a breach of the data protection principles by the data controller. The Court's decision did not necessarily prevent the documents, if material to the data subject's claim under section 13 or 14 of the 1998 Act, from being disclosed in the course of the subsequent proceedings. **10.35**

Right of access

The fourth issue in *Durant v Financial Services Authority* [2004] FSR 28 at 573 is by what principles a court should be guided in exercising its discretion under **10.44** section 7(9) of the 1998 Act to order a data controller who has wrongfully refused a request for information under section 7(1) to comply with the request. Auld LJ confined himself to saying that he agreed with the recent observations of Munby J in *R (Lord) v Secretary of State for the Home Department* [2003] EWHC 2073 at [160] that the discretion conferred by section 7(9) is general and untrammelled. The *Lord* case was a successful application for judicial review by a prisoner seeking disclosure under the 1998 Act of confidential prison records.

Right to prevent processing for the purpose of direct marketing

10.51 Individuals have the right under section 11 of the 1998 Act to prevent processing for the purpose of direct marketing. Note that, following the decision of the High Court in *R (Robertson) v Wakefield Metropolitan Council* [2002] QB 1052, this includes not only direct marketing by the data controller, but any disclosure by the data controller to third parties who may use the information for direct marketing.

Exemptions

10.69 The Information Commissioner has issued decision notices in the cases of *Standards Board for England*, case reference FS50064699 (1 August 2005), and *Corby Borough Council*, case reference FS50062124 (25 August 2005), involving data protection. For further discussion of these cases, see Supplement paras 7.77I and 7.77R.

11

MEDICAL RECORDS

F. Confidentiality

The following new heading and paragraph come after paragraph 11.80 of the Main Work:

The Care Record Guarantee

To allay concerns about possible unauthorized uses of the nationwide patient **11.80A**
record electronic database being rolled out from 2006, the Department of Health has published a list of commitments under the title *The NHS Care Record Guarantee*. There are twelve commitments in all, relating to patients' access to their own records and control over others' access to their records, and the ways in which access will be monitored and policed. They are as follows:

(1) When we receive a request from you in writing, we must normally give you access to everything we have recorded about you. However, we may not give you confidential information about other people, or information that a health professional considers likely to cause serious harm to the physical or mental health of you or someone else. This applies to paper and electronic records.

If you ask us to, we will also let other people see health records about you. Wherever possible, we will make your health records available to you free of charge or at a minimum charge, as allowed by law. We will provide other ways for you to apply to see your records if you cannot do so in writing. We will provide information in a format that is accessible to you (for example, in large type if you are partially sighted).

(2) When we provide health care, we will share health records about you with the people providing care or checking its quality. They must keep the information confidential, whether shared using the computer system or in any other way (such as on paper). We will aim to share only as much information as people need to know to play their part in your health care.

(3) We will not share information outside the NHS (particularly with other government agencies) that identifies you for any other reason, unless:
- you give us specific permission;
- we have to do this by law; or
- we have good reason to believe that failing to share the information would put someone else at risk.

If we share information without your permission, we will make sure that we follow the NHS confidentiality code of practice and other national guidelines on best practice . . .

(4) Under current law, no-one can make decisions about sharing health information about you on your behalf. At the moment, the only exceptions to this are parents or legal guardians, or people with powers under mental health law. However, if you are not able to make decisions about sharing information, a senior health care professional involved in your care may consider it to be in your best interests to share information. This judgment should take account of the views of relatives and carers, and any views you have already recorded.

(5) Sometimes your health care will be provided by members of a care team, which might include people from other services, such as social services or education. We will tell you if this is the case. When it could be in your best interests for us to share health information with organisations outside the NHS, we will agree this with you beforehand. If you don't agree, we will discuss with you the possible effect this may have on your care and alternatives.

(6) You can choose not to have information in your electronic care records shared. In helping you decide, we will discuss with you how this may affect our ability to provide you with care or treatment, and any alternatives available to you.

(7) We will deal fairly and efficiently with your questions, concerns and complaints about how we use information about you . . .

(8) We will take appropriate steps to make sure information about you is accurate. You will be given opportunities to check records about you and point out any mistakes. We would normally correct factual mistakes. If you are not happy with an opinion or comment that has been recorded, we will add your comments to the record. If you are suffering distress or harm as a result of information being held in your record, you can apply to have the information amended or deleted.

(9) We will make sure, through contract terms and staff training, that everyone who works in or on behalf of the NHS understands their duty of confidentiality, what it means in practice and how it applies to all parts of their work. Organisations under contract to the NHS must follow the same policies and controls as we do. We will enforce this duty at all times.

(10) We will take appropriate steps to make sure we hold records about you—both paper and electronic—securely and only make them available to people who have a right to see them.

(11) We will keep a record of everyone who looks at the information the NHS Care Records Service holds about you. You will be able to ask for a list of everyone who has looked at records about you and when they did so. There may be times when someone will need to look at information about you without having been given permission to do so beforehand. This may be justifiable, for example, if you need emergency care. We will tell you if the action cannot be justified.

(12) We will take action when someone deliberately looks at records about you without permission or good reason. This can include disciplinary action, ending a contract, firing an employee or bringing criminal charges.

13

WHISTLE-BLOWING

B. Mandatory Whistle-blowing

Pension schemes

The wide-ranging reforms effected by the Pensions Act 2004 involve the transfer of the Occupational Pensions Regulatory Authority's functions to the new Pensions Regulator as from 6 April 2005, SI 2005/275. Section 70 of the 2004 Act, which came into force on the same day, imposes a requirement on persons involved in the administration of occupational and personal pension schemes, or in advising the trustees or managers of such a scheme (whether in the capacity of auditor, actuary, lawyer, or otherwise), and (in relation to occupational pension schemes) on the employers concerned, to report in writing to the Regulator in certain circumstances. These occur where such a person has reasonable cause to believe that a legal duty relevant to the administration of the scheme in question has not been or is not being complied with, and the failure to comply is likely to be of material significance to the Regulator in the exercise of its functions. Anyone **13.04–13.05** who breaches the section 70 requirement without reasonable excuse is liable to a penalty under the Pensions Act 1995, section 10. The Regulator is required by section 90(2) of the 2004 Act to issue a code of practice relating to the discharge of the section 70 duty, which has to be laid before Parliament. The *Pensions Regulator Code of Practice: Reporting breaches of the law* also came into effect on 6 April 2005. The new reporting regime is thus considerably broader than that which existed under the Pensions Act 1995, section 48, which is repealed subject to savings and transitional provisions (SI 2005/695).

Effect of the Financial Services and Markets Act 2000

13.11 See now, too, the Financial Services and Markets Act 2000 (Communications by Actuaries) Regulations 2003, SI 2003/1294, which came into force on 1 September 2003. They prescribe circumstances in which an actuary is required to communicate to the Financial Services Authority information or opinion on matters of which he has become aware in the course of acting for an authorized person (or a person with close links to an authorized person). They are, in summary, that he reasonably believes that:

(a) there is or has been (or may be or have been) a contravention of a requirement under the Financial Services and Markets Act 2000, or an offence which the Authority has power to prosecute under that Act, which might be of material significance to the Authority in deciding whether to exercise any of its functions in relation to the authorized person;
(b) his information or opinion might be of material significance to the Authority in determining whether that person satisfies the threshold conditions;
(c) (where applicable) there is a significant risk that the authorized person is, or may be or become, unable to meet its liabilities attributable to long-term insurance contracts, or that the interests of long-term insurance policy holders have not been or may not be properly taken into account.

C. The Public Interest Disclosure Act 1998

Timing of disclosures

13.20 Contrast *Pinnington v Swansea City and County Council* [2005] ICR 685. On 2 July 1998 Mrs Pinnington had been suspended from her job for breach of confidence. On 3 July 1999 she was dismissed on the separate ground of incapability due to illness. The case reached the Court of Appeal on the issue of whether she had a cause of action under the Employment Rights Act 1996, section 47B (see Main Work paras 13.70–13.77). She claimed that she had been subjected to detriment on the ground that she had made a protected disclosure. The Court of

Appeal affirmed that a disclosure can be protected notwithstanding that it occurred before 2 July 1999, but held that a cause of action will only accrue under section 47B in respect of such a disclosure if both the detriment and the employer's act (or deliberate failure to act) which inflicted the detriment occurred after the provision came into effect, in accordance with the general presumption against retrospectivity of legislation. Not terminating Mrs Pinnington's suspension on 2 July 1999 involved no deliberate failure to act on the part of her employer. However, Mummery LJ observed that had the decision to dismiss her on other grounds not been taken, the employer might have been under a duty to revisit the question of continuing her suspension in the light of the new legislation.

Excepted categories of worker

Section 43KA of the Employment Rights Act 1996, extending the scope of the public interest disclosure legislation to the police, was brought into force on 1 April 2004 by the Police Reform Act 2002 (Commencement No 8) Order 2004, SI 2004/913. **13.23**

Qualifying disclosures

The word 'likely' in section 43B(1)(b) has been interpreted by the Employment Appeal Tribunal in *Kraus v Penna plc* [2004] IRLR 260 as requiring more than a mere possibility or risk of non-compliance with a legal obligation. It was held that the information disclosed should, in the reasonable belief of the worker making the disclosure at the time it is made, tend to show that it is probable or more probable than not that non-compliance will occur. 'Likely' must bear the same meaning throughout section 43B(1), so the decision is also authority on the meaning of the word in paragraphs (a) and (c)–(f). It was also held in that case that 'legal obligation' in section 43B(1)(b) means an actual legal obligation binding upon the person whose past, present or anticipated act or omission is the subject of the disclosure. If no such obligation exists as a matter of law, the worker cannot claim the protection of the legislation, even if he reasonably believes that it does. **13.26**

In *Darnton v University of Surrey* [2003] ICR 615, the Employment Appeal Tribunal allowed Mr Darnton's appeal on the basis that in rejecting his claim to have been dismissed for making a protected disclosure, the tribunal had asked the wrong question: not whether he had held the reasonable belief that what he was disclosing tended to show a relevant failure, but whether the factual allegations he had made were correct. They did not accept the submission made on his behalf that the worker's belief in the truth of the factual allegations he makes (as opposed to what the allegations 'tend to show') is irrelevant to the issue of whether he has the reasonable belief called for by section 43B(1), and relevant only to the **13.29** question of whether he is acting in good faith (as to which, see Main Work paras 13.35–13.40 and Supplement paras 13.40A–13.40D).

> In our opinion, the determination of the factual accuracy of the disclosure by the tribunal will, in many cases, be an important tool in determining whether the worker held the reasonable belief that the disclosure tended to show a relevant failure. Thus, if an employment tribunal find that an employee's factual allegation of something he claims to have seen himself is false, that will be highly relevant to the question of the worker's reasonable belief. It is extremely difficult to see how a worker can reasonably believe that an allegation tends to show that there has been a relevant failure if he knew or believed that the factual basis was false...as a matter of both law and common sense all circumstances must be considered together in determining whether the worker holds the reasonable belief. The circumstances will include his belief in the factual basis of the information disclosed as well as what those facts tend to show. The more the worker claims to have direct knowledge of the matters which are the subject of the disclosure, the more relevant will be his belief in the truth of what he says in determining whether he holds that reasonable belief.

However:

> ...reasonable belief must be based on facts as understood by the worker, not as actually found to be the case.

Good faith

13.37 And see *Darnton v University of Surrey* [2003] ICR 615. The Employment Appeal Tribunal said that there was no justification for importing into the general definition of a 'qualifying disclosure' in section 43B words which Parliament chose not to enact there (namely that the worker must believe that the information disclosed and the allegations contained in it are substantially true), in contrast to their express inclusion in sections 43F, 43G and 43H in relation to some qualifying disclosures only. Whether or not the worker has a belief in the factual basis of the information disclosed is, nonetheless, relevant when considering whether he has the reasonable belief for which section 43B calls, namely that the information tends to show a relevant failure. See the passage from the judgment quoted in Supplement para 13.29 above.

The following new paragraphs come after paragraph 13.40 of the Main Work:

13.40A The Court of Appeal has now endorsed the approach to the interpretation of the expression 'in good faith' suggested in the Main Work, namely that a disclosure will not be protected if the dominant (or predominant) motive for making it 'was not directed to remedying the wrongs identified in section 43B, but was an ulterior motive unrelated to the statutory objectives'.

13.40B Those words are taken from the judgment of Wall LJ in *Street v Derbyshire Unemployed Workers' Centre* [2005] ICR 97 at [73]. Mrs Street had been dismissed for making allegations against her manager of misconduct amounting to breach of his legal obligations to his employer, the allegations having been made both internally (to a member of the Centre's management committee) and externally (to one of the local authorities funding the Centre). She claimed the protection of the Employment Rights Act 1996, sections 43C, 43G and 103A (see Main Work paras 13.41 and 13.45–13.54). The employment tribunal held that none of her disclosures was protected because none had been made in good faith, notwithstanding its finding in her favour that all the other criteria for the application of section 43G were satisfied, including the existence of a reasonable belief on her part in the substantial truth of the allegations.

The Employment Appeal Tribunal and the Court of Appeal in turn upheld the distinction drawn by the tribunal between the requirement for such a reasonable belief and the requirement of 'good faith'. Although they overlap, the latter adds something to the former. The tribunal was entitled to consider Mrs Street's reasons for making the disclosures and, on finding as a fact that what had motivated her was personal antagonism towards the manager, to reject her claim. **13.40C**

The Court of Appeal declined to attempt to define what might constitute ulterior motivation or bad faith, Wall LJ expressing confidence in the ability of tribunals to identify and evaluate it on the facts of each individual case ([74]). Whether the nature or degree of any ulterior motive found amounts to bad faith is a matter for the tribunal to assess on a broad and commonsense basis, according to Auld LJ ([52–53]). But both Lords Justices acknowledged the reality that even a worker who is driven by concern to right or prevent a wrong may feel some antagonism towards the wrongdoer, and concluded that to amount to bad faith, the ulterior motive must be not just present, but predominant. **13.40D**

Disclosure to prescribed persons—section 43F

The Public Interest Disclosure (Prescribed Persons) Order 1999 was amended in 2003 by the substitution of a fresh list of prescribed persons and matters (SI 2003/1993). It has been further amended by SI 2004/664 (substituting the new Commissions for Healthcare Audit and Inspection and Social Care Inspection for the former National Care Standards Commission), and SI 2004/3265 (adding the Independent Police Complaints Commission). **13.44**

Rights and remedies

Remedies for unfair dismissal: compensation

The House of Lords has since clarified the position in *Dunnachie v Kingston upon Hull City Council* [2005] 1 AC 226, reaffirming that a compensatory award for unfair dismissal under section 123 cannot be made in respect of non-pecuniary loss such as injury to feelings, humiliation, or distress. In contrast, compensation **13.67(g)** for injury to feelings can be awarded under the Employment Rights Act 1996, sections 47B and 49 where an employee is subjected to detriment for making a protected disclosure (see Main Work para 13.77, as updated below). However, those sections do not apply where the worker is an employee and 'the detriment... amounts to dismissal': section 47B(2). In *Melia v Magna Kansei Ltd* [2005] ICR 874, Mr Melia successfully claimed that he had been both subjected to a detriment and unfairly dismissed for making a protected disclosure, but appealed against the tribunal's decision on quantum. His complaint was that it had not awarded him compensation for injury to feelings under section 49 right up to November 2001 when he had resigned, but only up to June 2001. That was the point in time at which it found that the employer's conduct had progressed beyond inflicting detriment to constituting fundamental breach of contract, entitling Mr Melia to resign and claim constructive dismissal. The Employment Appeal Tribunal upheld the tribunal's approach.

Burden of proof

13.73 The words 'done on the ground that' were held by the Employment Appeal Tribunal in *London Borough of Harrow v Knight* [2003] IRLR 140 to mean that the fact of the protected disclosure having been made must have caused or influenced the employer to act (or not act) in the way complained of; to decide whether that was the case requires an analysis of the mental processes (conscious or unconscious) which caused the employer to behave as he did.

Meaning of 'detriment'

13.74 The House of Lords applied Brightman LJ's *dictum* in *Shamoon v Chief Constable of the Royal Ulster Constabulary* [2003] ICR 337, Lord Scott saying that the issue must be considered from the victim's point of view. He thought it enough 'if the victim's opinion that the treatment was to his or her detriment was a reasonable one to hold'. There is no need for the victim to demonstrate any physical or economic consequence.

Remedies for subjection to detriment

13.77 In *Virgo Fidelis Senior School v Boyle* [2004] ICR 1210, the Employment Appeal Tribunal held that detriment falling within section 47B was a form of discrimination, and as consistency should be maintained, so far as possible, throughout all areas of discrimination, the level of compensation for injury to feelings awarded to whistle-blowers should be assessed having regard to the guidelines laid down for assessing such compensation in sex and race discrimination cases in *Vento v Chief Constable of West Yorkshire Police* [2003] ICR 318 at 335–36. The Court of Appeal there identified three broad bands of compensation: £15,000–£25,000 for 'the most serious cases, such as where there has been a lengthy campaign of discriminatory harassment'; £5,000–£15,000 for 'serious cases'; and £500–£5,000 for 'less serious cases, such as where the act of discrimination is an isolated or one-off occurrence'. Awards of less than £500 are to be avoided, as being too low to be a proper recognition of injury to feelings; awards exceeding £25,000 should be made only 'in the most exceptional case'. The Employment Appeal Tribunal held that Mr Boyle's case, albeit 'very serious', did not fall in that last category, and reduced the tribunal's award under this head from £42,500 to £25,000. However, it allowed Mr Boyle's cross-appeal against the tribunal's refusal of aggravated damages. Applying the Court of Appeal's *dictum* in *Vento* (that the decision whether or not to award aggravated damages in a discrimination case, and if so in what amount, must depend on the particular circumstances of the discrimination and on the way in which the complaint of discrimination has been handled), it awarded him an additional sum of £10,000 on that account. On the other hand, his claim for exemplary damages failed. The Employment Appeal Tribunal saw no reason why in principle such an award could not be made under the legislation, but found that Mr Boyle's employer was not acting as a servant or agent exercising executive power derived from the government, central or local, and its actions could not be characterized as oppressive, arbitrary or unconstitutional.

The following new paragraph comes after paragraph 13.77 of the Main Work:

Statutory dispute resolution procedures

Regard should now also be had to the provisions of Part 3 of the Employment Act 2002 and the Employment Act 2002 (Dispute Resolution) Regulations 2004, SI 2004/752. Failure to comply with an applicable statutory dispute resolution procedure may affect the employee's right to present a complaint to an employment tribunal under the Employment Rights Act 1996, section 111 or section 48, or the measure of available compensation. **13.77A**

14

MONEY LAUNDERING

C. Domestic Legislation

The Money Laundering Regulations 1993, together with the Financial Services and Markets Act 2000 (Regulations relating to Money Laundering) Regulations 2001, SI 2001/1819, and the Money Laundering Regulations 2001, SI 2001/3641, were revoked and replaced by the Money Laundering Regulations 2003, SI 2003/3075. **14.16**

The Proceeds of Crime Act 2002

The following new paragraphs come after paragraph 14.34 of the Main Work:

The interpretation of section 328 and its applicability in the context of legal proceedings arose for consideration in *Bowman v Fels* [2005] 1 WLR 3083. The dispute between claimant and defendant concerned the beneficial ownership of a property registered in the defendant's name. On seeing his disclosure documents, the claimant's solicitors suspected that he had included the cost of work on the **14.34A** property in his business accounts and VAT returns, although it had no connection with his business. They formed the view that before they took any further steps in the action, they ought to notify the National Criminal Intelligence Service and ask for its consent. This caused a delay, and the solicitors obtained an adjournment of the trial date without the defendant being told the reason. He applied for that order to be set aside. By the time the question of whether the claimant's solicitors' approach had been correct reached the Court of Appeal, the proceedings had settled, but the Court considered it to be of sufficient public importance for the hearing to proceed.

14.34B The conclusion arrived at by the Court of Appeal was that section 328 had not applied in the circumstances to require the claimant's solicitors to disclose their suspicions; they had been free to continue with the ordinary conduct of the action, and there had been no proper basis for an adjournment or good reason to conceal from the defendant the grounds on which they sought one. Properly interpreted, section 328 was not intended to cover the ordinary conduct of litigation by legal professionals. As a matter of language, neither an order nor a judgment, nor a step taken in proceedings with a view to obtaining one, would be described as an 'arrangement'. Article 7 of Council Directive 91/30/EEC (as amended), on which section 328 is based, cannot have been intended to include the conduct of litigation in the concept of 'carrying out a transaction'—even if assets which happened to be the proceeds of money laundering might be the subject of claims in the proceedings, or be retained or used to satisfy a liability according to the outcome of the proceedings. Had it been so intended, it would have contained provisions for the protection of legal professionals similar to those in Article 6. Similarly, the absence from section 328 of any protection equivalent to that conferred in section 330 on legal advisers (see Main Work para 14.54) supported a restricted interpretation of 'being concerned in an arrangement'. Much stronger and clearer language would have been required to indicate a legislative intention that legal professional privilege, and the implied undertaking not to disclose documents obtained on discovery to third parties, should be overridden. Indeed, the recitals to Council Directive 2001/97/EC (which amended the 1991 Directive) had expressly stated that it would not be appropriate to put legal professionals under an obligation to report suspicions of money laundering in respect of activities associated with existing or contemplated judicial proceedings.

14.34C The Court regarded settlement of legal proceedings as an integral part of the ordinary conduct of civil litigation and as such outside the scope of section 328. That means there is a distinction between consensual steps (including a settlement) taken in an ordinary litigious context and consensual arrangements independent of litigation. But that, according to the Court, is a distinction inherent in both the 2001 Directive and the 2002 Act.

15

LOCAL GOVERNMENT

A. Introduction

n1 For the Commission's final report, see *In the Public Interest: Publication of Local Authority Inquiry Reports* (Law Com No 289, 2004). **15.01**

C. Duties and Discretions of Local Authorities to Disclose Information

Subsequent court decisions

The following new paragraphs come after paragraph 15.81 of the Main Work:

In *R (Ellis) v Chief Constable of Essex Police* [2003] 2 FLR 566, Lord Woolf CJ (sitting in the Divisional Court with Goldring J) drew attention to the fact that **15.81A** the *North Wales* case had been decided before the Human Rights Act 1998 came into force. The change made by the Act, he said (at 577), was that where human rights were at stake the Court's task was no longer 'merely supervisory and confined to the *Wednesbury* test but now involved a more intensive review to establish whether the limitation of the right in issue was necessary in a democratic society and whether the interference was proportionate to the legitimate aim being pursued'.

15.81B Lord Woolf's point in *Ellis* serves only to strengthen what is clearly the effect of the earlier cases: that an authority considering the disclosure of information of the kind discussed here must weigh very carefully the particular circumstances of the case and the respective rights of all the parties. The cases show, unsurprisingly, that this is a far from easy task.

D. Publication of Local Authority Reports

15.86 **n1** For the Commission's final report, see *In the Public Interest: Publication of Local Authority Inquiry Reports* (Law Com No 289, 2004). The Commission's recommendations include provisions for local authority special inquiries and for the extension of statutory qualified privilege to such special inquiries and to certain ad hoc inquiries.

16

THE ENVIRONMENT AND OTHER STATUTES

A. The Environment

The 2002 draft directive on public environmental information

The European Parliament and the Council of the European Union adopted Council Directive 2003/4/EC on public access to environmental information on 28 January 2003. For the text of the Directive, see Supplement Appendix G1. This replaces the 2002 draft Directive discussed in Main Work paras 16.70–16.72. Directive 2003/4/EC was passed to implement the obligations assumed under the Aarhus Convention, for discussion of which see Main Work paras 16.50–16.69. **16.70**

The 2002 Draft Regulations

The 2002 draft Regulations discussed in Main Work paras 16.73–16.89 have been replaced by the Environmental Information Regulations 2004, SI 2004 No 3391, which were made on 21 December 2004 and came into force on **16.73**

1 January 2005. For the text of the Regulations ('the EIR'), see Supplement Appendix G2. The EIR implement Council Directive 2003/4/EC. Access to environmental information is dealt with outside the 2000 Act under the EIR. The EIR are supplemented by a Code of Practice issued by the Secretary of State in February 2005 under regulation 16. For the text of the Code of Practice ('the Code'), see Supplement Appendix G3. The foreword to the Code lists the main differences between the regimes established by the 2000 Act and the EIR. That is a good place to start. The main differences listed in the Code are:

(a) the range of bodies covered by the EIR is wider than the authorities subject to the 2000 Act. This is to allow for consistency with the Directive. The EIR extend to public utilities and certain public–private partnerships and private companies, in the water, waste, transport, and energy sectors;
(b) requests for environmental information, unlike requests under the 2000 Act, do not need to be in writing;
(c) under the EIR, the information held by a public authority includes information held on behalf of any other person;
(d) a public authority has a duty to provide assistance and advice. If the authority, in exercise of this duty, seeks more particulars from the applicant under the EIR, it must do so within 20 working days of the request;
(e) the time limits for responding to a request apply to all requests: there is no extension of time because the public interest has to be considered. Regulation 7 allows an extension from 20 to 40 working days for complex and high-volume requests;
(f) no exception is made for requests that will involve costs in excess of the *appropriate limit* within the meaning of the Freedom of Information and Data Protection (Appropriate Limit and Fees) Regulations 2004. Except in specified limited circumstances, all requests must be dealt with and any charges imposed must be reasonable;
(g) there are differences between the exceptions available under the EIR and the exemptions under the 2000 Act: the public interest test applies to all exceptions under the EIR, but it only applies to qualified exemptions under the 2000 Act, and the substantive exceptions in regulation 12(5) only apply to the extent that the disclosure would have an adverse effect on the matters listed, while only some of the exemptions under the Act are subject to a prejudice test;
(h) the requirement for public authorities to have a complaints and reconsideration procedure to deal with representations alleging non-compliance is mandatory under the EIR.

The following new paragraphs replace paragraphs 16.73–16.89 of the Main Work.

The 2004 EIR

Definitions

Under regulation 2(1), *environmental information* has the same meaning as in Article 2(1) of Council Directive 2003/4/EC, namely any information in written, visual, aural, electronic, or any other material form, on: **16.73A**

(a) the state of the elements of the environment, such as air and atmosphere, water, soil, land, landscape and natural sites including wetlands, coastal and marine areas, biological diversity and its components, including genetically modified organisms, and the interaction among those elements;
(b) factors, such as substances, energy, noise, radiation, or waste, including radioactive waste, emissions, discharges and other releases into the environment, affecting or likely to affect the elements of the environment referred to in (a);
(c) measures (including administrative measures) such as policies, legislation, plans, programmes, environmental agreements, and activities affecting or likely to affect the elements and factors referred to in (a) and (b), as well as measures and activities designed to protect those elements;
(d) reports on the implementation of environmental legislation;
(e) cost–benefit and other economic analyses and assumptions used within the framework of the measures and activities referred to in (c); and
(f) the state of human health and safety, including the contamination of the food chain, where relevant, conditions of human life, cultural sites and built structures inasmuch as they are or may be affected by the state of the elements of the environment referred to in (a) or, through those elements, by any of the matters referred to in (b) and (c).

The Department for Environment, Food and Rural Affairs ('DEFRA') has published guidance on the EIR on its website at http://www.defra.gov.uk/corporate/opengov/eir/guidance/index.htm. The guidance makes the following comments on the definition: **16.73B**

> *Air* in paragraph (a) of the definition should be taken to include the air within buildings and other natural and man-made structures above or below ground and in air conditioning systems;
>
> *Water* in paragraph (a) should be taken to include underground and surface waters (both natural and in man-made structures) sewage and foul water; the latter [surface waters] to include inland waters (ie rivers, canals, lakes) estuaries and seas; water tables, and aquifers;
>
> *Soil* in paragraph (a) should be taken to include the *in situ* upper layer of the mantle rock in which plants grow;
>
> *Land* and *Landscape* in paragraph (a) should be taken to include all land surfaces, buildings, caves, and underground strata. Land covered by water is also included;
>
> A *natural site* in paragraph (a) should be taken to include areas identified by reason of their flora, fauna, geological, or physiographical features (eg Sites of Special

Scientific Interest) or general environmental quality (eg Areas of Outstanding Natural Beauty);

Biological diversity in paragraph (a) should be taken to include species both living and dead;

Human health and safety and *conditions of human life* in paragraph (f) include human response to physical, chemical, and biological agents delivered through environmental media of water, air, land, and biodiversity etc;

Built structures in paragraph (f) should be taken to include structures, roads, and other infrastructures created by mankind and includes ancient and historic monuments;

The *state* in paragraph (f) should be taken to include physical, chemical, electro-magnetic, radiological, and biological conditions at any moment in time;

Emissions in paragraph (b) includes *discharges and other releases into the environment*, wherever they occur, and should be taken to include the direct or indirect release of substances, liquids, gases, radiation, vibrations, light, or noise from individual or diffuse sources into or onto air, water, or land;

Measures in paragraph (c) include administrative measures and environmental management programmes such as permit schemes, management contracts, land-use planning regimes and permits, regeneration and transport development plans and proposals;

Economic analyses in paragraph (e) include financial analyses;

Affect and *affecting* throughout the definition include direct and indirect effects.

16.73C Experience from the implementation of the earlier environmental information regime has established that *environmental information* is interpreted very broadly. The Government has treated all information relating to GM crop trials, to pesticide testing, to diseased cattle, and to land use planning (including the reasons for decisions to approve as well as to refuse planning permission) as environmental information. It will be seen that the definition covers many of the matters for which local government is responsible.

16.73D The definition of environmental information in the 1992 regulations was tested in the domestic and European courts. Although the definition in the EIR is different, these cases (which are discussed at Main Work paras 16.39–16.47) still provide useful guidance on how to approach the definition of environmental information.

16.73E The definition of *public authorities* in regulation 2(2) is wider than the definition in the 2000 Act and includes bodies such as privatized water authorities and power companies. *Public authority* means:

(a) government departments;
(b) other public authorities set out in the first Schedule to the 2000 Act. There are some slight modifications. The special forces of the Crown and any unit assisting GCHQ are included; any body or office holder who is included in

the list in relation only to information of a specified description (eg the BBC for purposes other than journalism art or literature) is excluded;

(c) any other body or other person that carries out functions of public administration;

(d) any other body or other person that is under the control of a person falling within sub-paragraphs (a),(b), or (c) and:
  (i) has public responsibilities relating to the environment;
  (ii) exercises functions of a public nature relating to the environment; or
  (iii) provides public services relating to the environment.

Functions in (c) and (d) is taken to include the provision of services. *Control* in (d) is taken to mean a relationship constituted by statute, regulations, rights, licence, contracts, or other matters which either separately or jointly confer the possibility of directly or indirectly exercising a decisive influence on a body: DEFRA's guidance, ch 2, paras 2.3 and 2.4. **16.73F**

The EIR do not apply to any public authority when it is acting in a judicial or legislative capacity: regulation 3(3). The Regulations do not extend to Scottish public authorities; those public authorities are subject to the Environmental Regulations (Scotland) 2004. **16.73G**

Further general guidance on who is covered by the Regulations is to be found in ch 2 of DEFRA's guidance. **16.73H**

Dissemination of environmental information

Regulation 4 requires public authorities to publish environmental information which they hold and to make it available to the public by electronic means which are easily accessible. Authorities are required to publish the information referred to in Article 7(2) of the Directive and the facts, and analyses of facts, which they consider relevant and important in framing major environmental policy proposals. **16.73I**

Article 7(2) is in these terms: **16.73J**

> The information to be made available and disseminated shall be updated as appropriate and shall include at least:
> (a) texts of international treaties, conventions or agreements, and of Community, national, regional or local legislation on the environment or relating to it;
> (b) policies, plans and programmes relating to the environment;
> (c) progress reports on the implementation of items referred to in (a) and (b) when prepared or held in electronic form by public authorities;
> (d) the reports on the state of the environment referred to in paragraph 3 (these are reports to be prepared on the initiative of governments at least once in every four years on the quality of, and pressures on, the environment);
> (e) data or summaries of data derived from the monitoring of activities affecting, or likely to affect the environment;

(f) authorizations with a significant impact on the environment and environmental agreements or a reference to a place where such information can be requested or found in the framework of article 3 [ie under the disclosure provisions of the EIR];

(g) environmental impact studies and risk assessments concerning the environmental elements referred to in article 2(1)(a) [Article 2(1) contains the definition of 'environmental information'] or a reference to the place where the information can be requested or found in the framework of article 3 [ie under the disclosure provisions].

16.73K Further general guidance is to be found in ch 5 of DEFRA's guidance on proactive dissemination.

Obligation to make information available on request

16.73L Regulations 5 and 6 oblige public authorities, upon receiving a request, to make environmental information available in the form requested and without an interest having to be stated, unless it is reasonable for the authority to make it available in another form or format, or the information is already publicly available and easily accessible in another form or format.

Time limits

16.73M Information has to be made available as soon as possible and no later than 20 working days after the date of receipt of the request. The public authority may extend the period of 20 working days to 40 working days if it reasonably believes that the complexity and volume of the information requested means that it is impracticable either to comply with the request within the earlier period or to make a decision to refuse to do so.

Charging

16.73N Under regulation 8(2) a public authority is not allowed to make any charge for allowing an applicant:

(a) access to any public registers or lists of environmental information which the authority holds; or

(b) to examine the information requested at the place which the public authority makes available for that examination.

16.73O Subject to that, a public authority is allowed to charge for supplying information, but the charge shall not exceed an amount which the public authority is satisfied is a reasonable amount: regulation 8(3). A public authority is required to publish and make available to applicants:

(a) a schedule of charges; and

(b) information on the circumstances in which a charge may be made or waived: regulation 8(8).

In the decision notice in the case of *South Holland District Council*, case reference FAC0065281 (16 May 2005), the Information Commissioner rejected a complaint that the fee to be charged by the Council was excessive. The applicant sought information concerning the proposed erection of 13 industrial wind turbines on Bicker Fen. The information requested consisted of 264 A4 pages and 32 A3 pages. The charge made by the Council for providing copies of this information was £25. The Commissioner's decision was that this was a reasonable amount. **16.73P**

Duty to provide advice and assistance

The EIR require public authorities to provide advice and assistance to those who propose to make or have made a request for environmental information. Guidance on this is given in paragraphs 8–20 of the Code. **16.73Q**

Transfer of a request

Regulation 10 of the EIR provides for the transfer of a request from one body to another. Guidance on this is given in paragraphs 31–39 of the Code. **16.73R**

Further general guidance on handling requests for environmental information is contained in ch 7 of DEFRA's guidance. **16.73S**

Representations and reconsideration

Regulation 11 provides that an internal procedure for handling complaints must be provided by each public authority. Wherever possible, complaints must be handled by someone other than the person who dealt with the request. Appeals can be made to the Information Commissioner if the outcome of the internal review is unsatisfactory. The procedure for handling complaints is set out in paragraphs 58–67 of the Code and the Information Commissioner has also published his expectations of review procedures: **16.73T**

> Once an authority has received your complaint, as a matter of good practice they should send you an acknowledgement stating when they expect to respond in full. If the authority is not able to meet their expected response date (as stated in the acknowledgment) they should inform you of this, and explain the reasons for the delay. An authority must review a decision as soon as possible and in every case within 40 working days of receipt of the complaint. If, following the review, the decision is to release information previously withheld, the Commissioner expects public authorities to release the information as soon as possible, and at the latest within 40 working days of the decision.
>
> The review should be carried out impartially by someone who was not party to the original decision, and who has the authority to reverse/amend the previous outcome where necessary.
>
> An authority cannot charge for carrying out an internal review.
>
> When a response is sent, as a matter of good practice the authority should repeat details of your right to appeal to the Commissioner.

16.73U Further general guidance is given on complaints and reconsideration in ch 8 of DEFRA's guidance.

Exceptions

16.73V The consultation paper which preceded the EIR said that the main difference between the draft Regulations and the 2000 Act was in the treatment of exceptions or exemptions. The differences between the EIR and the Act are striking. The Regulations contain a presumption in favour of disclosure of environmental information. The substantive exceptions only apply where disclosure would have an adverse effect, and there is a public interest test for all exceptions. If this is the right approach for environmental information, it is difficult to see why it is not the right approach for all information. Perhaps in the future the best solution may be to bring the exemptions in the Act into line with the EIR.

16.73W DEFRA's guidance on refusal is contained in ch 7. It starts:

> The regulations contain a presumption in favour of disclosure of environmental information. Refusal is only permissible on the limited grounds set out in the Regulations. These include some circumstances where information cannot be released, for example, because a public authority does not hold the information or because the request is formulated in too general a manner.
>
> In these cases the public authority will provide advice and assistance. In all cases where an exception applies, the grounds for refusal must be interpreted in a restrictive way, taking into account the public interest served by disclosure.
>
> Information relating to emissions into the environment is subject to more limited exceptions.
>
> Wherever a request for environmental information concerns a mixture of information that can be released and information which it would not be in the public interest to release, the information that can be supplied must be separated out and made available.
>
> Refusals must be communicated as soon as possible.

16.73X The exceptions are set out in regulation 12 in the following terms:

> (1) Subject to paragraphs (2), (3) and (9), a public authority may refuse to disclose environmental information requested if:
> (a) an exception to disclosure applies under paragraphs (4) or (5); and
> (b) in all the circumstances of the case, the public interest in maintaining the exception outweighs the public interest in disclosing the information.
>
> (2) A public authority shall apply a presumption in favour of disclosure.
>
> (3) To the extent that information requested includes personal data of which the applicant is not the data subject, the personal data shall not be disclosed otherwise than in accordance with regulation 13 [see Supplement para 16.73Z].
>
> (4) For the purposes of paragraph (1)(a), a public authority may refuse to disclose information to the extent that–
> (a) it does not hold that information when an applicant's request is received;
> (b) the request for information is manifestly unreasonable;

(c) the request for information is formulated in too general a manner and the public authority has complied with regulation 9 [advice and assistance];
(d) the request relates to material which is still in the course of completion, to unfinished documents or to incomplete data; or
(e) the request involves the disclosure of internal communications.

(5) For the purposes of paragraph (1)(a) a public authority may refuse to disclose information to the extent that its disclosure would adversely affect–
(a) international relations, defence, national security, or public safety;
(b) the course of justice, the ability of a person to receive a fair trial or the ability of a public authority to conduct an inquiry of a criminal or disciplinary nature;
(c) intellectual property rights;
(d) the confidentiality of the proceedings of that or any other public authority where such confidentiality is provided by law;
(e) the confidentiality of commercial or industrial information where such confidentiality is provided by law to protect a legitimate economic interest;
(f) the interests of the person who provided the information where that person–
(i) was not under, and could not have been put under, any legal obligation to supply it to that or any other public authority;
(ii) did not supply it in circumstances such that that or any other public authority is entitled apart from the Regulations to disclose it; and
(iii) has not consented to its disclosure;
(g) the protection of the environment to which the information relates.

(6) For the purposes of paragraph (1), a public authority may respond to a request by neither confirming nor denying whether such information exists and is held by the public authority, whether or not it holds such information, if that confirmation or denial would involve the disclosure of information which would adversely affect any of the interests referred to in paragraph (5)(a) [international relations, defence, national security, or public safety] and would not be in the public interest under paragraph (1)(b).

(7) For the purposes of a response under paragraph (6) whether information exists and is held by the public authority is itself the disclosure of information.

(8) For the purposes of paragraph 4(e), internal communications includes communications between government departments.

(9) To the extent that the environmental information to be disclosed relates to information on emissions, a public authority shall not be entitled to refuse to disclose that information under an exception referred to in paragraphs 5(d) to (g) [confidentiality, third parties, and protection of the environment to which the information relates].

(10) For the purposes of paragraphs (5)(b),(d) and (f), references to a public authority shall include references to a Scottish public authority.

(11) Nothing in these Regulations shall authorize a refusal to make available any environmental information contained in or otherwise held with other information which is withheld by virtue of these Regulations unless it is not reasonably capable of being separated from the other information for the purpose of making available that information.

16.73Y The Information Commissioner has issued a decision notice in the case of *Bridgnorth District Council*, case reference FS50062329 (12 July 2005) involving regulations 12(5)(b) and 12(5)(f). For further discussion of this case, see Supplement para 7.77A. Further general guidance on refusals is given in ch 7 of DEFRA's guidance.

Personal data

16.73Z Regulation 13 makes provision for exceptions to the disclosure of environmental information which includes personal data of which the person requesting the information is not the data subject. It provides that the personal data shall not be disclosed if that would breach the data protection principles set out in Part 1 of Schedule 1 to the Data Protection Act 1998 [see Main Work paras 10.16–10.34]. It also provides that the personal data must not be disclosed if the individual who is the subject of the personal data has properly given notice that disclosure would cause unwarranted substantial damage or distress and there is no overriding public interest in disclosure. It also provides that there must be no disclosure if the individual who is the subject of the personal data would not be entitled to have access to the data under section 7(1) of the Data Protection Act 1998 and there is no overriding public interest in disclosure.

Ministerial certificates

16.73AA Regulation 15 provides that a Minister of the Crown may certify that a refusal to disclose information under regulation 12(1) is because the disclosure would adversely affect national security and would not be in the public interest. A Minister of the Crown means a Cabinet Minister or the Attorney-General. Such a certificate shall be conclusive evidence of the matters it states and may identify the information to which it relates in general terms.

Code of practice and historical records

16.73AB Part 4 of the EIR deals with the code of practice and historical records. They are dealt with in similar terms to the 2000 Act.

Enforcement, appeals and offences

Part 5 of the EIR provides a proper system of review and enforcement. In effect, the appeal and enforcement provisions of the 2000 Act are applied indirectly to requests for environmental information. Section 77 of the 2000 Act has been amended so that the offence of altering records with intent to prevent disclosure applies to environmental information. **16.73AC**

17

IMPLICATIONS FOR BUSINESS

E. Access to and Protection of Business Information

Experience of the United States of America

The following new paragraphs come after paragraph 17.63 of the Main Work:

In early 2000, both the US Department of Justice ('DOJ') and the Department of Defense ('DOD') issued internal memoranda disagreeing with the *McDonnell* decision. Notwithstanding the DOD and DOJ memoranda, the US District Court for the District of Columbia overturned the General Services Administration's decision to release detailed pricing information pursuant to a FOIA request, and in the process held that agencies may not release unit pricing information pursuant to a FOIA request if the information is confidential or trade secret information under Exemption 4: *MCI Worldcom, Inc v General Services Administration* 165 F Supp 2d 28 (DDC 2001). **17.63A**

Most recently, in another case involving McDonnell Douglas (*McDonnell Douglas Corp v US Department of the Air Force* 375 F 3d 1182 (DC Cir 2004), the DC **17.63B**

Circuit held that certain line item and option year prices in a contract awarded by the US Air Force for the maintenance and repair of aircraft were within the scope of Exemption 4. The court agreed with McDonnell Douglas that disclosure of the option year prices was likely to cause it substantial competitive harm because disclosure would significantly increase the probability that its competitors would underbid McDonnell Douglas's prices if the Air Force competed for the contract again. Accordingly, the DC Circuit held that the Air Force's decision to release the option year pricing was contrary to law. In addition, in deciding whether it would prevent the Air Force from releasing the prices for vendor pricing line items, the DC Circuit rejected the Air Force's argument that McDonnell Douglas was unlikely to suffer substantial harm. The Air Force had contended that McDonnell Douglas's competitors could not derive the percentage by which McDonnell Douglas marks up the bids it receives from subcontractors with any degree of certainty. The DC Circuit opined that the Air Force's reasoning was neither as compelling as that of McDonnell Douglas nor as well reasoned, logical, or consistent, and held that the Air Force's decision to release the information was arbitrary and capricious.

18

FREEDOM OF INFORMATION IN COMMERCIAL DISPUTES

B. The Disclosure of Documents

The grounds for withholding inspection or disclosure

Legal professional privilege

The following new paragraphs come after paragraph 18.46 of the Main Work: **18.46A**

The *Three Rivers* litigation (in which the Bank of England is being sued for misfeasance in public office in respect of its supervision of BCCI) has thrown up questions as to the scope of legal advice privilege.

In *Three Rivers District Council and others v Governor and Company of the Bank of England (No 5)* [2003] QB 1556, the Bank of England relied upon 'legal advice privilege' in answer to an application for disclosure of documents prepared by the Bank's employees or ex-employees and produced to the Bingham Inquiry Unit (a body of Bank officials appointed to deal on its behalf with all communications between the Bank and the Bingham Inquiry), whether prepared for submission to or at the direction of the solicitors retained by the Unit or not. Litigation privilege could not be claimed because the Bingham Inquiry was a private non-statutory inquiry which did not constitute adversarial proceedings. **18.46B**

18.46C The Court of Appeal decided that for the purposes of legal advice privilege, unlike litigation privilege, information provided to solicitors is only privileged if it is provided by the true client. In that case the Inquiry Unit was the client and information provided by an employee or ex-employee or officer or ex-officers stood in the same position as information provided by an independent third party. This was not appealed to the House of Lords and remains the law.

18.46D Mann J observed in *USP Strategies Plc and another v London General Holdings Ltd and others* (1 March 2004) that this does not mean that legal advice privilege is restricted to communications between solicitor and client or vice versa, with the result that communication of that legal advice to a third party will not be privileged. The Court of Appeal was concerned with information prepared for the purpose of giving instructions which were to lead to advice. The Court of Appeal made clear that the privilege would extend to documents evidencing communications passing between solicitor and client. This would catch, so Mann J held, disclosures of that advice whether internally or to third parties, subject to the issue of whether the disclosure amounted to a waiver of privilege. It is not inevitable that there will be waiver. The communication may be subject to a confidentiality which maintains the privilege as against the rest of the world.

18.46E The decision of the House of Lords in *Three Rivers District Council and others v Governor and Company of the Bank of England (No 6)* [2005] 1 AC 610 was concerned with an application by the claimants for disclosure of communications passing between the Bingham Inquiry Unit and its solicitors during the course of the inquiry.

18.46F The judge hearing the application found that the solicitors had been advising the Bank on how to present evidence in a manner least likely to attract criticism. He decided that the Bank could claim legal advice privilege only in respect of solicitor–client communications exchanged for the purpose of seeking advice as to the Bank's rights and obligations. The privilege was not available in respect of communications relating to the seeking or obtaining of advice or assistance on the presentation of evidence to the inquiry.

18.46G The Court of Appeal dismissed the appeal ([2004] QB 916). Its decision was that legal advice privilege applied to obtaining advice from a lawyer about legal rights and liabilities, and advice as to how the Bank should present its case to the inquiry so as to lead to as favourable an outcome as possible was not within that category. It was necessary to show that this was the dominant purpose but, if it was, broad protection would be given to communications within that solicitor–client relationship which were ancillary to that purpose.

18.46H The House of Lords allowed the appeal and held that legal advice privilege applied. It was desirable as a matter of public policy that communications between clients and their lawyers for the purpose of obtaining legal advice should be privileged from discovery, notwithstanding that as a result cases might have to be decided in the absence of relevant probative material. 'Legal advice' is not confined to telling the client the law, but includes advising upon what should prudently and sensibly be done in a 'relevant legal context', which would include the presentation of a case to an inquiry by someone whose conduct might be criticized by the inquiry. Lord Scott said that 'communications between clients and lawyers, whereby the clients are hoping for the assistance of the lawyers' legal skills in the management of their [the clients'] affairs, should be secure against the possibility of any scrutiny from others' (at [34]).

Lord Rodger said that what mattered was that Freshfields was instructed 'to carry out a function which necessarily involved the use of their legal skills if it was to be performed properly' and therefore the communications were concerned with obtaining 'legal advice' in the broader sense in which it should be understood for the purposes of legal advice privilege (at [60]). Lord Carswell considered that legal professional privilege does not stem from litigation, as the Court of Appeal held, but is a more general privilege based on the relationship of lawyer and client which sub-divides into legal advice privilege and litigation privilege. **18.46I**

Lord Brown agreed and added the following remarks specifically related to inquiries (at [120]): **18.46J**

> I would go so far as to state as a general principle that the process by which a client seeks and obtains his lawyer's assistance in the presentation of his case for the purposes of any formal inquiry—whether concerned with public law or private law issues, whether adversarial or inquisitorial in form, whether held in public or in private, whether or not directly affecting his rights or liabilities—attracts legal advice privilege. Such assistance to my mind clearly has the character of legal business. It is precisely the sort of professional service for which lawyers are ordinarily employed by virtue of their expertise and experience. Indeed, it falls squarely within Dr Johnson's description of a lawyer's function...

Dr Johnson's description (as quoted by Lord Carswell in [114]) reads as follows:

> As it rarely happens that a man is fit to plead his own cause, lawyers are a class of the community who, by study and experience, have acquired the art and power of arranging evidence, and of applying to the points at issue what the law has settled. A lawyer is to do for his client all that his client might fairly do for himself, if he could (*Boswell, Life of Johnson*, ed Birkbeck Hill (1950), vol 5, p 26).

20

PRIVACY AND CONFIDENTIALITY

A. Introduction

Is there today a right of privacy in English law?

The argument was taken a stage further when *Wainwright v Home Office* was considered on appeal in the House of Lords, where Lord Hoffmann concluded by rejecting **20.03**

> the invitation to declare that since at the latest 1950 [ie when the UK signed the European Convention] there has been a previously unknown tort of invasion of privacy.

The claimants accordingly lost their appeal on the privacy issue. For further consideration of this decision, see Supplement para 20.89A.

D. Protection of Privacy

The Human Rights Act 1998

20.50 The interplay of Articles 8, 10, and 13 of the European Convention is further considered in *Theakston v MGN Ltd* [2002] EMLR 398, and *Campbell v MGN Ltd* [2004] 2 AC 457, as is section 12 of the Human Rights Act 1998 which applies if a court is considering whether to grant any relief which, if granted, might affect the exercise of the Convention right to freedom of expression: see also *Jagger v News of the World, The Times*, 10 March 2005. For further discussion of these cases, see Supplement paras 20.93A–20.93F.

E. The New Cases

Wainwright v Home Office

The following new paragraphs come after paragraph 20.89 of the Main Work:

20.89A In their appeal to the House of Lords (*Wainwright v Home Office* [2004] 2 AC 406), on the privacy issue the claimants placed particular reliance on Sedley LJ's judgment in *Douglas v Hello* [2001] QB 967 (see Main Work paras 20.53–20.60). In a detailed consideration of that judgment Lord Hoffmann commented as follows (at [28]–[34]):

> 28. Sedley LJ drew attention to the way in which the development of the law of confidence had attenuated the need for a relationship of confidence between the recipient of the confidential information and the person from whom it was obtained—a development which enabled the UK Government to persuade the European Human Rights Commission in *Earl Spencer v United Kingdom* (1998) 25 EHRR CD 105 that English law of confidence provided an adequate remedy to restrain the publication of private information about the applicants' marriage and medical condition and photographs taken with a telephoto lens. These developments showed that the basic value protected by the law in such cases was privacy. Sedley LJ said, at p 1001, paragraph 126:
>
>> What a concept of privacy does, however, is accord recognition to the fact that the law has to protect not only those people whose trust has been abused but those who simply find themselves subjected to an unwanted intrusion into their personal lives. The law no longer needs to construct an artificial relationship of confidentiality between the intruder and the victim: it can recognise privacy itself as a legal principle drawn from the fundamental value of personal autonomy.
>
> 29. I read these remarks as suggesting that, in relation to the publication of personal information obtained by intrusion, the common law of breach of confidence has reached the point at which a confidential relationship has become unnecessary. As the underlying value protected is privacy, the action might as well be renamed invasion of privacy. 'To say this' said Sedley LJ at p 1001, paragraph 125, 'is in my

> belief to say little, save by way of a label, that our courts have not said already over the years.'
>
> 30. I do not understand Sedley LJ to have been advocating the creation of a high-level principle of invasion of privacy. His observations are in my opinion no more (although certainly no less) than a plea for the extension and possibly renaming of the old action for breach of confidence. As Buxton LJ pointed out in this case in the Court of Appeal [2002] QB 1334, 1361–1362, paragraphs 96–99, such an extension would go further than any English court has yet gone and would be contrary to some cases (such as *Kaye v Robertson* [1991] FSR 62) in which it positively declined to do so. The question must wait for another day. But Sedley LJ's dictum does not support a principle of privacy so abstract as to include the circumstances of the present case.
>
> 31. There seems to me a great difference between identifying privacy as a value which underlies the existence of a rule of law (and may point the direction in which the law should develop) and privacy as a principle of law in itself. The English common law is familiar with the notion of underlying values—principles only in the broadest sense—which direct its development. A famous example is *Derbyshire County Council v Times Newspapers Ltd* [1993] AC 534, in which freedom of speech was the underlying value which supported the decision to lay down the specific rule that a local authority could not sue for libel. But no one has suggested that freedom of speech is in itself a legal principle which is capable of sufficient definition to enable one to deduce specific rules to be applied in concrete cases. That is not the way the common law works.
>
> ...
>
> 34. Furthermore, the coming into force of the Human Rights Act 1998 weakens the argument for saying that a general tort of invasion of privacy is needed to fill gaps in existing remedies. Sections 6 and 7 of the Act are in themselves substantial gap fillers; if it is indeed the case that a person's rights under article 8 have been infringed by a public authority, he will have a statutory remedy...

Lord Hoffmann concluded at [35] by rejecting **20.89B**

> the invitation to declare that since at the latest 1950 [ie when the UK signed the European Convention] there has been a previously unknown tort of invasion of privacy.

The claimants accordingly lost their appeal on the privacy issue.

A v B plc

The following new paragraphs come after paragraph 20.93 of the Main Work:

Theakston v MGN Ltd

In *Theakston v MGN Ltd* [2002] EMLR 398 the claimant had visited a brothel **20.93A** and engaged in sexual activity with at least three prostitutes. One of them sold her story and some photographs to the defendant, which published the *Sunday People*. The claimant applied for an interim injunction to restrain publication on the grounds of breach of confidence and invasion of privacy. Ouseley J granted an injunction to restrain publication of the photographs but refused to restrain publication of the story. The judge said that by virtue of section 12(4) of the Human Rights Act 1998 the court had to have regard to the Article 10(1) right to freedom of expression, not just of the *Sunday People* but also of the prostitute who had information of a journalistic nature which she wished to impart. In the circumstances of the case the balance between the competing Article 10 and Article 8 rights would be struck by refusing an injunction with regard to the basic facts and by granting an injunction to restrain publication of the photographs.

Campbell v MGN Ltd

20.93B In *Campbell v MGN Ltd* [2004] 2 AC 457 Naomi Campbell sued the defendant, as publisher of the *Mirror*, for damages and an injunction. Her action was for breach of confidence. An additional claim for breach of the duty under section 4(4) of the Data Protection Act 1998 was agreed to have added nothing to the breach of confidence claim: [2004] 2 AC 494 at [130]. Ms Campbell had volunteered information to the media about her private life, and had said, publicly but untruthfully, that she did not take drugs. In the relevant articles the *Mirror* disclosed her drug addiction and the fact that she was receiving therapy through a named self-help group. The newspaper gave details of group meetings and showed photographs of her in the street as she was leaving a group meeting. In bringing her action Ms Campbell accepted that the newspaper was entitled to publish the fact of her drug addiction and the bare fact that she was receiving treatment, but she alleged that the *Mirror* had acted in breach of confidence by obtaining and publishing (a) the additional details of her therapy at the group meetings; and (b) the photographs, which had been taken covertly. The newspaper's defence was that (i) it was entitled, in the public interest, to publish the information in order to correct the claimant's misleading public statements; and (ii) the information published about her treatment was peripheral and not sufficiently significant to amount to a breach of the duty of confidence.

20.93C Morland J gave judgment for the claimant, holding that the information complained of was confidential and that (having regard to section 12(4) of the Human Rights Act 1998 and balancing Articles 8 and 10) publication was not justified in the public interest. The Court of Appeal unanimously allowed the newspaper's appeal, agreeing that the disclosure of the additional information complained of was peripheral and that a reasonable person of ordinary sensibilities would not find its disclosure offensive; the publicized information was a legitimate part of the journalistic package designed to demonstrate, with the detail necessary to carry credibility, that the claimant had deceived the public; and accordingly publication was justified in the public interest.

20.93D The House of Lords allowed Ms Campbell's appeal (Lord Nicholls and Lord Hoffmann dissenting): [2004] 2 AC 457. The majority (Baroness Hale and Lords

Hope and Carswell) took the view that the threshold test as to whether information was private was to ask whether a reasonable person of ordinary sensibilities, if placed in the same situation as the subject of the disclosure, rather than its recipient, would find the disclosure offensive; that, since the details of the claimant's therapy for her drug addiction related to the condition of her physical and mental health and the treatment she was receiving for it, they were akin to the private and confidential information contained in medical records and their publication required special justification; that the assurances of privacy, confidentiality, and anonymity were essential to the type of treatment that the claimant was undergoing, so that a person in her position would find disclosure highly offensive, and might also be deterred from continuing with the therapy, thereby causing a setback to recovery; that therefore the details of the claimant's therapy constituted private information which gave rise to a duty of confidentiality; that the publication of that information went beyond disclosure which was necessary to add credibility to the legitimate story that the claimant had deceived the public and went beyond the journalistic margin of appreciation allowed to a free press; that although the photographs of the claimant were taken in a public place, the context in which they were used and linked to the articles added to the overall intrusion into the claimant's private life; that, looking at the publication as a whole and taking account of all the circumstances, the claimant's right pursuant to Article 8 to respect for her private life outweighed the newspaper's right pursuant to Article 10 to freedom of expression; and that, accordingly, publication of the additional information and the accompanying photographs constituted an unjustified infringement of the claimant's right to privacy for which she was entitled to damages.

In the course of her litigation Ms Campbell found four judges in her favour and five against her, though she won a majority where it mattered most. Beyond the general and familiar point about the hazards of litigation, however, the judgments reveal that the Article 8 and Article 10 rights may be found to be almost evenly balanced, so that there is a particular difficulty in predicting which way the scales will be tipped. **20.93E**

Jagger v News of the World

More recently, the High Court has found that Elizabeth Jagger (daughter of Mick) and Calum Best (son of George) had 'a legitimate expectation of privacy' when their 'sexual activities' just inside the closed doors of the Kabaret's Prophecy nightclub were filmed, as they became aware when a series of 'rather indistinct stills' from a security camera appeared on the front page of the *News of the World* (*The Times*, 10 March 2005). Miss Jagger claimed breach of copyright, and of her rights to data protection, her right to respect for private life under the European Convention and her rights at common law. She sought and obtained an interim **20.93F** injunction against the club's manager and any other unknown defendant who might have supplied the footage to the *News of the World* (the manager denied that he did so) preventing any further publication of the closed-circuit television images or any stills from the film footage. Bell J said:

> Although the claimant may be said to be guilty of misconduct in a most general sense, she was not in my view on the present information guilty of such moral turpitude as to prevent her seeking her remedy from the court. I can see no legitimate public interest in further dissemination of the images, which could serve only to humiliate the claimant for the prurient interest of others.

He concluded that the balance between the claimant's rights and the manager's rights to freedom of expression came down firmly in favour of restricting publication.

Conclusions

20.97 **n113** and see *Princess Caroline von Hannover v Germany* (2005) 40 EHRR 1.

20.99 The House of Lords has now had the opportunity of considering the questions raised in this chapter in *Wainwright* [2004] 2 AC 406 and *Campbell v MGN Ltd* [2004] 2 AC 457 but they have yet to reach a final conclusion. The authors therefore offer some further, necessarily *interim*, conclusions in the following new paragraphs.

20.99A The breach of confidence cases considered here suggest that English law may provide effective protection against 'invasion of privacy' even though there is no separate tort of that name. Whether or not privacy is an 'underlying value' which may 'point the direction in which the law should develop' (*Wainwright v Home Office* [2004] 2 AC 406 at 423), the courts are obliged to identify privacy rights under Article 8(1) and balance them where appropriate against 'the rights and freedoms of others' under Article 8(2) and the freedom of expression rights under Article 10(1). The outcome of the balancing exercise may sometimes be difficult to predict, but (in breach of confidence cases) that would not justify a conclusion that privacy interests were unprotected.

20.99B The position is not so clear, however, where the claimants cannot bring their claim within the boundaries of breach of confidence. *Wainwright* [2004] 2 AC 406 (the strip search case) is such an example. It is true that the searches took place in 1997 before the Human Rights Act 1998 had been passed (and long before it came into force). And it is true that in the Court of Appeal Buxton LJ expressed the view ([2002] QB 1334 at 1352 [62]), that the claimants would have had a strong case for relief under section 7 if the Human Rights Act had been in force, 'by reason of a public authority's lack of regard for Article 8…'. However, Lord Hoffmann (referring to Buxton LJ's view) is 'not so sure…Article 8 may justify a monetary remedy for an intentional invasion of privacy by a public authority, even if no damage is suffered other than distress for which damages are not ordinarily recoverable. It does not follow that a merely negligent act should, contrary to general principle, give rise to a claim for damages for distress because it affects privacy rather than some other interest like bodily safety…': [2004] 2 AC 406 at 427 [51].

While it would be prudent to await some further privacy decisions outside the boundaries of breach of confidence in order to see whether the courts tend to reinforce Buxton LJ's confidence or Lord Hoffmann's doubts, the recent Court of Appeal decision (on the substantive appeal) in *Douglas v Hello* (2005) EWCA Civ 595, 18 May 2005, appears to support the approach of Buxton LJ. The Court of Appeal, referring to Princess Caroline of Monaco's complaints of press photographs which (she successfully contended) invaded her privacy (*Princess Caroline von Hannover v Germany* (2005) 40 EHRR 1), noted (at [57]) that 'the ECtHR has recognised an obligation on member states to protect one individual from an unjustified invasion of private life by another individual and an obligation on the courts of a member state to interpret legislation in a way that will achieve that result'. As to what is encompassed by 'private life', the ECtHR said ((2005) 40 EHRR 1 at [50]) that 'private life, in the Court's view, includes a person's physical and psychological integrity'. 20.99C

21

THE HUMAN RIGHTS ACT 1998

B. The European Convention for the Protection of Human Rights and Fundamental Freedoms

Main provisions

The decision of the Court of Appeal in *R (Morgan Grenfell Ltd) v Special Commissioners of Income Tax* has been reversed by the House of Lords: [2003] **21.12**

1 AC 563. The Inland Revenue sought disclosure by Morgan Grenfell of instructions to counsel and counsel's advice on a lease-back scheme under section 20(1) of the Taxes and Management Act 1970. The House of Lords held that Morgan Grenfell could rely on legal professional privilege. Legal professional privilege was a fundamental human right that could only be overridden by express words or necessary implication, and neither could be found in section 20. The case was cited in the Main Work as an illustration of the fact that respect for private and family life and freedom of expression are qualified rights. The rights are qualified rights but the *Morgan Grenfell* case is no longer an example of this.

n15 *R v Shayler* is now reported at [2003] 1 AC 247.

Free speech purists were dismayed by the controversial decision of the House of Lords in *R (Pro Life Alliance) v BBC* [2004] 1 AC 185, which demonstrates again that the right to freedom of expression under Article 10 is a qualified right. The claimant was entitled to a party election broadcast in Wales in the 2001 General Election. It submitted for broadcasting a video that contained graphic footage of an actual abortion, including images of aborted foetuses. The BBC refused transmission of the video on the grounds of taste and decency, concluding that they would be offensive to public feeling and would thus contravene its agreement with the Secretary of State and section 6(1)(a) of the Broadcasting Act 1990. The Judge refused the claimant's application for permission to apply for judicial review of the decision to refuse transmission. The Court of Appeal allowed an appeal by the claimant. The House of Lords allowed the appeal by the BBC. The House held that on the basis accepted by the claimant, that party political broadcasts were subject to the same restriction on transmission of offensive material as other programmes, there had been no ground for interfering with the decision of the BBC that, applying the standards laid down by Parliament, the claimant's video should not be transmitted; and that its decision had not been a discriminatory, arbitrary, or unreasonable denial of the right to freedom of expression under Article 10(2) of the Convention.

C. The Human Rights Act 1998

Legislation to be construed as compatible with Convention rights

21.19 *A v Secretary of State for the Home Department* HL(E) [2005] 2 AC 68 (the *Bellmarsh* case) is an example of the courts making a declaration of incompatibility. Following large-scale terrorist attacks in the US on 11 September 2001 the UK Government concluded that there was a public emergency threatening the life of the nation within the meaning of Article 15 of the Convention. Accordingly the Government made the Human Rights Act 1998 (Designed Derogation)

Order 2001, designating the UK's proposed derogation from the right to personal liberty guaranteed by Article 5(1) of the Convention. The Government also, by section 23 of the Anti-terrorism, Crime and Security Act 2001, provided for the detention of non-nationals if the Home Secretary believed that their presence in the United Kingdom was a risk to national security and he suspected that they were terrorists who, for the time being, could not be deported because of fears for their safety or other practical considerations. The nine appellants were detained under the 2001 Act.

When their appeal reached the House of Lords Lord Bingham set out the role of the court at [42]:

> ...the appellants are in my opinion entitled to invite the courts to review, on proportionality grounds, the Derogation Order and the compatibility with the Convention of section 23 and the courts are not effectively precluded by any doctrine of deference from scrutinising the issues raised. It also follows that I do not accept the full breadth of the Attorney General's submissions. I do not in particular accept the distinction he drew between democratic institutions and the courts. It is of course true that the judges in this country are not elected and are not answerable to Parliament. It is also of course true, as pointed out in paragraph 29 above, that Parliament, the executive and the courts have different functions. But the function of the independent judges charged to interpret and apply the law is universally recognised as a cardinal feature of the modern democratic state, a cornerstone of the rule of law itself. The Attorney General is fully entitled to insist on the proper limits of judicial authority, but he is wrong to stigmatize judicial decision-making as in some way undemocratic. It is particularly inappropriate in a case such as the present in which Parliament has expressly legislated in section 6 of the 1998 Act to render unlawful any act of a public authority, including a court, incompatible with a Convention right, has required courts (in section 2) to take account of relevant Strasbourg jurisprudence, has (in section 3) required courts, so far as possible, to give effect to Convention rights and has conferred a right of appeal on derogation issues. The effect is not of course to override the sovereign legislative authority of the Queen in Parliament, since if primary legislation is declared to be incompatible the validity of the legislation is unaffected (section 4(6)) and the remedy lies with the appropriate minister (section 10) who is answerable to Parliament. The 1998 Act gives the courts a very specific, wholly democratic, mandate. As Professor Jowell has put it 'The courts are charged by Parliament with delineating the boundaries of a rights-based democracy' ('Judicial Deference: servility, civility or institutional capacity?' [2003] PL 592, 597). See also Clayton, 'Judicial deference and democratic dialogue: the legitimacy of judicial intervention under the Human Rights Act 1998' [2004] PL 33.

The House of Lords, sitting as a nine-judge panel, held (Lord Walker dissenting) that the Derogation Order would be quashed and section 23 of the 2001 Act would be declared to be incompatible with Articles 5 and 14 of the Convention.

Proceedings and remedies

n37 The decision of the Court of Appeal in *Marcic v Thames Water Utilities Ltd* **21.27**
has been reversed by the House of Lords: [2004] 2 AC 42. The House of Lords

held that a sewerage undertaker was subject to an elaborate scheme of regulation under the Water Industry Act 1991 which included an independent regulator with powers of enforcement whose decisions were subject to judicial review. The House found that the statutory scheme provided a procedure for making complaints to the regulator which the claimant had chosen not to pursue. It said that a balance had to be struck between the interests of a person subject to sewer flooding and the interests of those, including other customers of the sewerage undertaker, who would have to finance the cost of constructing more sewers. The House concluded that such a balancing exercise was better undertaken by an industry regulator than a court and that the common law should not impose on a sewerage undertaker obligations which would be inconsistent with the statutory scheme since that would run counter to the will of Parliament. Members of the House of Lords held that a cause of action in nuisance would be inconsistent with the statutory scheme; that given the need to balance competing interests and the claimant's rights under the Convention, the statutory scheme was compatible with the claimant's rights under the Convention; and that accordingly the claimant could sustain neither a claim in nuisance against the defendant nor a claim under the Human Rights Act 1998. Lord Hoffmann drew attention to the decision of the European Court of Human Rights in *Hatton v United Kingdom* (2003) 37 EHRR 611 (the case about noise at Heathrow) where the court made it clear that the Convention does not accord absolute protection to property or even to residential premises. It requires a fair balance to be struck between the interests of persons whose homes and property are affected and the interests of other people such as customers and the general public. Damages will only be awarded under the Human Rights Act where they are necessary to provide just satisfaction for the successful claimant.

D. Enforcing the Convention Against Individuals

How far does the Convention apply to rights between individuals?

21.30 In *Von Hannover v Germany* (2005) 40 EHRR 1 the Strasbourg Court reiterated (at [57]) what it had said in *X and Y v The Netherlands* (1985) 8 EHRR 235, adding that the possible adoption of measures designed to secure respect for private life between individuals also applies to the protection of a person's picture against abuse by others.

21.33 n42 Buxton LJ's reservation in *Wainwright v Home Office* is now reported at [2002] QB 1334, 1360. The Court of Appeal's decision was upheld by the House of Lords: [2004] 2 AC 406.

21.38 n50 *A v B plc* is now reported at [2003] QB 195 (see 202 at [4]).

E. A Convention Right to Information?

Is there a Convention right to freedom of information?

The following new paragraph comes after paragraph 21.43 of the Main Work:

In *Brinks v Netherlands* (2005) 41 EHRR SE5, the Strasbourg Court stated that **21.43A** the storing by a public authority of information relating to a person's private life, the use of it, and the refusal to disclose that information to the person concerned amount to an interference with the right to respect for private life secured in Article 8. However, on the particular facts of that case it found there to be no violation of the Article. The applicant's complaint was that he had been granted access to only some of the information held about him by the Netherlands National Security Service ('the BVD'), namely outdated information which contained no third-party personal data and could give no insight into BVD sources, working methods, and current level of knowledge. The Court accepted that the decision not to give any further disclosure had been taken on the basis that it could harm the functioning of the BVD and thus the security of the State, attracting the exemption from disclosure conferred by the Government Information (Public Access) Act 1991, section 10 (see Main Work para 25.187). It went on to conclude that the resultant interference with the applicant's right to respect for his private life was not disproportionate to the legitimate aim pursued and was 'necessary in a democratic society' within the meaning of Article 8(2). While reiterating that in order for systems of secret surveillance to be compatible with Article 8 they must contain safeguards established by law which involve effective supervision of the relevant services' activities, normally by the judiciary, the Court found that the two-tier appeal system provided for by the Dutch Administrative Law Act 1994 (see Main Work para 25.193) met those requirements.

F. Conflicting Rights

Section 12 raises the threshold test for interlocutory injunctions

The meaning of 'likely' in section 12(3) was considered further by the House of **21.60** Lords in *Cream Holdings Ltd v Banerjee* [2005] 1 AC 253. The claimants were a group of companies which had begun as the *Cream* nightclub in Liverpool and had grown and diversified to become a substantial and newsworthy Liverpool business whose activities included staging large events such as dance festivals, franchising their brand name and logo and merchandising clothes and other items. Ms Banerjee, the first defendant, was a chartered accountant who, from February 1998, was the financial controller of one of the companies in the Cream group. The second defendant was the publisher of the *Daily Post* and the *Liverpool Echo*. In January 2001 Ms Banerjee was dismissed by the Cream group. When she left she took with her copies of documents which she claimed to show illegal and improper activities on the part of the Cream group. She passed these documents to the *Liverpool Echo*. In June 2002 the *Echo* published articles about alleged corruption involving a director of the Cream group and a local council official.

A few days later, the Cream group sought an interim injunction to restrain publication of any further confidential information given to the *Echo* by Ms Banerjee. In the High Court Lloyd J granted an interim injunction, holding that there were seriously arguable issues either way on whether the defence would succeed, and that the balance of convenience favoured the grant of relief. He held that the Cream group had established the necessary likelihood of a permanent injunction under section 12(3) of the Human Rights Act in that it had a real prospect of success. On the defendant's appeal ([2003] Ch 650) all three judges agreed with Lloyd J that the test to be applied was that of a real prospect of success. Simon Brown LJ and Arden LJ concluded that, on the material before him, Lloyd J was entitled to have concluded that the claimants had a real prospect of success at trial, and the appeal was dismissed. Sedley LJ, in a strong dissenting opinion, could see 'no real possibility of the claimants succeeding at trial'. He concluded that the essential story was in his view 'one which, whatever its source, no court could properly suppress': [2003] Ch 650 at 676–677 [86]–[92].

The House of Lords unanimously allowed the appeal: [2005] 1 AC 253. Lord Nicholls, agreeing with Sedley LJ, said that 'the principal happenings the *Echo* wishes to publish are clearly matters of serious public interest…[Given that public interest] I am firmly of the view that the Cream group's prospects of success at trial are not sufficiently likely to justify making an interim restraint order in this case': [2005] 1 AC 253, at 262–263, [24] and [25].

As to the meaning of the word 'likely' in section 12(3), Lord Nicholls held:

(a) The principal purpose of section 12(3) was to buttress the protection afforded to freedom of speech at the interlocutory stage. It sought to do so by setting a higher threshold for the grant of interlocutory injunctions against the media than the guideline of 'a serious question to be tried' or a 'real prospect' of success, as set out in *American Cyanamid Co v Ethicon Ltd* [1975] AC 396.

(b) The *Echo* had submitted that 'likely' in section 12(3) means 'more likely than not'. Although that meaning would be consistent with the underlying Parliamentary intention of emphasizing the importance of freedom of expression, it could not have been intended by Parliament to apply to all cases of interim prior restraint, since (for example) it would preclude the court from granting an interim injunction in some circumstances where it was plain that injunctive relief should be granted as a temporary measure.

(c) The degree of likelihood of success at the trial needed to satisfy section 12(3) depended on the circumstances of the case. The intention of Parliament was that 'likely' should have an extended meaning which set as a normal prerequisite to the grant of an injunction before trial a likelihood of success at the trial higher than the *American Cyanamid* standard but permitted the court to dispense with the higher standard where particular circumstances made this necessary.

(d) The general approach was that courts should be exceedingly slow to make interim restraint orders where the applicant had not satisfied the court that he would be more likely than not to succeed at trial. In general, that would be the threshold an applicant had to cross, before the court embarked on the exercise of its discretion.

(e) There were cases, however, where a lesser degree of likelihood of success would suffice. Circumstances where this might be the case included cases where the potential adverse effects of disclosure were particularly grave or where a short-lived injunction was needed to enable the court to hear and give proper consideration to the application for interim relief.

The judgment is one which the media may well find more cheering for its support for freedom of expression than for its explanation of the statutory position. Unless a clear pattern emerges in court decisions applying the *Cream Holdings* principles, it may be difficult to predict whether a particular case falls within the general approach of 'more likely than not' or into the category of cases 'where a lesser degree of likelihood of success would suffice'.

Many of the conditional exemptions to the 2000 Act only apply if the disclosure of information 'would, or would be likely' to prejudice the interest identified in the particular exemption. It remains to be seen whether the courts will derive any assistance in construing 'likely' in the context of exemptions from the principles stated in *Cream Holdings*.

Balancing conflicting rights

nn81 and 82: The Court of Appeal's decision in *A v B plc* is now reported at [2003] QB 195; see 208, [11(xii)] and 209, [11(xiii)]. **21.68–21.69**

The relationship between the law of defamation and Article 10 was considered by the Strasbourg Court in *Steel and Morris v United Kingdom* (2005) 41 EHRR 403, the case arising out of McDonalds' libel action against two activists from London Greenpeace (a small group unconnected with Greenpeace International). The Court found unanimously that the denial of legal aid to the applicants had deprived them of the opportunity to present their case effectively before the national court and contributed to an unacceptable inequality. There had therefore been a violation of Article 6(1). **21.69**

The Court also found a violation of Article 10. The Court recalled that it had long held that political expression, including expression on matters of public interest and concern, required a high level of protection under Article 10: see, for example *Thorgeir Thorgeirson v Iceland* (1992) 14 EHRR 843. The United Kingdom Government had contended that, as the applicants were not journalists, they should not attract the high level of protection afforded to the press under Article 10. However in a democratic society even small informal campaign groups, such as London Greenpeace, had to be able to carry on their activities effectively.

The Court said that the State enjoyed a margin of appreciation as to the means it provided under domestic law to enable a company to challenge the truth, and limit the damage, of allegations which risked harming its reputation. If, however, a State decided to provide such a remedy to a corporate body, it was essential, in order to safeguard the countervailing interests in free expression and open debate, that a measure of procedural fairness and equality of arms was provided for. The lack of procedural fairness and equality between McDonalds and the applicants gave rise to a breach of Article 10.

The following new paragraphs come after paragraph 21.69 of the Main Work:

21.69A The interplay between Articles 8 and 10 has been illuminated by the House of Lords' two recent decisions in *Campbell v MGN Ltd* [2004] 2 AC 457 and *In re S (A Child)(Identification: Restrictions on Publication)* [2005] 1 AC 593, and the decision of the Strasbourg Court in *Von Hannover v Germany* (2005) 40 EHRR 1.

21.69B In *Campbell v MGN Ltd* Naomi Campbell sued the publisher of the *Daily Mirror* for damages and an injunction. The *Mirror* had published articles disclosing Ms Campbell's drug addiction and the fact that she was receiving therapy through a named self-help group. The newspaper gave details of the group meetings and showed photographs of her in the street as she was leaving a group meeting. The majority in the House of Lords held that Ms Campbell's right pursuant to Article 8 to respect for her private life outweighed the newspaper's right pursuant to Article 10 to freedom of expression, and that, accordingly, publication of the additional information about the self-help group and the accompanying photographs constituted an unjustified infringement of the claimant's right to privacy for which she was entitled to damages. For the impact of the case on the law of confidentiality, see Supplement paras 20.93B–20.93E.

21.69C In the course of her litigation Ms Campbell found four judges in her favour and five judges against her, though she won a majority where it mattered most. Lord Steyn, commenting on *Campbell v MGN Ltd* in *Re S*, said at [2005] 1 AC 593, 603 at [17]:

> For present purposes the decision of the House on the facts of *Campbell* and the differences between the majority and the minority are not material. What does, however, emerge clearly from the opinions are four propositions. First, neither article

> has *as such* precedence over the other. Secondly, where the values under the two articles are in conflict, an intense focus on the comparative importance of the specific rights being claimed in the individual case is necessary. Thirdly, the justifications for interfering with or restricting each right must be taken into account. Finally the proportionality test must be applied to each. For convenience I will call this the ultimate balancing test.

It is necessary to break off from the opinion of Lord Steyn to state the facts in *Re S*.

Following the death of his brother, care proceedings were brought in relation to S, then a boy aged five. His parents separated and he went to live with his father. His brother's death was found to have been caused by salt poisoning and the mother was indicted for murder. Hedley J, the Judge hearing the care proceedings, made an order prohibiting any identification of S by name or the school he attended and preventing any publication in a report of the criminal trial of the name or photograph of the mother or the deceased child. On the application of a newspaper the Judge varied the order so as to allow reports of the criminal trial to contain names or photographs of the mother or the deceased child. The Court of Appeal, by a majority, Hale LJ dissenting, held that the interference with S's rights to respect to private and family life under Article 8 of the European Convention was proportionate and justified in the light of public interest and the rights of the press under Article 10 and accordingly affirmed the Judge's order. The House of Lords dismissed the appeal. The only substantial opinion is that of Lord Steyn. **21.69D**

Lord Steyn's observations on Articles 8 and 10 in paragraphs 24–31 of his judgment are instructive and worth setting out at length: **21.69E**

> *Article 8*
> 24. On the evidence it can readily be accepted that article 8 is engaged. Hedley J observed, at paragraph 18, 'that these will be dreadfully painful times for the child'. Everybody will sympathise with that observation.
>
> 25. But it is necessary to measure the nature of the impact of the trial on the child. He will not be involved in the trial as a witness or otherwise. It will not be necessary to refer to him. No photograph of him will be published. There will be no reference to his private life or upbringing. Unavoidably his mother must be tried for murder and that must be a deeply hurtful experience for the child. The impact upon him is, however, essentially indirect.
>
> 26. While article 8(1) is engaged, and none of the factors in article 8(2) justifies the interference, it is necessary to assess realistically the nature of the relief sought. This is an application for an injunction beyond the scope of section 39 [of the Children and Young Persons Act 1933], the remedy provided by Parliament to protect juveniles directly affected by criminal proceedings. No such injunction has in the past been granted under the inherent jurisdiction or under the provisions of the ECHR. There is no decision of the Strasbourg Court granting injunctive relief to non parties, juvenile or adult, in respect of publication of criminal proceedings...The verdict of experience appears to be that such a development is a step too far.
>
> 27. The interference with article 8 rights, however distressing for the child, is not of the same order when compared with cases of juveniles, who are directly involved in

criminal trials. In saying this I have not overlooked the fact that the mother, the defendant in the criminal trial, has waived her right to a completely public trial, and supports the appeal of the child. In a case such as the present her stance can only be of limited weight.

Article 10

28. Article 10 is also engaged. This case is concerned with the freedom of the press, subject to limited statutory restrictions, to report the proceedings at a criminal trial without restriction. It is necessary to assess the importance of this freedom. I start with a general proposition. In *Reynolds v Times Newspapers Ltd* [2001] 2 AC 127, 200 Lord Nicholls of Birkenhead described the position:

> It is through the mass media that most people today obtain their information on political matters. Without freedom of expression by the media, freedom of expression would be a hollow concept. The interest of a democratic society in ensuring a free press weighs heavily in the balance in deciding whether any curtailment of this freedom bears a reasonable relationship to the purpose of the curtailment.

These observations apply with equal force to the freedom of the press to report criminal trials in progress and after verdict.

Lord Steyn then refers with approval to a passage in the judgment of Lord Woolf MR in *R v Legal Aid Board, Ex p Kaim Todner* [1999] QB 966, 977. Lord Steyn continues:

30. Dealing with the relative importance of the freedom of the press to report the proceedings in a criminal trial Hale LJ drew a distinction. She observed [2004] Fam 43, 73 paragraph 56:

> The court must consider what restriction, if any, is needed to meet the legitimate aim of protecting the rights of CS. If prohibiting publication of the family name and photographs is needed, the court must consider how great an impact that will in fact have upon the freedom protected by article 10. It is relevant here that restrictions on the identification of defendants before conviction are by no means unprecedented. The situation may well change if and when the mother is convicted. There is a much greater public interest in knowing the names of persons convicted of serious crime than of those who are merely suspected or charged. These considerations are also relevant to the extent of the interference with CS's rights.

I cannot accept these observations without substantial qualification. A criminal trial is a public event. The principle of open justice puts, as has often been said, the judge and all who participate in the trial under intense scrutiny. The glare of contemporaneous publicity ensures that trials are properly conducted. It is a valuable check on the criminal process. Moreover, the public interest may be as much involved in the circumstances of a remarkable acquittal as in a surprising conviction. Informed public debate is necessary about all matters. Full contemporaneous reporting of criminal trials in progress promotes public confidence in the administration of justice. It promotes the values of the rule of law.

31. For these reasons I would, therefore attribute greater importance to the freedom of the press to report the progress of a criminal trial without any restraint than Hale LJ did.

The effect of the House of Lords' decision was that there was no injunction in respect of publication of the identity of the defendant or of photographs of the defendant or her deceased son. **21.69F**

In *Von Hannover v Germany* Princess Caroline of Monaco sought to restrain the publication of photographs of herself in the German press which she said infringed her right to protection of her private life and her right to control her image. The Court considered that the decisive factor in balancing the protection of private life against freedom of expression should lie in the contribution that the published photographs and articles make to a public debate of general interest. The Court found in this case that they made no such contribution since the applicant exercised no official function and the photographs and articles related exclusively to her private life. The Court considered that the public did not have a legitimate interest in knowing where the applicant was and how she behaved generally in her private life, and this was so even if she appeared in places which could not always be described as secluded and despite the fact that she was well known to the public. The Court concluded that even if such a public interest existed, as did a commercial interest of the magazines in publishing the photographs, these interests must on the facts of this case yield to the applicant's right to have effective protection of her private life. The Court found a breach of Article 8. **21.69G**

The House of Lords decision in *In re S (A Child) (Identification: Restrictions on publication)* [see Supplement paras 21.69C–21.69F] was considered by Sir Mark Potter, President in *In re W (Children) (Identification: Restrictions on publication) The Times*, 21 July 2005, where he said the case before him raised, in substantially different circumstances, issues similar to those considered in *Re S*. The local authority in care proceedings sought an injunction prohibiting any identification or location of the mother or the father of the children concerned. The local authority was concerned about the adverse effects upon the viability of the placement of two children whose mother suffered from HIV. The mother was at the time awaiting sentence, having pleaded guilty to a charge under section 20 of the Offences against the Person Act 1861 alleging that she had knowingly infected the father of one of the children with the virus. **21.69H**

The President set out the reasoning of Lord Steyn in *Re S* at some length because it had been suggested by at least one commentator that the House of Lords, while on the one hand acknowledging and accepting the new methodology required by the Human Rights Convention, as scheduled to the Human Rights Act 1998, as explained in *Campbell v MGN plc* [see Supplement paras 21.69B and 21.69C] had on the other hand effectively restored the presumptive priority of Article 10 which in *Campbell* they were at pains to reject. **21.69I**

The President did not read Lord Steyn's judgment in that way. Paragraphs [17] and [23] of the judgment were clear as to the approach to be followed in such **21.69J** cases. There was an express approval of the methodology in *Campbell* in which it was made clear that each Article propounded a fundamental right which there was a pressing social need to protect. Equally, each Article qualified the right it propounded so far as it was lawful, necessary and proportionate to do so in order to accommodate the other. The exercise to be performed was one of parallel analysis in which the starting point was presumptive parity.

21.69K The President said that Lord Steyn acknowledged that although it was the ordinary rule that the press, as public watchdog, could report everything that took place in a criminal court, that rule might none the less be displaced in unusual and exceptional circumstances. He said that clarification of the distinctions between *Re S and Re W* brought out vividly the factors which, if sufficiently established by the evidence, would militate in favour of recognizing and supporting the Article 8 rights of the children by the grant of the injunction sought.

21.69L The President concluded by considering the matter in the terms of section 12(4)(a) of the 1998 Act:

(i) this did not appear to be a case where the identity of the mother or any link with the children had yet become available to the public at large;
(ii) it was in the public interest for the identity of the mother to be published given the general rule that unfettered freedom to report criminal proceedings and give publicity to the identity of the defendant was in the public interest. However, a knowledge of that identity was not essential in order to give the public an adequate account or understanding of the trial or issues involved for the purposes of open justice or general discussion. Nor was any breach of Article 6 rights to a fair trial involved.

After careful consideration, the President decided to grant the injunction sought.

G. Judicial Review and Proportionality

The common law of human rights

21.86 In *R (Association of British Civilian Internees: Far East Region) v Secretary of State for Defence* [2003] QB 1397 (the case about *ex gratia* compensation for British civilians interned by the Japanese in the Second World War) the Court of Appeal considered the *dicta* of Lord Cooke of Thorndon in *R (Daly) v Secretary of State for the Home Department* [2001] 2 AC 532, 548–549. Dyson LJ delivered the judgment of the court and at [34] said:

> Support for the recognition of proportionality as part of English domestic law in cases which do not involve Community law or the Convention is to be found in paragraph 51 of the speech of Lord Slynn of Hadley in *R (Alconbury Development Ltd) v Secretary of State for the Environment, Transport and the Regions* [2003] 2 AC 295,

> 320–321; and in the speech of Lord Cooke of Thorndon in *R (Daly) v Secretary of State for the Home Department* [2001] AC 532, 548–9, paragraph 32. See also de Smith, Woolf & Jowell, *Judicial Review of Administrative Action* 5th edition (1995) p 606. It seems to us that the case for this is indeed a strong one. As Lord Slynn points out, trying to keep the *Wednesbury* principle and proportionality in separate compartments is unnecessary and confusing. The criteria of proportionality are more precise and sophisticated: see Lord Steyn in the *Daly* case, at pp 547–548, paragraph 27. It is true that sometimes proportionality may require the reviewing court to assess for itself the balance that has been struck by the decision-maker, and that may produce a different result from one that would be arrived at on the application of the *Wednesbury* test. But the strictness of the *Wednesbury* test has been relaxed in recent years even in areas that have nothing to do with fundamental rights: see the discussion in Craig, *Administrative Law*, 4th edition (1999) pp 582–584. The *Wednesbury* test is moving closer to proportionality and in some cases it is not possible to see any daylight between the two tests: see Lord Hoffmann's Third John Maurice Kelly Lecture 1996 *A sense of proportionality*, at p 13. Although we did not hear argument on the point, we have difficulty in seeing what justification there now is for retaining the *Wednesbury* test.

The Court of Appeal, however, decided that laying the *Wednesbury* test to rest was a step that could only be taken by the House of Lords: see [37].

In *R (ProLife Alliance) v BBC* [2004] 1 AC 185 Lord Walker of Gestingthorpe suggested that the House of Lords should be cautious in attempting any comprehensive statement of principle. Lord Walker also lent his support to Lord Hoffmann in another important discussion about the Human Rights Act. Lord Hoffmann addressed the notion of judicial deference. His comment at [75] deserves repetition: **21.91**

> Although the word 'deference' is now very popular in describing the relationship between the judicial and the other branches of government, I do not think that its overtones of servility, or perhaps gracious concession, are appropriate to describe what is happening.

Instead, he insisted that the question of which branch of government has decision-making power in any particular instance, and what the legal limits of that power are, is squarely a question of law, which must be decided by the courts.

Lord Walker at [144] agreed and added some interesting comments on a article by Richard Edwards (*Judicial Deference under the Human Rights Act* (2002) 65 MLR 859) which discusses the notion of human rights legislation as formalizing a constitutional dialogue between different branches of government, with each branch being in a sense accountable to the other. Lord Walker says the elements Mr Edwards put forward as his basis for a principled approach (largely drawing on Canadian jurisprudence: legislative context, the importance of Convention rights in a democracy, mediation between different groups in society, respect for legislation based on considered balancing of interests, recognition of 'holistic' policy areas which are not readily justiciable, and respect for legislation representing the democratic will on moral and ethical questions) appear to him by no means dissimilar from the principles which do emerge from the *Daly* case and other recent decisions of the House of Lords.

Lord Walker concludes:

> The *Wednesbury* test…for all its defects, had the advantage of simplicity, and it might be thought unsatisfactory that it must now be replaced (when human rights are in play) by a much more complex and contextually sensitive approach. But the scope and reach of the 1998 Act is so extensive that there is no alternative. It might be a mistake, at this stage in the bedding-down of the 1998 Act, for your Lordships' House to go too far in attempting any comprehensive statement of principle. But it is clear that any simple 'one size fits all' formulation of the test would be impossible.

Judicial review and the Freedom of Information Act

21.95 The future of the *Wednesbury* principle is, as indicated in Supplement paras 12.86 and 12.91, uncertain. It remains likely, however, as suggested in the Main Work, that where the courts are concerned, whether on appeal on a point of law or on an application for judicial review, to consider not just rights under the Freedom of Information Act, but also rights to information under Article 8, and possibly Article 10, the courts will apply the higher test laid down in *R (Daly) v Secretary of State for the Home Department*.

22

SCOTLAND

E. The Scottish Act

(1) The right of access to information held by Scottish public authorities

Exempt information

The first group of absolute exemptions: information otherwise available

In *Re L and Lothian and Borders Safety Camera Partnership*, a decision of the Scottish Information Commissioner no 001/2005 (17 May 2005), Mr L asked to see the calibration certificate for equipment used in an alleged speeding offence. The Partnership eventually supplied the information, after the matter had been referred to the Commissioner. Mr L asked for a decision as to whether the Partnership had acted correctly. **22.45**

The Scottish Information Commissioner, in his analysis and findings, said that he wanted to comment on the Partnership's claim that the information need not have been supplied as it was otherwise accessible by virtue of being posted on its website, thus qualifying for exemption under section 25. The Commissioner found that the calibration sheet was not in fact present on the Partnership's website at the date of the request but went on to ask whether, if it had been on the site, it would have been regarded as otherwise accessible. The Partnership argued that as most people have access to the internet, then information posted on a website is accessible.

However, the Commissioner said that the most recent information on data trends available from the Scottish Household Survey shows that in Scotland only 45% of adults access the internet for personal use. The Commissioner continued:

> This hides a wide disparity between income groups and types of household. The Social Justice Annual Report for 2003 provides percentages of households with home internet access...Access in the least deprived homes is 51%; for the most deprived 20%. As might be expected an even greater disparity is evident when specific household income is considered. 63% of households with an income of over £20,000 have home internet access. This falls to 11% for households with an income of less than £6,000. Finally the type of household also has a bearing. Only 27% of single parents have home internet access whilst single pensioners barely register with 3%.
>
> In my view therefore it is not yet possible to say that information which is solely provided on a website is reasonably accessible to people in Scotland.

22.46 In *Re S and Miss S and the Scottish Legal Aid Board*, a decision of the Scottish Information Commissioner no 005/2005 (30 June 2005), the Commissioner had to consider section 38 of the Scottish Act (the personal data exemption). Mr S contacted the Scottish Legal Aid Board by email on behalf of himself and his daughter. He made five requests relating to a decision about legal aid for a case with which he and his daughter were involved.

The second question, which was the question which raised issues of general interest, sought the names of all legal aid employees involved in the decision to provide the legal firms Balfour Manson, solicitors, and Cook Stevenson, solicitors, with legal aid in the case of *S v S*. The Board confirmed that it held the information but considered it exempt under section 38.

Section 38 exempts information from disclosure if it is personal data and disclosure would contravene any of the data protection principles. The question the Commissioner had to consider was whether the release of the employees' names in connection with decisions they had taken at work would be fair and lawful.

The Commissioner took into account the guidance given by the Information Commissioner for the UK, who is responsible for regulating the Data Protection Act in Scotland. The guidance is that in general senior staff and those in public-facing roles should expect that information about them will be available to the public. The Commissioner also took account of the decision of the Irish Information Commissioner (Case no 991436) in which she directed the release of the names of members of *An Garda Siochana* (police) which appeared in Health Board records in connection with an investigation in a child care case. The Irish

Commissioner found that the identity of a *Garda*, as the *Garda* who was involved in particular matters in the course of his or her official duties, was not personal information about the *Garda*. She also considered it relevant that these were members of the national police force and its officers were public servants.

In *Re S and Miss S and the Scottish Legal Aid Board* the Board's staff were aware of a policy decision taken several years ago that all decisions within legal aid cases were to be treated as decisions of the Board. This had given rise to an expectation that the names of individual employees would not be released. The Scottish Commissioner found that the Board dealt with a range of members of the public, including applicants for legal aid, people in receipt of legal aid, opponents of those applying for or in receipt of legal aid, those accused of or convicted of criminal offences and victims of crime. Emotions were often highly charged and feelings of anger or grievance were often focused on decision-makers. This sometimes resulted in transference of the individual's sense of grievance or anger to the Board and its staff, and from time to time this had manifested itself in the form of actual abuse or threats of violence against staff. The Commissioner said that the Board had provided him with examples of incidents, all reported to the police, which showed their concern that access to names of staff could place them in danger was not simply theoretical. The Commissioner therefore accepted that were the Board to release the names of staff involved in making particular decisions this would not constitute fair processing of data, and that the Board had correctly applied the exemption in section 38. The Commissioner also decided that the authority's claim that it did not hold much of the other information which the applicants sought was well founded.

Another case in which the Information Commissioner found that section 38 had been correctly applied is *Re Q and the Scottish Executive*. This is a decision of the Scottish Information Commissioner, no 006/2005 (30 June 2005), following a request for information relating to Mr Q's unsuccessful application to join the Scottish Local Authorities Remuneration Committee. Mr Q asked for: (i) details of where he had failed to meet the person specification; (ii) where his experience and referees fell short; and (iii) details of other candidates being interviewed, in order to match their suitability for interview. The Scottish Executive gave the applicant the personal data which they had about him and declined to give him personal data about third parties as that would have breached the data protection principles.

The second group of absolute exemptions: where a rule of law is recognized as over-riding the duty of disclosure

The text in the Main Work is incorrect in suggesting that the exemption for informa- **22.49**
tion in respect of which a claim to confidentiality of communications could be maintained in legal proceedings is an absolute exemption. It is a conditional

exemption, as is made clear in *Re David Emslie and Communities Scotland*, a decision of the Scottish Information Commissioner, no 023/2005 (19 August 2005). Mr Emslie submitted an information request to the Scottish Executive on 17 January 2005. The request was passed to Communities Scotland, an agency of the Scottish Executive. The request related to allegations of fraud made by Mr Emslie in relation to Grampian Housing Association and to his request that Communities Scotland investigate his allegations. Information was provided to Mr Emslie in response to his request, but copies of correspondence between Communities Scotland and a legal adviser were withheld.

The first record withheld from Mr Emslie was an email from a solicitor for the Scotland Office. The email was a factual report of a telephone conversation which the solicitor had with Mr Emslie. The solicitor did not act for Communities Scotland or the Scottish Executive, but the email was passed to Communities Scotland and this resulted in any confidential status the email may have had being lost. The Scottish Executive subsequently accepted that the email should be released to Mr Emslie.

The second and third records withheld from Mr Emslie comprised a request for legal advice from Communities Scotland to its solicitors and the legal advice in response to this request. The Commissioner pointed out that the Scottish Act has brought many changes to public life in Scotland, not least that for the first time communications between a legal adviser and a public authority client may be made public if it is in the public interest for those communications to be released. The Commissioner added:

> The courts have long recognised the strong public interest in maintaining the right to confidentiality of communications between legal adviser and client on administration of justice grounds. Many of the arguments in favour of maintaining confidentiality of communications were discussed towards the end of last year in a House of Lords case *Three Rivers Council and others v Governor and Company of the Bank of England (No.6)* [2005] AC 610.
>
> There will always be a strong public interest in maintaining the right to confidentiality between legal adviser and client. As a result, I am likely only to order the release of such communications in highly compelling cases…As a result, I do not require the request for advice or the legal advice itself to be released.

Government policy and public affairs in Scotland

22.73 *Re John Hodgson (Chairman of the Skye Windfarm Action Group Ltd) and the Scottish Executive*, a decision of the Scottish Information Commissioner, no 015/2005 (21 July 2005), concerned a request for correspondence and other information relating to the Edinbane wind farm proposal. The Scottish Executive claimed that the information was exempt under section 30(a),(b), and (c) of the Scottish Act. The Executive argued that the disclosure of internal consideration and the views of a particular Minister would undermine collective responsibility of the Cabinet and would, or would be likely to, prejudice substantially the effective conduct of public affairs. In addition it was considered that the release of the information could prejudice substantially the Highland Council's consideration of the planning application for the wind farm, which was understood to be still before the authority for determination.

At the review stage the Scottish Executive released much of the information sought and dropped its reliance on section 30(a). The investigation focused on the remaining information withheld from the applicant:

(a) background information from the Scottish Executive planning officer (four pages);
(b) internal exchanges of correspondence about the planning process for the Edinbane wind farm proposal; and
(c) internal exchanges on the subject of Mr and Mrs Hodgson's correspondence with the Executive (five pages).

The Scottish Information Commissioner, in his analysis and findings, said that the documents in (a) consisted of factual background notes from the Scottish Executive planning officers and that those listed under (b) were mainly routine exchanges of correspondence between officials in which advice was sought when drafting replies to enquirers about the wind farm proposal.

The Commissioner said:

> In my view the standard to be met in applying the tests in sections 30(b)(i) and 30(b)(ii) is high. To qualify for the exemptions in 30(b)(i) and 30(b)(ii) the information withheld does not just have to constitute either 'advice' or 'opinion', but the public authority must show that the release of the information would inhibit substantially the provision of advice or the exchange of views…
>
> The four memoranda from the Scottish Executive planner which have been withheld simply provide factual background information about the proposed wind farm development and the status of the planning application before the Highland Council. I reject the argument that the release of such factual content is likely to inhibit substantially the provision of advice or the exchange of views.

The Commissioner reached a similar conclusion about the exchange of correspondence. The Scottish Executive was required to provide the applicant with the information specified after redacting personal data relating to other correspondents.

Law enforcement

Under section 35(2) of the Scottish Act, information is exempt (subject to the public interest test) if the disclosure of it would, or would be likely to, prejudice substantially the exercise by a public authority of its functions for various specified regulatory purposes. In *Re Mrs S and the Scottish Commission for Regulation of* **22.92**

Care, a decision of the Scottish Information Commissioner, no 007/2005 (6 July 2005), the Commissioner said:

> In order for a public authority to argue that the release of information would prejudice substantially the interest in question it must be able to show that the damage caused by disclosing the information requested would be real or very likely, not hypothetical. The harm caused must be significant, not marginal, and it would have to occur in the near future not in some distant time.

Mrs S, who had applied to be a childminder, requested a list of questions and answers used by the Care Commission officers when conducting a fit person assessment. The main role of the Care Commission is to regulate care services in Scotland and to work to improve the quality of those services. When someone applies to be a childminder they would be both a provider and a manager of services. In order to assess the fitness of a person for the role, an interview is conducted by Care Commission staff. The fitness test to be applied covers character and integrity, physical and mental fitness, qualifications, skills and experience. If a person is not considered fit for the role the Care Commission can refuse registration.

The Scottish Information Commissioner said that he was satisfied that a fit person assessment serves as a core part of the Care Commission's statutory duty to check that people are fit persons to provide or manage care services in Scotland. He decided that the provision of the questions and answers of a fit person assessment to applicants and managers in advance of an interview would serve to defeat the very purpose of such an assessment and would prejudice substantially the authority's ability to exercise its functions, such as its regulatory duty to assess a service provider's fitness to be authorized to provide or manage a care service. Disclosure would not be in the public interest.

Re T and Glasgow City Council, a decision of the Scottish Information Commissioner, no 022/2005 (19 August 2005), raised the exemptions in section 34(1) (information held for the purposes of an investigation) and section 35(1) (whether disclosure would prejudice substantially the prevention or detection of crime, the apprehension or prosecution of offenders, or the administration of justice). Mr T requested information about the Chirnsyde Community Initiative, and in particular its co-ordinator. Mr T and others had previously raised with the Council allegations against this individual, which had been passed on to the Strathclyde Police.

Mr T sought, among other information, the following:

(a) the name of the police officer who stated that Strathclyde Police had no concern about the co-ordinator or his involvement with the Initiative;
(b) the rank of this police officer;
(c) the division of this police officer;

(d) the date on which the information was received by the Council; and
(e) the name of the individual at the Council to whom this information was disclosed.

The Council confirmed that it did hold the relevant information but sought to rely on the exemptions in section 34(1), section 35(1), section 36(2) (release of the information would entail an actionable breach of confidence), and section 38(1) (the data protection exemption). The Council concluded that the public interest in withholding the information prevailed.

The Scottish Information Commissioner held that the communications in question related to information about the outcome of investigations conducted by the police and were therefore likely to fall within the scope of section 34(1). However, the Commissioner found that Mr T had not sought access to the content of these communications but only to the identities of the individuals who exchanged them and confirmation of when they were made. The Commissioner therefore did not accept that the information had ever been held by the police for the purposes of its investigations into allegations relating to the Initiative. Nor did he accept that releasing details of the individuals imparting and receiving advice could lead to a substantial prejudice to law enforcement functions. The Commissioner also said that while there was an occasion when some of the information conveyed to the Council was clearly identified as being confidential in nature, he did not accept that the exemption in section 36 applied to the particular information sought by Mr T. The Commissioner did not therefore find it necessary to consider the public interest test.

The Commissioner then turned to the personal information exemption. He cited with approval the Court of Appeal's decision in the English case of *Durant v Financial Services Authority* [2004] FSR 28, 573 (discussed at Supplement paras 10.08B–10.08H) and concluded that if he accepted that the release of information would affect the individual members of staff, he must treat the information as personal data. The Commissioner said:

> In this case, I do not accept the Council's contention that release of identities will affect the individuals' private lives in this way. I am aware that complaints about the Initiative and its co-ordinator have in the past led to stories being published in both the national and local press. Some of this coverage has made allegations relating to individuals associated with both the Strathclyde Police and the Council. It is possible that the information released as a result of this decision will lead to further media interest in the issues surrounding the Initiative, and the naming of those involved. However, I do not regard the possibility of media interest as constituting a sufficient reason for withholding the information requested (information which is no more than the identification of officials between whom an acknowledged exchange took place) and am not satisfied on the basis of the information before me, that individuals' private lives would be affected.

The Commissioner required the Council to release the information.

Commerce

22.95 *Re Kelly and South Ayrshire Council*, a decision of the Scottish Information Commissioner, no 025/2005 (26 August 2005), is a case about section 33(1)(b), substantial prejudice to commercial interests. Mr Kelly of Robert C Kelly Ltd, an independent theatrical production house, requested information about the Gaiety Theatre at Ayr. He wanted to know the total seats sold and the value of those sales in relation to the annual pantomime and the summer seasons over the period from 1998 to 2005. The Council gave the figures for the years 1998–2001, but refused to release those for the later years, claiming that to do so would prejudice substantially the commercial interests of the Gaiety Theatre and the Council.

Even though this information, if released, would simply provide aggregate totals, the Council argued that a chain of events would be likely to follow from release. First of all, it said, a competitor theatre would analyze the information for each year to establish which shows, cast members, marketing strategies, etc proved effective and which ones did not. It would then use this analysis in building its own strategies for developing and marketing future shows. As a result, the competitor would gain customers at the expense of the Gaiety Theatre, thereby reducing its income and ability to offer high-quality shows in future. The Commissioner commented that although the Council suggested a possible chain of events, it provided no evidence of its likelihood.

The Commissioner added:

> Furthermore, it seems to me unlikely that the potential chain of events described by the Council would be possible on the basis of information about tickets sold and the income from these. With this information, it is feasible that a competitor could establish an understanding of the relative success of shows over the years. However from such aggregate figures, it would be difficult to conclude whether a show's success was a result of casting, production, its marketing or any other factor that distinguishes it from previous productions.

The Commissioner said that he was of the view that the Council had not demonstrated that real harm could occur as a result of the release of the information sought by Mr Kelly, and even if it did, the Council had not demonstrated that the harm would be substantial. The Commissioner therefore required the Council to release the information sought by Mr Kelly for the years 2002–2005.

The environment

22.98 The Scottish Ministers made the Environmental Information (Scotland) Regulations 2004, SSI 2004/520, on 30 November 2004 and the regulations came into force on 1 January 2005. These regulations implement Directive 2003/4/EC on public access to environmental information as regards Scottish public authorities which are defined in regulation 2.

Regulation 2 also defines 'environmental information' which has the same meaning as in Article 2(1) of the Directive. The definition which is also used in the EIR for England and Wales is discussed further at Supplement paras 16.73–16.73D.

The duty to make environmental information available on request is in regulation 5 and it is subject to the exceptions in regulation 10. Regulation 10, paragraphs (1)–(6), is in the following terms:

(1) A Scottish public authority may refuse a request to make environmental information available if–
  (a) there is an exception to disclosure under paragraphs (4) and (5); and
  (b) in all the circumstances, the public interest in making the information available is outweighed by that in maintaining the exception.

(2) In considering the application of the exception referred to in paragraphs (4) and (5) a Scottish public authority shall–
  (a) interpret those paragraphs in a restrictive way; and
  (b) apply a presumption in favour of disclosure.

(3) Where the environmental information requested includes personal data, the authority shall not make those personal data available otherwise than in accordance with regulation 11.

(4) A Scottish public authority may refuse to make environmental information available to the extent that–
  (a) it does not hold that information when an applicant's request is received;
  (b) the request for information is manifestly unreasonable;
  (c) the request for information is formulated in too general a manner and the authority has complied with its duty [to provide advice and assistance] in regulation 9;
  (d) the request relates to material which is still in the course of completion, to unfinished documents or to incomplete data; or
  (e) the request involves making available internal communications.

(5) A Scottish public authority may refuse to make environmental information available to the extent that its disclosure would, or would be likely to, prejudice substantially–
  (a) international relations, defence, national security, or public safety;
  (b) the course of justice, the ability of a person to receive a fair trial, or the ability of any public authority to conduct an inquiry of a criminal or disciplinary nature;
  (c) intellectual property rights;
  (d) the confidentiality of the proceedings of any public authority where such confidentiality is provided for by law;
  (e) the confidentiality of commercial or industrial information where such confidentiality is provided for by law to protect a legitimate interest;
  (f) the interest of the person who provided the information where that person–
    (i) was not under, and could not have been put under, any legal obligation to supply the information;
    (ii) did not supply it in circumstances such that it could, apart from these Regulations, be made available; and
    (iii) has not consented to its disclosure; or
  (g) the protection of the environment to which the information relates.

(6) To the extent that the environmental information to be made available relates to information on emissions, a Scottish public authority shall not be entitled to refuse to make it available except under an exception referred to in paragraph 5(d) to (g).

The comparable provisions in the EIR for England and Wales are set out and discussed at Supplement paragraphs 16.73V–16.73Y.

The following new heading and paragraphs come after paragraph 22.109 of the Main Work:

The Scottish Information Commissioner's briefing papers

22.109A The Scottish Information Commissioner has produced briefing papers on the following subjects:

(a) section 25—information otherwise accessible;
(b) section 26—prohibitions on disclosure;
(c) section 27—information intended for future publication;
(d) section 28—relations within the United Kingdom;
(e) section 29—formulation of Scottish Administration policy, etc;
(f) section 31—national security and defence;
(g) section 32—international relations;
(h) section 33—commercial interests and the economy;
(i) section 34—investigations by Scottish Public Authorities and proceedings arising out of such investigations;
(j) section 35—law enforcement;
(k) section 36—confidentiality;
(l) section 37—court records;
(m) section 39—health, safety, and the environment;
(n) section 40—audit function;
(o) section 41—communications with Her Majesty, etc and honours;
(p) the public interest test.

These briefing notes are published on the Scottish Information Commissioner's website and can be downloaded at http://www.itspublicknowledge.info/legislation/briefings.

(2) Environmental information

22.110 The Scottish Ministers made the Environmental Information (Scotland) Regulations 2004, SSI 2004/520, on 30 November 2004 and the regulations came into force on 1 January 2005. These regulations implement Directive 2003/4/EC on public access to environmental information as regards Scottish public authorities, which are defined in regulation 2. The regulations are discussed at Supplement para 22.98.

(5) Procedure and enforcement

Responses to requests

Fees notices

The Scottish Ministers have made the Freedom of Information (Fees for Required Disclosure) (Scotland) Regulations 2004, SSI 2004/467. **22.165**

Under regulation 3(1) the 'projected costs' means the total costs, whether direct or indirect, which a Scottish public authority reasonably estimates in accordance with the regulation that it is likely to incur in locating, retrieving and providing such information in accordance with the Act. Under regulation 3(2), in estimating projected costs:

(a) no account shall be taken of costs incurred in determining–
  (i) whether the authority holds the information specified in the request; or
  (ii) whether the person seeking the information is entitled to receive the requested information or, if not so entitled, should nevertheless be provided with it or should be refused it; and
(b) any estimate of the cost of staff time in locating, retrieving or providing the information shall not exceed £15 per hour per member of staff.

Regulation 4(2) provides that where the projected costs do not exceed £100, no fee shall be payable. Regulation 4(3) provides that where the projected costs exceed £100 but do not exceed the prescribed amount, the fee shall not exceed 10% of the difference between the projected costs and £100.

Section 12(1) of the Scottish Act provides that no disclosure need be made where the costs exceed the prescribed amount. Regulation 5 provides that the prescribed amount is £600. The Freedom of Information (Fees for Disclosure under section 13) (Scotland) Regulations, SSI 2004/376, make provision for the fees which may be charged in such a case.

APPENDIX D1

Secretary of State for Constitutional Affairs' Code of Practice on the Discharge of Public Authorities' Functions under Part I of the Freedom of Information Act 2000

ISSUED UNDER SECTION 45 OF THE ACT

NOVEMBER 2004

PRESENTED TO PARLIAMENT BY THE
SECRETARY OF STATE FOR CONSTITUTIONAL AFFAIRS
PURSUANT TO SECTION 45(5) OF THE
FREEDOM OF INFORMATION ACT 2000

Foreword

Introduction

1. The Code of Practice, to which this is a foreword, fulfils the duty of the Secretary of State set out in section 45 of the Freedom of Information Act 2000, to provide guidance to public authorities as to the practice which it would, in his opinion, be desirable for them to follow in connection with the discharge of their functions under Part I of the Act. It is envisaged that Regulations to be made with respect to environmental information will make provision for the issue by the Secretary of State of a Code of Practice applying to the discharge of authorities' functions under those Regulations.
2. This foreword does not form part of the Code itself.
3. The Government is committed to greater openness in the public sector. The Freedom of Information Act will further this aim by helping to transform the culture of the public sector to one of greater openness, enabling members of the public to better understand the decisions of public authorities, and ensuring that services provided by the public sector are seen to be efficiently and properly delivered. Conformity with the Code will assist this.

4. The aims of the Code are to:
   - facilitate the disclosure of information under the Act by setting out good administrative practice that it is desirable for public authorities to follow when handling requests for information, including, where appropriate, the transfer of a request to a different authority;
   - protect the interests of applicants by setting out standards for the provision of advice which it would be good practice to make available to them and to encourage the development of effective means of complaining about decisions taken under the Act;
   - facilitate consideration by public authorities of the interests of third parties who may be affected by any decision to disclose information, by setting standards for consultation; and
   - promote consideration by public authorities of the implications for Freedom of Information before agreeing to confidentiality provisions in contracts and accepting information in confidence from a third party more generally.

Role of the Information Commissioner

5. The Information Commissioner has a duty under section 47 of the Act to promote the following of good practice by public authorities, and in particular to promote observance of the requirements of the Act and of the provisions of this Code of Practice. The Act confers a number of powers on him to enable him to carry out that duty specifically in relation to the Code.

Practice recommendations

6. If it appears to the Commissioner that the practice of a public authority in relation to the exercise of its functions under the Act does not conform with that proposed in this Code of Practice, he may give to the authority a recommendation, under section 48 (known as a 'practice recommendation'), specifying the steps which should, in his opinion, be taken for promoting such conformity.
7. A practice recommendation must be given in writing and must refer to the particular provisions of the Code of Practice with which, in the Commissioner's opinion, the public authority's practice does not conform. A practice recommendation is simply a recommendation and cannot be directly enforced by the Information Commissioner. However, a failure to comply with a practice recommendation may lead to a failure to comply with the Act. Further, a failure to take account of a practice recommendation may lead to an adverse comment in a report to Parliament by the Commissioner.
8. It should be noted that because the provisions of the Act relating to the general right of access will not be brought into force until 1 January 2005, the Commissioner's powers to issue practice recommendations in relation to the handling of individual requests for information under the general rights of access will not take effect before that date.

Decision and Enforcement Notices

9. The Commissioner may also refer to non-compliance with the Code in decision notices issued as a result of a complaint under s.50 of the Act and enforcement notices issued under s.52 of the Act where, irrespective of any complaints that may have been received, the Commissioner considers that a public authority has failed to comply with any requirement of Part 1 of the Act. Where relevant, the Commissioner will make reference to the specific provisions of the Code in specifying the steps to be taken to ensure compliance with the Act.

Information Notices

10. If the Information Commissioner reasonably requires any information for the purpose of determining whether the practice of a public authority conforms to the Code, under section 51 of the Act he may serve an "information notice" on the authority, requiring it to provide specified information relating to its conformity with the Code.

Compliance with notices

11. Under the provisions of section 54 of the Act, if a public authority fails to comply with a decision, information or enforcement notice, the Commissioner may certify in writing to the court that the public authority has failed to comply with that notice. The court may then inquire into the matter and, after hearing any witnesses who may be produced against or on behalf of, the public authority, and after hearing any statement that may be offered in defence, deal with the authority as if it had committed a contempt of court.

PART I OF THE FREEDOM OF INFORMATION ACT

12. The Code provides guidance on good practice for public authorities in connection with the discharge of their functions under Part I of the Act. The main features of Part I Freedom of Information Act 2000 are:

- general rights of access in relation to recorded information held by public authorities, subject to certain conditions and exemptions;
- in cases where access to information is refused in reliance on an exemption from disclosure, a duty on public authorities to give reasons for that refusal;
- a duty to provide reasonable advice and assistance to applicants approaching public authorities seeking information;
- a duty on every public authority to adopt and maintain a publication scheme, approved by the Commissioner, which relates to the publication of information by the authority, and to publish information in accordance with the scheme (an authority may adopt a model publication scheme approved by the Commissioner).

Duty to provide advice and assistance

13. Section 16 of the Act places a duty on public authorities to provide reasonable advice and assistance to applicants. A public authority is to be taken to have complied with this duty in any particular case if it has conformed with the provisions of this Code in relation to the provision of advice and assistance in that case. The duty to assist and advise is enforceable by the Information Commissioner. If a public authority fails in its statutory duty, the Commissioner may issue a decision notice under section 50, or an enforcement notice under section 52.

14. Public authorities should not forget that other Acts of Parliament may be relevant to the way in which authorities provide advice and assistance to applicants or potential applicants, e.g. the Disability Discrimination Act 1995 and the Race Relations Act 1976 (as amended by the Race Relations (Amendment) Act 2000).

PROCEDURES AND TRAINING

15. All communications in writing to a public authority, including those transmitted by electronic means, may contain or amount to requests for information within the meaning of the Act, and so must be dealt with in accordance with the provisions of the Act. While in many cases such requests will be dealt with in the course of normal business, it is essential that public authorities dealing with correspondence, or which otherwise may be required to provide information, have in place procedures for taking decisions at appropriate levels, and ensure that sufficient staff are familiar with the requirements of the Act and the Codes of Practice issued under its provisions. Staff dealing with correspondence should also take account of any relevant guidance on good practice issued by the Commissioner. Authorities should ensure that proper training is provided in this regard. Larger authorities should ensure that they have a central core of staff with particular expertise in Freedom of Information who can provide expert advice to other members of staff as needed.

16. In planning and delivering training authorities should be aware of other provisions affecting the disclosure of information such as Environmental Information Regulations and the Data Protection Act 1998.

Further Guidance

17. The DCA has produced a suite of guidance which provides advice for public authorities in order to help them fulfil their obligations under the Freedom of Information Act. Of particular relevance to authorities will be the Guidance on Processing Requests, which provides detailed advice on handling requests for information. The suite of guidance also includes detailed guidance on the application of exemptions. This should be referred to for further guidance on the factors which should be taken into account when considering whether exemptions apply.
18. The Information Commissioner's Office have also issued 'Awareness Guides' on its website. Again, these Awareness Guides provide detailed, practical guidance on best practice which should be followed by public authorities. The Commissioner will also publish the internal advice developed for use by complaint caseworkers and summaries of complaint cases considered by the Commissioner and the Tribunal.
19. More specialist advice on the Act is also available from representative bodies (for instance the Local Government Association and the Association of Chief Police Officers) and by Government Departments for small public authorities falling within their general policy areas (for instance the DfES for schools).

CODE OF PRACTICE

(Freedom of Information Act 2000, section 45)

Guidance to public authorities as to the practice which it would be desirable for them to follow in connection with the discharge of their functions under Part I of the Freedom of Information Act 2000

Having consulted the Information Commissioner, this Code of Practice is issued by the Secretary of State for Constitutional Affairs under section 45 of the Freedom of Information Act 2000 (c.36) on 25 November 2004. The Code provides guidance to public authorities, as defined in the Act, as to the practice which it would, in the Secretary of State's opinion, be desirable for them to follow in connection with the discharge of their functions under Part I of the Act.

Laid before Parliament on 25 November 2004 pursuant to section 45(5) of the Freedom of Information Act 2000.

I Introduction

1. This Code of Practice provides guidance to public authorities as to the practice which it would, in the opinion of the Secretary of State for Constitutional Affairs, be desirable for them to follow in connection with the discharge of their functions under Part I (Access to information held by public authorities) of the Freedom of Information Act 2000 ('the Act').
2. Words and expressions used in this Code have the same meaning as the same words and expressions used in the Act.

II The Provision of Advice and Assistance to Persons Making Requests for Information

3. The following paragraphs of this Code apply in relation to the provision of advice and assistance to persons who propose to make, or have made, requests for information to public authorities. They are intended to provide guidance to public authorities as to the practice which it would be desirable for them to follow in the discharge of their duty under section 16 of the Act.

Advice and assistance to those proposing to make requests

4. Public authorities should publish their procedures for dealing with requests for information. Consideration should be given to including in these procedures a statement of:
   - what the public authority's usual procedure will be where it does not hold the information requested (see also III—'Transferring requests for information'); and
   - when the public authority may need to consult other public authorities and/or third parties in order to reach a decision on whether the requested information can be released (see also IV—'Consultation with third parties').
5. The procedures should include an address or addresses (including an e-mail address where possible) to which applicants may direct requests for information or for assistance. A telephone number should also be provided, where possible that of a named individual who can provide assistance. These procedures should be referred to in the authority's publication scheme.
6. Staff working in public authorities in contact with the public should bear in mind that not everyone will be aware of the Act, or Regulations made under it, and they will need where appropriate to draw these to the attention of potential applicants who appear unaware of them.
7. Where a person is unable to frame his or her request in writing, the public authority should ensure that appropriate assistance is given to enable that person to make a request for information. Depending on the circumstances, consideration should be given to:
   - advising the person that another person or agency (such as a Citizens Advice Bureau) may be able to assist them with the application, or make the application on their behalf;
   - in exceptional circumstances, offering to take a note of the application over the telephone and then send the note to the applicant for confirmation (in which case the written note of the telephone request, once verified by the applicant and returned, would constitute a written request for information and the statutory time limit for reply would begin when the written confirmation was received).

This list is not exhaustive, and public authorities should be flexible in offering advice and assistance most appropriate to the circumstances of the applicant.

Clarifying the request

8. A request for information must adequately specify and describe the information sought by the applicant. Public authorities are entitled to ask for more detail, if needed, to enable them to identify and locate the information sought. Authorities should, as far as reasonably practicable, provide assistance to the applicant to enable him or her to describe more clearly the information requested.
9. Authorities should be aware that the aim of providing assistance is to clarify the nature of the information sought, not to determine the aims or motivation of the applicant. Care should be taken not to give the applicant the impression that he or she is obliged to disclose the nature of his or her interest as a precondition to exercising the rights of access, or that he or she will be treated differently if he or she does (or does not). Public authorities should be prepared to explain to the applicant why they are asking for more information. It is important that the applicant is contacted as soon as possible, preferably by telephone, fax or e-mail, where more information is needed to clarify what is sought.
10. Appropriate assistance in this instance might include:
    - providing an outline of the different kinds of information which might meet the terms of the request;
    - providing access to detailed catalogues and indexes, where these are available, to help the applicant ascertain the nature and extent of the information held by the authority;
    - providing a general response to the request setting out options for further information which could be provided on request.

This list is not exhaustive, and public authorities should be flexible in offering advice and assistance most appropriate to the circumstances of the applicant.

11. In seeking to clarify what is sought, public authorities should bear in mind that applicants cannot reasonably be expected to possess identifiers such as a file reference number, or a description of a particular record, unless this information is made available by the authority for the use of applicants.

Limits to advice and assistance

12. If, following the provision of such assistance, the applicant still fails to describe the information requested in a way which would enable the authority to identify and locate it, the authority is not expected to seek further clarification. The authority should disclose any information relating to the application which has been successfully identified and found for which it does not propose to claim an exemption. It should also explain to the applicant why it cannot take the request any further and provide details of the authority's complaints procedure and the applicant's rights under section 50 of the Act (see 'Complaints Procedure' in section VI).

Advice and assistance and fees

13. Where the applicant indicates that he or she is not prepared to pay the fee notified in any fees notice given to the applicant, the authority should consider whether there is any information that may be of interest to the applicant that is available free of charge.

14. Where an authority is not obliged to comply with a request for information because, under section 12(1) and regulations made under section 12, the cost of complying would exceed the 'appropriate limit' (i.e. cost threshold) the authority should consider providing an indication of what, if any, information could be provided within the cost ceiling. The authority should also consider advising the applicant that by reforming or re-focusing their request, information may be able to be supplied for a lower, or no, fee.

15. An authority is not expected to provide assistance to applicants whose requests are vexatious within the meaning of section 14 of the Act. Guidance on what constitutes a vexatious request can be found in the DCA Handbook—*Guidance on Processing Requests*. The Information Commissioner has also issued advice on dealing with vexatious and repetitious requests.

III Transferring Requests for Information

16. The following paragraphs apply in any case in which a public authority is not able to comply with a request (or to comply with it in full) because it does not hold the information requested, and proposes, in accordance with section 1(1)(a), to confirm that it does not hold that information.

17. If the authority has reason to believe that some or all of the information requested, but which it does not hold, is held by another public authority, the authority should consider what would be the most helpful way of assisting the applicant with his or her request.

18. In most cases this is likely to involve:
    - contacting the applicant and informing him or her that the information requested may be held by another public authority;
    - suggesting that the applicant re-applies to the authority which the original authority believes may hold the information; and
    - providing him or her with contact details for that authority.

19. However, in some cases the authority to which the original request is made may consider it to be more appropriate to transfer the request to another authority in respect of the information which it does not hold. In such cases, the authority should consult the other authority with a view to ascertaining whether it does in fact hold the information and, if so, whether it is obliged

to confirm this under section 1(1) of the Act. If that is the case, the first authority should proceed to consider transferring the request. A request (or part of a request) should not be transferred without confirmation by the second authority that it holds the information, and will confirm as much to the applicant on receipt of a request.

20. Before transferring a request for information to another authority, the original authority should consider:
    - whether a transfer is appropriate; and if so
    - whether the applicant is likely to have any grounds to object to the transfer. If the authority reasonably concludes that the applicant is not likely to object, it may transfer the request without going back to the applicant, but should tell him or her it has done so.
21. Where there are reasonable grounds to believe an applicant is likely to object, the authority should only transfer the request to another authority with his or her consent. If the authority is in any doubt, it may prefer to advise the applicant to make a new request to the other authority, and to inform the applicant that the other authority has confirmed that it holds the information.
22. Where a request or part of a request is transferred from one public authority to another, the receiving authority should comply with its obligations under Part I of the Act in the same way as it would in the case of a request that is received direct from an applicant. The time for complying with such a request should be calculated by regarding the date of transfer as the date of receipt of the request.
23. All transfers of requests should take place as soon as is practicable, and the applicant must be informed as soon as possible once this has been done.
24. Where a public authority is unable either to advise the applicant which public authority holds, or may hold, the requested information or to facilitate the transfer of the request to another authority (or considers it inappropriate to do so) it should consider what advice, if any, it can provide to the applicant to enable him or her to pursue his or her request.

IV Consultation with Third Parties

25. There are many circumstances in which:
    - requests for information may relate to persons other than the applicant and the authority; or
    - disclosure of information is likely to affect the interests of persons other than the applicant or the authority.
26. It is highly recommended that public authorities take appropriate steps to ensure that such third parties, and those who supply public authorities with information, are aware of the public authority's duty to comply with the Freedom of Information Act, and that therefore information will have to be disclosed upon request unless an exemption applies.
27. In some cases it will be necessary to consult, directly and individually, with such persons in order to determine whether or not an exemption applies to the information requested, or in order to reach a view on whether the obligations in section 1 of the Act arise in relation to that information. But in a range of other circumstances it will be good practice to do so; for example, where a public authority proposes to disclose information relating to third parties, or information which is likely to affect their interests, reasonable steps should, where appropriate, be taken to give them advance notice, or failing that, to draw it to their attention afterwards.
28. In some cases, it may also be appropriate to consult such third parties about such matters as whether any further explanatory material or advice should be given to the applicant together with the information in question. Such advice may, for example, refer to any restrictions (including copyright restrictions) which may exist as to the subsequent use which may be made of such information.

29. No decision to release information which has been supplied by one government department to another should be taken without first notifying, and where appropriate consulting, the department from which the information originated.
30. Where information to be disclosed relates to a number of third parties, or the interests of a number of third parties may be affected by a disclosure, and those parties have a representative organisation which can express views on behalf of those parties, the authority may consider whether it would be sufficient to notify or consult with that representative organisation. If there is no representative organisation, the authority may consider that it would be sufficient to notify or consult with a representative sample of the third parties in question.

V Freedom of Information and Confidentiality Obligations

31. Public authorities should bear clearly in mind their obligations under the Freedom of Information Act when preparing to enter into contracts which may contain terms relating to the disclosure of information by them.
32. When entering into contracts with non-public authority contractors, public authorities may be asked to accept confidentiality clauses, for example to the effect that information relating to the terms of the contract, its value and performance will not be disclosed. Public authorities should carefully consider the compatibility of such terms with their obligations under the Act. It is important that both the public authority and the contractor are aware of the limits placed by the Act on the enforceability of such confidentiality clauses.
33. The Act does, however, recognise that there will be circumstances and respects in which the preservation of confidentiality between public authority and contractor is appropriate, and must be maintained, in the public interest.
34. Where there is good reason, as recognised by the terms of the exemption provisions of the Act, to include non-disclosure provisions in a contract, public authorities should consider the desirability where possible of making express provision in the contract identifying the information which should not be disclosed and the reasons for confidentiality. Consideration may also be given to including provision in contracts as to when consultation with third parties will be necessary or appropriate before the information is disclosed.
35. Similar considerations will apply to the offering or acceptance of confidentiality obligations by public authorities in non-contractual circumstances. There will be circumstances in which such obligations will be an appropriate part of the acquisition of information from third parties and will be protected by the terms of the exemption provisions of the Act. But again, it will be important that both the public authority and the third party are aware of the limits placed by the Act on the enforceability of expectations of confidentiality, and for authorities to ensure that such expectations are created only where to do so is consistent with their obligations under the Act.

VI Complaints Procedure

36. Each public authority should have a procedure in place for dealing with complaints in relation to its handling of requests for information. The same procedure could also usefully handle complaints in relation to the authority's publication scheme. If the complaints cannot be dealt with swiftly and satisfactorily on an informal basis, the public authority should inform persons if approached by them of the details of its internal complaints procedure, and how to contact the Information Commissioner, if the complainant wishes to write to him about the matter.
37. When communicating any decision made to refusing a request, in reliance on an exemption provision, public authorities are obliged, under section 17(7) of the Act to notify the applicant of particulars of the procedure provided by the public authority for dealing with complaints (or to state that it does not have one). In doing so, they should provide full details of their own

complaints procedure, including how to make a complaint and inform the applicant of the right to complain to the Commissioner under section 50 if he or she is still dissatisfied following the authority's review.

38. Any written reply from the applicant (including one transmitted by electronic means) expressing dissatisfaction with an authority's response to a request for information should be treated as a complaint, as should any written communication from a person who considers that the authority is not complying with its publication scheme. These communications should be handled in accordance with the authority's complaints procedure, even if, in the case of a request for information under the general rights of access, the applicant does not expressly state his or her desire for the authority to review its decision or its handling of the application.

39. The complaints procedure should provide a fair and thorough review of handling issues and of decisions taken pursuant to the Act, including decisions taken about where the public interest lies in respect of exempt information. It should enable a fresh decision to be taken on a reconsideration of all the factors relevant to the issue. Complaints procedures should be as clear and simple as possible. They should encourage a prompt determination of the complaint.

40. Where the complaint concerns a request for information under the general rights of access, the review should be undertaken by someone senior to the person who took the original decision, where this is reasonably practicable. The public authority should in any event undertake a full re-evaluation of the case, taking into account the matters raised by the investigation of the complaint.

41. In all cases, complaints should be acknowledged promptly and the complainant should be informed of the authority's target date for determining the complaint. Where it is apparent that determination of the complaint will take longer than the target time (for example because of the complexity of the particular case), the authority should inform the applicant and explain the reason for the delay. The complainant should always be informed of the outcome of his or her complaint.

42. Authorities should set their own target times for dealing with complaints; these should be reasonable, and subject to regular review. Each public authority should publish its target times for determining complaints and information as to how successful it is with meeting those targets.

43. Records should be kept of all complaints and of their outcome. Authorities should have procedures in place for monitoring complaints and for reviewing, and, if necessary, amending, procedures for dealing with requests for information where such action is indicated by more than occasional reversals of initial decisions.

44. Where the outcome of a complaint is a decision that information should be disclosed which was previously withheld, the information in question should be disclosed as soon as practicable and the applicant should be informed how soon this will be.

45. Where the outcome of a complaint is that the procedures within an authority have not been properly followed by the authority's staff, the authority should apologise to the applicant. The authority should also take appropriate steps to prevent similar errors occurring in future.

46. Where the outcome of a complaint is that an initial decision to withhold information is upheld, or is otherwise in the authority's favour, the applicant should be informed of his or her right to apply to the Commissioner, and be given details of how to make an application, for a decision on whether the request for information has been dealt with in accordance with the requirements of Part I of the Act.

APPENDIX G1

Directive 2003/4/EC of the European Parliament and of the Council of 28 January 2003

ON PUBLIC ACCESS TO ENVIRONMENTAL INFORMATION AND REPEALING COUNCIL DIRECTIVE 90/313/EEC

THE EUROPEAN PARLIAMENT AND THE COUNCIL OF THE EUROPEAN UNION,

Having regard to the Treaty establishing the European Community, and in particular Article 175(1) thereof,

Having regard to the proposal from the Commission,

Having regard to the opinion of the European Economic and Social Committee,

Having regard to the opinion of the Committee of the Regions,

Acting in accordance with the procedure laid down in Article 251 of the Treaty in the light of the joint text approved by the Conciliation Committee on 8 November 2002,

Whereas:

(1) Increased public access to environmental information and the dissemination of such information contribute to a greater awareness of environmental matters, a free exchange of views, more effective participation by the public in environmental decision-making and, eventually, to a better environment.

(2) Council Directive 90/313/EEC of 7 June 1990 on the freedom of access to information on the environment initiated a process of change in the manner in which public authorities approach the issue of openness and transparency, establishing measures for the exercise of the right of public access to environmental information which should be developed and continued. This Directive expands the existing access granted under Directive 90/313/EEC.

(3) Article 8 of that Directive requires Member States to report to the Commission on the experience gained, in the light of which the Commission is required to make a report to the European Parliament and to the Council together with any proposal for revision of the Directive which it may consider appropriate.

(4) The report produced under Article 8 of that Directive identifies concrete problems encountered in the practical application of the Directive.

(5) On 25 June 1998 the European Community signed the UN/ECE Convention on Access to Information, Public Participation in Decision-Making and Access to Justice in Environmental Matters ('the Aarhus Convention'). Provisions of Community law must be consistent with that Convention with a view to its conclusion by the European Community.

(6) It is appropriate in the interest of increased transparency to replace Directive 90/313/EEC rather than to amend it, so as to provide interested parties with a single, clear and coherent legislative text.

(7) Disparities between the laws in force in the Member States concerning access to environmental information held by public authorities can create inequality within the Community as regards access to such information or as regards conditions of competition.

(8) It is necessary to ensure that any natural and legal person has a right of access to environmental information held by or for public authorities without his having to state an interest.

(9) It is also necessary that public authorities make available and disseminate environmental information to the general public to the widest extent possible, in particular by using information and communication technologies. The future development of these technologies should be taken into account in the reporting on, and reviewing of, this Directive.

(10) The definition of environmental information should be clarified so as to encompass information in any form on the state of the environment, on factors, measures or activities affecting or likely to affect the environment or designed to protect it, on cost–benefit and economic analyses used within the framework of such measures or activities and also information on the state of human health and safety, including the contamination of the food chain, conditions of human life, cultural sites and built structures in as much as they are, or may be, affected by any of those matters.

(11) To take account of the principle in Article 6 of the Treaty, that environmental protection requirements should be integrated into the definition and implementation of Community policies and activities, the definition of public authorities should be expanded so as to encompass government or other public administration at national, regional or local level whether or not they have specific responsibilities for the environment. The definition should likewise be expanded to include other persons or bodies performing public administrative functions in relation to the environment under national law, as well as other persons or bodies acting under their control and having public responsibilities or functions in relation to the environment.

(12) Environmental information which is physically held by other bodies on behalf of public authorities should also fall within the scope of this Directive.

(13) Environmental information should be made available to applicants as soon as possible and within a reasonable time and having regard to any timescale specified by the applicant.

(14) Public authorities should make environmental information available in the form or format requested by an applicant unless it is already publicly available in another form or format or it is reasonable to make it available in another form or format. In addition, public authorities should be required to make all reasonable efforts to maintain the environmental information held by or for them in forms or formats that are readily reproducible and accessible by electronic means.

(15) Member States should determine the practical arrangements under which such information is effectively made available. These arrangements shall guarantee that the information is effectively and easily accessible and progressively becomes available to the public through public telecommunications networks, including publicly accessible lists of public authorities and registers or lists of environmental information held by or for public authorities.

(16) The right to information means that the disclosure of information should be the general rule and that public authorities should be permitted to refuse a request for environmental information in specific and clearly defined cases. Grounds for refusal should be interpreted in a restrictive way, whereby the public interest served by disclosure should be weighed against the interest served by the refusal. The reasons for a refusal should be provided to the applicant within the time limit laid down in this Directive.

(17) Public authorities should make environmental information available in part where it is possible to separate out any information falling within the scope of the exceptions from the rest of the information requested.

(18) Public authorities should be able to make a charge for supplying environmental information but such a charge should be reasonable. This implies that, as a general rule, charges may not exceed actual costs of producing the material in question. Instances where advance payment will be required should be limited. In particular cases, where public authorities make available environmental information on a commercial basis, and where this is necessary in order to guarantee the continuation of collecting and publishing such information, a market-based charge is considered to be reasonable; an advance payment may be required. A schedule of charges should be published and made available to applicants together with information on the circumstances in which a charge may be levied or waived.

(19) Applicants should be able to seek an administrative or judicial review of the acts or omissions of a public authority in relation to a request.

(20) Public authorities should seek to guarantee that when environmental information is compiled by them or on their behalf, the information is comprehensible, accurate and comparable. As this is an important factor in assessing the quality of the information supplied the method used in compiling the information should also be disclosed upon request.

(21) In order to increase public awareness in environmental matters and to improve environmental protection, public authorities should, as appropriate, make available and disseminate information on the environment which is relevant to their functions, in particular by means of computer telecommunication and/or electronic technology, where available.

(22) This Directive should be evaluated every four years, after its entry into force, in the light of experience and after submission of the relevant reports by the Member States, and be subject to revision on that basis. The Commission should submit an evaluation report to the European Parliament and the Council.

(23) Since the objectives of the proposed Directive cannot be sufficiently achieved by the Member States and can therefore be better achieved at Community level, the Community may adopt measures, in accordance with the principle of subsidiarity as set out in Article 5 of the Treaty. In accordance with the principle of proportionality, as set out in that Article, this Directive does not go beyond what is necessary in order to achieve those objectives.

(24) The provisions of this Directive shall not affect the right of a Member State to maintain or introduce measures providing for broader access to information than required by this Directive,

Have adopted this directive:

Article 1

Objectives

The objectives of this Directive are:

(a) to guarantee the right of access to environmental information held by or for public authorities and to set out the basic terms and conditions of, and practical arrangements for, its exercise; and

(b) to ensure that, as a matter of course, environmental information is progressively made available and disseminated to the public in order to achieve the widest possible systematic availability and dissemination to the public of environmental information. To this end the use, in particular, of computer telecommunication and/or electronic technology, where available, shall be promoted.

Article 2

Definitions

For the purposes of this Directive:

1. 'Environmental information' shall mean any information in written, visual, aural, electronic or any other material form on:

   (a) the state of the elements of the environment, such as air and atmosphere, water, soil, land, landscape and natural sites including wetlands, coastal and marine areas, biological diversity and its components, including genetically modified organisms, and the interaction among these elements;

   (b) factors, such as substances, energy, noise, radiation or waste, including radioactive waste, emissions, discharges and other releases into the environment, affecting or likely to affect the elements of the environment referred to in (a);

   (c) measures (including administrative measures), such as policies, legislation, plans, programmes, environmental agreements, and activities affecting or likely to affect the elements and factors referred to in (a) and (b) as well as measures or activities designed to protect those elements;

   (d) reports on the implementation of environmental legislation;

(e) cost–benefit and other economic analyses and assumptions used within the framework of the measures and activities referred to in (c); and
(f) the state of human health and safety, including the contamination of the food chain, where relevant, conditions of human life, cultural sites and built structures inasmuch as they are or may be affected by the state of the elements of the environment referred to in (a) or, through those elements, by any of the matters referred to in (b) and (c).

2. 'Public authority' shall mean:

(a) government or other public administration, including public advisory bodies, at national, regional or local level;
(b) any natural or legal person performing public administrative functions under national law, including specific duties, activities or services in relation to the environment; and
(c) any natural or legal person having public responsibilities or functions, or providing public services, relating to the environment under the control of a body or person falling within (a) or (b).

Member States may provide that this definition shall not include bodies or institutions when acting in a judicial or legislative capacity. If their constitutional provisions at the date of adoption of this Directive make no provision for a review procedure within the meaning of Article 6, Member States may exclude those bodies or institutions from that definition.

3. 'Information held by a public authority' shall mean environmental information in its possession which has been produced or received by that authority.

4. 'Information held for a public authority' shall mean environmental information which is physically held by a natural or legal person on behalf of a public authority.

5. 'Applicant' shall mean any natural or legal person requesting environmental information.

6. 'Public' shall mean one or more natural or legal persons, and, in accordance with national legislation or practice, their associations, organisations or groups.

Article 3

Access to environmental information upon request

1. Member States shall ensure that public authorities are required, in accordance with the provisions of this Directive, to make available environmental information held by or for them to any applicant at his request and without his having to state an interest.

2. Subject to Article 4 and having regard to any timescale specified by the applicant, environmental information shall be made available to an applicant:

(a) as soon as possible or, at the latest, within one month after the receipt by the public authority referred to in paragraph 1 of the applicant's request; or
(b) within two months after the receipt of the request by the public authority if the volume and the complexity of the information is such that the one-month period referred to in (a) cannot be complied with. In such cases, the applicant shall be informed as soon as possible, and in any case before the end of that one-month period, of any such extension and of the reasons for it.

3. If a request is formulated in too general a manner, the public authority shall as soon as possible, and at the latest within the timeframe laid down in paragraph 2(a), ask the applicant to specify the request and shall assist the applicant in doing so, e.g. by providing information on the use of the public registers referred to in paragraph 5(c). The public authorities may, where they deem it appropriate, refuse the request under Article 4(1)(c).

4. Where an applicant requests a public authority to make environmental information available in a specific form or format (including in the form of copies), the public authority shall make it so available unless:

(a) it is already publicly available in another form or format, in particular under Article 7, which is easily accessible by applicants; or

(b) it is reasonable for the public authority to make it available in another form or format, in which case reasons shall be given for making it available in that form or format.

For the purposes of this paragraph, public authorities shall make all reasonable efforts to maintain environmental information held by or for them in forms or formats that are readily reproducible and accessible by computer telecommunications or by other electronic means. The reasons for a refusal to make information available, in full or in part, in the form or format requested shall be provided to the applicant within the time limit referred to in paragraph 2(a).

5. For the purposes of this Article, Member States shall ensure that:

(a) officials are required to support the public in seeking access to information;
(b) lists of public authorities are publicly accessible; and
(c) the practical arrangements are defined for ensuring that the right of access to environmental information can be effectively exercised, such as:—the designation of information officers;—the establishment and maintenance of facilities for the examination of the information required;—registers or lists of the environmental information held by public authorities or information points, with clear indications of where such information can be found. Member States shall ensure that public authorities inform the public adequately of the rights they enjoy as a result of this Directive and to an appropriate extent provide information, guidance and advice to this end.

Article 4
Exceptions

1. Member States may provide for a request for environmental information to be refused if:

(a) the information requested is not held by or for the public authority to which the request is addressed. In such a case, where that public authority is aware that the information is held by or for another public authority, it shall, as soon as possible, transfer the request to that other authority and inform the applicant accordingly or inform the applicant of the public authority to which it believes it is possible to apply for the information requested;
(b) the request is manifestly unreasonable;
(c) the request is formulated in too general a manner, taking into account Article 3(3);
(d) the request concerns material in the course of completion or unfinished documents or data;
(e) the request concerns internal communications, taking into account the public interest served by disclosure.

Where a request is refused on the basis that it concerns material in the course of completion, the public authority shall state the name of the authority preparing the material and the estimated time needed for completion.

2. Member States may provide for a request for environmental information to be refused if disclosure of the information would adversely affect:

(a) the confidentiality of the proceedings of public authorities, where such confidentiality is provided for by law;
(b) international relations, public security or national defence;
(c) the course of justice, the ability of any person to receive a fair trial or the ability of a public authority to conduct an enquiry of a criminal or disciplinary nature;
(d) the confidentiality of commercial or industrial information where such confidentiality is provided for by national or Community law to protect a legitimate economic interest, including the public interest in maintaining statistical confidentiality and tax secrecy;
(e) intellectual property rights;
(f) the confidentiality of personal data and/or files relating to a natural person where that person has not consented to the disclosure of the information to the public, where such confidentiality is provided for by national or Community law;

(g) the interests or protection of any person who supplied the information requested on a voluntary basis without being under, or capable of being put under, a legal obligation to do so, unless that person has consented to the release of the information concerned;
(h) the protection of the environment to which such information relates, such as the location of rare species.

The grounds for refusal mentioned in paragraphs 1 and 2 shall be interpreted in a restrictive way, taking into account for the particular case the public interest served by disclosure. In every particular case, the public interest served by disclosure shall be weighed against the interest served by the refusal. Member States may not, by virtue of paragraph 2(a), (d), (f), (g) and (h), provide for a request to be refused where the request relates to information on emissions into the environment. Within this framework, and for the purposes of the application of subparagraph (f), Member States shall ensure that the requirements of Directive 95/46/EC of the European Parliament and of the Council of 24 October 1995 on the protection of individuals with regard to the processing of personal data and on the free movement of such data are complied with.

3. Where a Member State provides for exceptions, it may draw up a publicly accessible list of criteria on the basis of which the authority concerned may decide how to handle requests.

4. Environmental information held by or for public authorities which has been requested by an applicant shall be made available in part where it is possible to separate out any information falling within the scope of paragraphs 1(d) and (e) or 2 from the rest of the information requested.

5. A refusal to make available all or part of the information requested shall be notified to the applicant in writing or electronically, if the request was in writing or if the applicant so requests, within the time limits referred to in Article 3(2)(a) or, as the case may be, (b). The notification shall state the reasons for the refusal and include information on the review procedure provided for in accordance with Article 6.

Article 5
Charges

1. Access to any public registers or lists established and maintained as mentioned in Article 3(5) and examination *in situ* of the information requested shall be free of charge.

2. Public authorities may make a charge for supplying any environmental information but such charge shall not exceed a reasonable amount.

3. Where charges are made, public authorities shall publish and make available to applicants a schedule of such charges as well as information on the circumstances in which a charge may be levied or waived.

Article 6
Access to justice

1. Member States shall ensure that any applicant who considers that his request for information has been ignored, wrongfully refused (whether in full or in part), inadequately answered or otherwise not dealt with in accordance with the provisions of Articles 3, 4 or 5, has access to a procedure in which the acts or omissions of the public authority concerned can be reconsidered by that or another public authority or reviewed administratively by an independent and impartial body established by law. Any such procedure shall be expeditious and either free of charge or inexpensive.

2. In addition to the review procedure referred to in paragraph 1, Member States shall ensure that an applicant has access to a review procedure before a court of law or another independent and impartial body established by law, in which the acts or omissions of the public authority concerned can be reviewed and whose decisions may become final. Member States may furthermore provide that third parties incriminated by the disclosure of information may also have access to legal recourse.

3. Final decisions under paragraph 2 shall be binding on the public authority holding the information. Reasons shall be stated in writing, at least where access to information is refused under this Article.

Article 7

Dissemination of environmental information

1. Member States shall take the necessary measures to ensure that public authorities organise the environmental information which is relevant to their functions and which is held by or for them, with a view to its active and systematic dissemination to the public, in particular by means of computer telecommunication and/or electronic technology, where available. The information made available by means of computer telecommunication and/or electronic technology need not include information collected before the entry into force of this Directive unless it is already available in electronic form. Member States shall ensure that environmental information progressively becomes available in electronic databases which are easily accessible to the public through public telecommunication networks.

2. The information to be made available and disseminated shall be updated as appropriate and shall include at least:

(a) texts of international treaties, conventions or agreements, and of Community, national, regional or local legislation, on the environment or relating to it;
(b) policies, plans and programmes relating to the environment;
(c) progress reports on the implementation of the items referred to in (a) and (b) when prepared or held in electronic form by public authorities;
(d) the reports on the state of the environment referred to in paragraph 3;
(e) data or summaries of data derived from the monitoring of activities affecting, or likely to affect, the environment;
(f) authorisations with a significant impact on the environment and environmental agreements or a reference to the place where such information can be requested or found in the framework of Article 3;
(g) environmental impact studies and risk assessments concerning the environmental elements referred to in Article 2(1)(a) or a reference to the place where the information can be requested or found in the framework of Article 3.

3. Without prejudice to any specific reporting obligations laid down by Community legislation, Member States shall take the necessary measures to ensure that national, and, where appropriate, regional or local reports on the state of the environment are published at regular intervals not exceeding four years; such reports shall include information on the quality of, and pressures on, the environment.

4. Without prejudice to any specific obligation laid down by Community legislation, Member States shall take the necessary measures to ensure that, in the event of an imminent threat to human health or the environment, whether caused by human activities or due to natural causes, all information held by or for public authorities which could enable the public likely to be affected to take measures to prevent or mitigate harm arising from the threat is disseminated, immediately and without delay.

5. The exceptions in Article 4(1) and (2) may apply in relation to the duties imposed by this Article.

6. Member States may satisfy the requirements of this Article by creating links to Internet sites where the information can be found.

Article 8

Quality of environmental information

1. Member States shall, so far as is within their power, ensure that any information that is compiled by them or on their behalf is up to date, accurate and comparable.

2. Upon request, public authorities shall reply to requests for information pursuant to Article 2(1)b, reporting to the applicant on the place where information, if available, can be found on the measurement procedures, including methods of analysis, sampling, and pre-treatment of samples, used in compiling the information, or referring to a standardised procedure used.

Article 9

Review procedure

1. Not later than 14 February 2009, Member States shall report on the experience gained in the application of this Directive. They shall communicate the report to the Commission not later than 14 August 2009. No later than 14 February 2004, the Commission shall forward to the Member States a guidance document setting out clearly the manner in which it wishes the Member States to report.

2. In the light of experience and taking into account developments in computer telecommunication and/or electronic technology, the Commission shall make a report to the European Parliament and to the Council together with any proposal for revision, which it may consider appropriate.

Article 10

Implementation

Member States shall bring into force the laws, regulations and administrative provisions necessary to comply with this Directive by 14 February 2005. They shall forthwith inform the Commission thereof. When Member States adopt these measures, they shall contain a reference to this Directive or shall be accompanied by such reference on the occasion of their official publication. The methods of making such reference shall be laid down by Member States.

Article 11

Repeal

Directive 90/313/EEC is hereby repealed with effect from 14 February 2005. References to the repealed Directive shall be construed as referring to this Directive and shall be read in accordance with the correlation table in the Annex.

Article 12

Entry into force

This Directive shall enter into force on the day of its publication in the *Official Journal of the European Union.*

Article 13

Addressees

This Directive is addressed to the Member States.

Done at Brussels, 28 January 2003.

For the European Parliament The President P. COX

For the Council The President G. PAPANDREOU

APPENDIX G2

The Environmental Information Regulations 2004 (SI 2004 No 3391)

Made *21st December 2004*

Coming into force *1st January 2005*

Whereas a draft of these Regulations has been approved by resolution of each House of Parliament in pursuance of paragraph 2(2) of Schedule 2 to the European Communities Act 1972;

Now, therefore, the Secretary of State, being a Minister designated for the purposes of section 2(2) of the European Communities Act 1972 in relation to freedom of access to, and dissemination of, information on the environment held by or for public authorities or other bodies, in exercise of the powers conferred on her by that section, makes the following Regulations:

Part 1
Introductory

Citation and commencement

1. These Regulations may be cited as the Environmental Information Regulations 2004 and shall come into force on 1st January 2005.

Interpretation

2.—(1) In these Regulations—

'the Act' means the Freedom of Information Act 2000;

'applicant', in relation to a request for environmental information, means the person who made the request;

'appropriate records authority', in relation to a transferred public record, has the same meaning as in section 15(5) of the Act;

'the Commissioner' means the Information Commissioner;

'the Directive' means Council Directive 2003/4/EC on public access to environmental information and repealing Council Directive 90/313/EEC;

'environmental information' has the same meaning as in Article 2(1) of the Directive, namely any information in written, visual, aural, electronic or any other material form on—

(a) the state of the elements of the environment, such as air and atmosphere, water, soil, land, landscape and natural sites including wetlands, coastal and marine areas, biological diversity and its components, including genetically modified organisms, and the interaction among these elements;

(b) factors, such as substances, energy, noise, radiation or waste, including radioactive waste, emissions, discharges and other releases into the environment, affecting or likely to affect the elements of the environment referred to in (a);

(c) measures (including administrative measures), such as policies, legislation, plans, programmes, environmental agreements, and activities affecting or likely to affect the elements and factors referred to in (a) and (b) as well as measures or activities designed to protect those elements;

(d) reports on the implementation of environmental legislation;

(e) cost–benefit and other economic analyses and assumptions used within the framework of the measures and activities referred to in (c); and

(f) the state of human health and safety, including the contamination of the food chain, where relevant, conditions of human life, cultural sites and built structures inasmuch as they are or may be affected by the state of the elements of the environment referred to in (a) or, through those elements, by any of the matters referred to in (b) and (c);

'historical record' has the same meaning as in section 62(1) of the Act;
'public authority' has the meaning given by paragraph (2);
'public record' has the same meaning as in section 84 of the Act;
'responsible authority', in relation to a transferred public record, has the same meaning as in section 15(5) of the Act;
'Scottish public authority' means—

(a) a body referred to in section 80(2) of the Act; and

(b) insofar as not such a body, a Scottish public authority as defined in section 3 of the Freedom of Information (Scotland) Act 2002;

'transferred public record' has the same meaning as in section 15(4) of the Act; and
'working day' has the same meaning as in section 10(6) of the Act.

(2) Subject to paragraph (3), 'public authority' means—

(a) government departments;

(b) any other public authority as defined in section 3(1) of the Act, disregarding for this purpose the exceptions in paragraph 6 of Schedule 1 to the Act, but excluding—

(i) any body or office-holder listed in Schedule 1 to the Act only in relation to information of a specified description; or

(ii) any person designated by Order under section 5 of the Act;

(c) any other body or other person, that carries out functions of public administration; or

(d) any other body or other person, that is under the control of a person falling within sub-paragraphs (a), (b) or (c) and—

(i) has public responsibilities relating to the environment;

(ii) exercises functions of a public nature relating to the environment; or

(iii) provides public services relating to the environment.

(3) Except as provided by regulation 12(10) a Scottish public authority is not a 'public authority' for the purpose of these Regulations.

(4) The following expressions have the same meaning in these Regulations as they have in the Data Protection Act 1998, namely—

(a) 'data' except that for the purposes of regulation 12(3) and regulation 13 a public authority referred to in the definition of data in paragraph (e) of section 1(1) of that Act means a public authority within the meaning of these Regulations;

(b) 'the data protection principles';

(c) 'data subject'; and

(d) 'personal data'.

(5) Except as provided by this regulation, expressions in these Regulations which appear in the Directive have the same meaning in these Regulations as they have in the Directive.

Application

3.—(1) Subject to paragraphs (3) and (4), these Regulations apply to public authorities.

(2) For the purposes of these Regulations, environmental information is held by a public authority if the information—

(a) is in the authority's possession and has been produced or received by the authority; or

(b) is held by another person on behalf of the authority.

(3) These Regulations shall not apply to any public authority to the extent that it is acting in a judicial or legislative capacity.

(4) These Regulations shall not apply to either House of Parliament to the extent required for the purpose of avoiding an infringement of the privileges of either House.

(5) Each government department is to be treated as a person separate from any other government department for the purposes of Parts 2, 4 and 5 of these Regulations.

Part 2

Access to Environmental Information held by Public Authorities

Dissemination of environmental information

4.—(1) Subject to paragraph (3), a public authority shall in respect of environmental information that it holds—

(a) progressively make the information available to the public by electronic means which are easily accessible; and

(b) take reasonable steps to organize the information relevant to its functions with a view to the active and systematic dissemination to the public of the information.

(2) For the purposes of paragraph (1) the use of electronic means to make information available or to organize information shall not be required in relation to information collected before 1st January 2005 in non-electronic form.

(3) Paragraph (1) shall not extend to making available or disseminating information which a public authority would be entitled to refuse to disclose under regulation 12.

(4) The information under paragraph (1) shall include at least—

(a) the information referred to in Article 7(2) of the Directive; and

(b) facts and analyses of facts which the public authority considers relevant and important in framing major environmental policy proposals.

Duty to make available environmental information on request

5.—(1) Subject to paragraph (3) and in accordance with paragraphs (2), (4), (5) and (6) and the remaining provisions of this Part and Part 3 of these Regulations, a public authority that holds environmental information shall make it available on request.

(2) Information shall be made available under paragraph (1) as soon as possible and no later than 20 working days after the date of receipt of the request.

(3) To the extent that the information requested includes personal data of which the applicant is the data subject, paragraph (1) shall not apply to those personal data.

(4) For the purposes of paragraph (1), where the information made available is compiled by or on behalf of the public authority it shall be up to date, accurate and comparable, so far as the public authority reasonably believes.

(5) Where a public authority makes available information in paragraph (b) of the definition of environmental information, and the applicant so requests, the public authority shall, insofar as it is able to do so, either inform the applicant of the place where information, if available, can be found on the measurement procedures, including methods of analysis, sampling and pre-treatment of samples, used in compiling the information, or refer the applicant to a standardized procedure used.

(6) Any enactment or rule of law that would prevent the disclosure of information in accordance with these Regulations shall not apply.

Form and format of information

6.—(1) Where an applicant requests that the information be made available in a particular form or format, a public authority shall make it so available, unless—

(a) it is reasonable for it to make the information available in another form or format; or

(b) the information is already publicly available and easily accessible to the applicant in another form or format.

(2) If the information is not made available in the form or format requested, the public authority shall—

(a) explain the reason for its decision as soon as possible and no later than 20 working days after the date of receipt of the request for the information;

(b) provide the explanation in writing if the applicant so requests; and

(c) inform the applicant of the provisions of regulation 11 and of the enforcement and appeal provisions of the Act applied by regulation 18.

Extension of time

7.—(1) Where a request is made under regulation 5, the public authority may extend the period of 20 working days referred to in the provisions in paragraph (2) to 40 working days if it reasonably believes that the complexity and volume of the information requested means that it is impracticable either to comply with the request within the earlier period or to make a decision to refuse to do so.

(2) The provisions referred to in paragraph (1) are—

(a) regulation 5(2);

(b) regulation 6(2)(a); and

(c) regulation 14(2).

(3) Where paragraph (1) applies the public authority shall notify the applicant accordingly as soon as possible and no later than 20 working days after the date of receipt of the request.

Charging

8.—(1) Subject to paragraphs (2) to (8), where a public authority makes environmental information available in accordance with regulation 5(1) the authority may charge the applicant for making the information available.

(2) A public authority shall not make any charge for allowing an applicant—

(a) to access any public registers or lists of environmental information held by the public authority; or

(b) to examine the information requested at the place which the public authority makes available for that examination.

(3) A charge under paragraph (1) shall not exceed an amount which the public authority is satisfied is a reasonable amount.

(4) A public authority may require advance payment of a charge for making environmental information available and if it does it shall, no later than 20 working days after the date of receipt of the request for the information, notify the applicant of this requirement and of the amount of the advance payment.

(5) Where a public authority has notified an applicant under paragraph (4) that advance payment is required, the public authority is not required—

(a) to make available the information requested; or

(b) to comply with regulations 6 or 14,

unless the charge is paid no later than 60 working days after the date on which it gave the notification.

(6) The period beginning with the day on which the notification of a requirement for an advance payment is made and ending on the day on which that payment is received by the public authority

is to be disregarded for the purposes of determining the period of 20 working days referred to in the provisions in paragraph (7), including any extension to those periods under regulation 7(1).

(7) The provisions referred to in paragraph (6) are—

(a) regulation 5(2);
(b) regulation 6(2)(a); and
(c) regulation 14(2).

(8) A public authority shall publish and make available to applicants—

(a) a schedule of its charges; and
(b) information on the circumstances in which a charge may be made or waived.

Advice and assistance

9.—(1) A public authority shall provide advice and assistance, so far as it would be reasonable to expect the authority to do so, to applicants and prospective applicants.

(2) Where a public authority decides that an applicant has formulated a request in too general a manner, it shall—

(a) ask the applicant as soon as possible and in any event no later than 20 working days after the date of receipt of the request, to provide more particulars in relation to the request; and
(b) assist the applicant in providing those particulars.

(3) Where a code of practice has been made under regulation 16, and to the extent that a public authority conforms to that code in relation to the provision of advice and assistance in a particular case, it shall be taken to have complied with paragraph (1) in relation to that case.

(4) Where paragraph (2) applies, in respect of the provisions in paragraph (5), the date on which the further particulars are received by the public authority shall be treated as the date after which the period of 20 working days referred to in those provisions shall be calculated.

(5) The provisions referred to in paragraph (4) are—

(a) regulation 5(2);
(b) regulation 6(2)(a); and
(c) regulation 14(2).

Transfer of a request

10.—(1) Where a public authority that receives a request for environmental information does not hold the information requested but believes that another public authority or a Scottish public authority holds the information, the public authority shall either—

(a) transfer the request to the other public authority or Scottish public authority; or
(b) supply the applicant with the name and address of that authority,

and inform the applicant accordingly with the refusal sent under regulation 14(1).

(2) Where a request is transferred to a public authority, for the purposes of the provisions referred to in paragraph (3) the request is received by that public authority on the date on which it receives the transferred request.

(3) The provisions referred to in paragraph (2) are—

(a) regulation 5(2);
(b) regulation 6(2)(a); and
(c) regulation 14(2).

Representations and reconsideration

11.—(1) Subject to paragraph (2), an applicant may make representations to a public authority in relation to the applicant's request for environmental information if it appears to the applicant that the authority has failed to comply with a requirement of these Regulations in relation to the request.

(2) Representations under paragraph (1) shall be made in writing to the public authority no later than 40 working days after the date on which the applicant believes that the public authority has failed to comply with the requirement.

(3) The public authority shall on receipt of the representations and free of charge—

(a) consider them and any supporting evidence produced by the applicant; and
(b) decide if it has complied with the requirement.

(4) A public authority shall notify the applicant of its decision under paragraph (3) as soon as possible and no later than 40 working days after the date of receipt of the representations.

(5) Where the public authority decides that it has failed to comply with these Regulations in relation to the request, the notification under paragraph (4) shall include a statement of—

(a) the failure to comply;
(b) the action the authority has decided to take to comply with the requirement; and
(c) the period within which that action is to be taken.

Part 3

Exceptions to the Duty to Disclose Environmental Information

Exceptions to the duty to disclose environmental information

12.—(1) Subject to paragraphs (2), (3) and (9), a public authority may refuse to disclose environmental information requested if—

(a) an exception to disclosure applies under paragraphs (4) or (5); and
(b) in all the circumstances of the case, the public interest in maintaining the exception outweighs the public interest in disclosing the information.

(2) A public authority shall apply a presumption in favour of disclosure.

(3) To the extent that the information requested includes personal data of which the applicant is not the data subject, the personal data shall not be disclosed otherwise than in accordance with regulation 13.

(4) For the purposes of paragraph (1)(a), a public authority may refuse to disclose information to the extent that—

(a) it does not hold that information when an applicant's request is received;
(b) the request for information is manifestly unreasonable;
(c) the request for information is formulated in too general a manner and the public authority has complied with regulation 9;
(d) the request relates to material which is still in the course of completion, to unfinished documents or to incomplete data; or
(e) the request involves the disclosure of internal communications.

(5) For the purposes of paragraph (1)(a), a public authority may refuse to disclose information to the extent that its disclosure would adversely affect—

(a) international relations, defence, national security or public safety;
(b) the course of justice, the ability of a person to receive a fair trial or the ability of a public authority to conduct an inquiry of a criminal or disciplinary nature;
(c) intellectual property rights;
(d) the confidentiality of the proceedings of that or any other public authority where such confidentiality is provided by law;
(e) the confidentiality of commercial or industrial information where such confidentiality is provided by law to protect a legitimate economic interest;
(f) the interests of the person who provided the information where that person—
    (i) was not under, and could not have been put under, any legal obligation to supply it to that or any other public authority;

(ii) did not supply it in circumstances such that that or any other public authority is entitled apart from these Regulations to disclose it; and

(iii) has not consented to its disclosure; or

(g) the protection of the environment to which the information relates.

(6) For the purposes of paragraph (1), a public authority may respond to a request by neither confirming nor denying whether such information exists and is held by the public authority, whether or not it holds such information, if that confirmation or denial would involve the disclosure of information which would adversely affect any of the interests referred to in paragraph (5)(a) and would not be in the public interest under paragraph (1)(b).

(7) For the purposes of a response under paragraph (6), whether information exists and is held by the public authority is itself the disclosure of information.

(8) For the purposes of paragraph (4)(e), internal communications includes communications between government departments.

(9) To the extent that the environmental information to be disclosed relates to information on emissions, a public authority shall not be entitled to refuse to disclose that information under an exception referred to in paragraphs (5)(d) to (g).

(10) For the purposes of paragraphs (5)(b), (d) and (f), references to a public authority shall include references to a Scottish public authority.

(11) Nothing in these Regulations shall authorize a refusal to make available any environmental information contained in or otherwise held with other information which is withheld by virtue of these Regulations unless it is not reasonably capable of being separated from the other information for the purpose of making available that information.

Personal data

13.—(1) To the extent that the information requested includes personal data of which the applicant is not the data subject and as respects which either the first or second condition below is satisfied, a public authority shall not disclose the personal data.

(2) The first condition is—

(a) in a case where the information falls within any of paragraphs (a) to (d) of the definition of 'data' in section 1(1) of the Data Protection Act 1998, that the disclosure of the information to a member of the public otherwise than under these Regulations would contravene—

(i) any of the data protection principles; or

(ii) section 10 of that Act (right to prevent processing likely to cause damage or distress) and in all the circumstances of the case, the public interest in not disclosing the information outweighs the public interest in disclosing it; and

(b) in any other case, that the disclosure of the information to a member of the public otherwise than under these Regulations would contravene any of the data protection principles if the exemptions in section 33A(1) of the Data Protection Act 1998 (which relate to manual data held by public authorities) were disregarded.

(3) The second condition is that by virtue of any provision of Part IV of the Data Protection Act 1998 the information is exempt from section 7(1) of that Act and, in all the circumstances of the case, the public interest in not disclosing the information outweighs the public interest in disclosing it.

(4) In determining whether anything done before 24th October 2007 would contravene any of the data protection principles, the exemptions in Part III of Schedule 8 to the Data Protection Act 1998 shall be disregarded.

(5) For the purposes of this regulation a public authority may respond to a request by neither confirming nor denying whether such information exists and is held by the public authority, whether or not it holds such information, to the extent that—

(a) the giving to a member of the public of the confirmation or denial would contravene any of the data protection principles or section 10 of the Data Protection Act 1998 or would do so if the exemptions in section 33A(1) of that Act were disregarded; or

(b) by virtue of any provision of Part IV of the Data Protection Act 1998, the information is exempt from section 7(1)(a) of that Act.

Refusal to disclose information

14.—(1) If a request for environmental information is refused by a public authority under regulations 12(1) or 13(1), the refusal shall be made in writing and comply with the following provisions of this regulation.

(2) The refusal shall be made as soon as possible and no later than 20 working days after the date of receipt of the request.

(3) The refusal shall specify the reasons not to disclose the information requested, including—

(a) any exception relied on under regulations 12(4), 12(5) or 13; and

(b) the matters the public authority considered in reaching its decision with respect to the public interest under regulation 12(1)(b) or, where these apply, regulations 13(2)(a)(ii) or 13(3).

(4) If the exception in regulation 12(4)(d) is specified in the refusal, the authority shall also specify, if known to the public authority, the name of any other public authority preparing the information and the estimated time in which the information will be finished or completed.

(5) The refusal shall inform the applicant—

(a) that he may make representations to the public authority under regulation 11; and

(b) of the enforcement and appeal provisions of the Act applied by regulation 18.

Ministerial certificates

15.—(1) A Minister of the Crown may certify that a refusal to disclose information under regulation 12(1) is because the disclosure—

(a) would adversely affect national security; and

(b) would not be in the public interest under regulation 12(1)(b).

(2) For the purposes of paragraph (1)—

(a) a Minister of the Crown may designate a person to certify the matters in that paragraph on his behalf; and

(b) a refusal to disclose information under regulation 12(1) includes a response under regulation 12(6).

(3) A certificate issued in accordance with paragraph (1)—

(a) shall be conclusive evidence of the matters in that paragraph; and

(b) may identify the information to which it relates in general terms.

(4) A document purporting to be a certificate under paragraph (1) shall be received in evidence and deemed to be such a certificate unless the contrary is proved.

(5) A document which purports to be certified by or on behalf of a Minister of the Crown as a true copy of a certificate issued by that Minister under paragraph (1) shall in any legal proceedings be evidence (or, in Scotland, sufficient evidence) of that certificate.

(6) In paragraphs (1), (2) and (5), a 'Minister of the Crown' has the same meaning as in section 25(3) of the Act.

Part 4
Code of Practice and Historical Records

Issue of a code of practice and functions of the Commissioner

16.—(1) The Secretary of State may issue, and may from time to time revise, a code of practice providing guidance to public authorities as to the practice which it would, in the Secretary of State's opinion, be desirable for them to follow in connection with the discharge of their functions under these Regulations.

(2) The code may make different provision for different public authorities.

(3) Before issuing or revising any code under this regulation, the Secretary of State shall consult the Commissioner.

(4) The Secretary of State shall lay before each House of Parliament any code issued or revised under this regulation.

(5) The general functions of the Commissioner under section 47 of the Act and the power of the Commissioner to give a practice recommendation under section 48 of the Act shall apply for the purposes of these Regulations as they apply for the purposes of the Act but with the modifications specified in paragraph (6).

(6) For the purposes of the application of sections 47 and 48 of the Act to these Regulations, any reference to—

(a) a public authority is a reference to a public authority within the meaning of these Regulations;

(b) the requirements or operation of the Act, or functions under the Act, includes a reference to the requirements or operation of these Regulations, or functions under these Regulations; and

(c) a code of practice made under section 45 of the Act includes a reference to a code of practice made under this regulation.

Historical and transferred public records

17.—(1) Where a request relates to information contained in a historical record other than one to which paragraph (2) applies and the public authority considers that it may be in the public interest to refuse to disclose that information under regulation 12(1)(b), the public authority shall consult—

(a) the Lord Chancellor, if it is a public record within the meaning of the Public Records Act 1958; or

(b) the appropriate Northern Ireland Minister, if it is a public record to which the Public Records Act (Northern Ireland) 1923 applies,

before it decides whether the information may or may not be disclosed.

(2) Where a request relates to information contained in a transferred public record, other than information which the responsible authority has designated as open information for the purposes of this regulation, the appropriate records authority shall consult the responsible authority on whether there may be an exception to disclosure of that information under regulation 12(5).

(3) If the appropriate records authority decides that such an exception applies—

(a) subject to paragraph (4), a determination on whether it may be in the public interest to refuse to disclose that information under regulation 12(1)(b) shall be made by the responsible authority;

(b) the responsible authority shall communicate its determination to the appropriate records authority within such time as is reasonable in all the circumstances; and

(c) the appropriate records authority shall comply with regulation 5 in accordance with that determination.

(4) Where a responsible authority is required to make a determination under paragraph (3), it shall consult—

(a) the Lord Chancellor, if the transferred public record is a public record within the meaning of the Public Records Act 1958; or
(b) the appropriate Northern Ireland Minister, if the transferred public record is a public record to which the Public Records Act (Northern Ireland) 1923 applies,

before it determines whether the information may or may not be disclosed.

(5) A responsible authority which is not a public authority under these Regulations shall be treated as a public authority for the purposes of—

(a) the obligations of a responsible authority under paragraphs (3)(a) and (b) and (4); and
(b) the imposition of any requirement to furnish information relating to compliance with regulation 5.

Part 5

Enforcement and Appeals, Offences, Amendment and Revocation

Enforcement and appeal provisions

18.—(1) The enforcement and appeals provisions of the Act shall apply for the purposes of these Regulations as they apply for the purposes of the Act but with the modifications specified in this regulation.

(2) In this regulation, 'the enforcement and appeals provisions of the Act' means—

(a) Part IV of the Act (enforcement), including Schedule 3 (powers of entry and inspection) which has effect by virtue of section 55 of the Act; and
(b) Part V of the Act (appeals).

(3) Part IV of the Act shall not apply in any case where a certificate has been issued in accordance with regulation 15(1).

(4) For the purposes of the application of the enforcement and appeals provisions of the Act—

(a) for any reference to—
    (i) 'this Act' there shall be substituted a reference to 'these Regulations'; and
    (ii) 'Part I' there shall be substituted a reference to 'Parts 2 and 3 of these Regulations';
(b) any reference to a public authority is a reference to a public authority within the meaning of these Regulations;
(c) for any reference to the code of practice under section 45 of the Act (issue of a code of practice by the Secretary of State) there shall be substituted a reference to any code of practice issued under regulation 16(1);
(d) in section 50(4) of the Act (contents of decision notice)—
    (i) in paragraph (a) for the reference to 'section 1(1)' there shall be substituted a reference to 'regulation 5(1)'; and
    (ii) in paragraph (b) for the references to 'sections 11 and 17' there shall be substituted references to 'regulations 6, 11 or 14';
(e) in section 56(1) of the Act (no action against public authority) for the words 'This Act does not confer' there shall be substituted the words 'These Regulations do not confer';
(f) in section 57(3)(a) of the Act (appeal against notices served under Part IV) for the reference to 'section 66' of the Act (decisions relating to certain transferred public records) there shall be substituted a reference to 'regulations 17(2) to (5)';
(g) in paragraph 1 of Schedule 3 to the Act (issue of warrants) for the reference to 'section 77' (offence of altering, etc. records with intent to prevent disclosure) there shall be substituted a reference to 'regulation 19'; and
(h) in paragraph 8 of Schedule 3 to the Act (matters exempt from inspection and seizure) for the reference to 'information which is exempt information by virtue of section 23(1) or

24(1)' (bodies and information relating to national security) there shall be substituted a reference to 'information whose disclosure would adversely affect national security'.

(5) In section 50(4)(a) of the Act (contents of decision notice) the reference to confirmation or denial applies to a response given by a public authority under regulation 12(6) or regulation 13(5).

(6) Section 53 of the Act (exception from duty to comply with decision notice or enforcement notice) applies to a decision notice or enforcement notice served under Part IV of the Act as applied to these Regulations on any of the public authorities referred to in section 53(1)(a); and in section 53(7) for the reference to 'exempt information' there shall be substituted a reference to 'information which may be refused under these Regulations'.

(7) Section 60 of the Act (appeals against national security certificate) shall apply with the following modifications—

(a) for the reference to a certificate under section 24(3) of the Act (national security) there shall be substituted a reference to a certificate issued in accordance with regulation 15(1);
(b) subsection (2) shall be omitted; and
(c) in subsection (3), for the words, 'the Minister did not have reasonable grounds for issuing the certificate' there shall be substituted the words 'the Minister or person designated by him did not have reasonable grounds for issuing the certificate under regulation 15(1)'.

(8) A person found guilty of an offence under paragraph 12 of Schedule 3 to the Act (offences relating to obstruction of the execution of a warrant) is liable on summary conviction to a fine not exceeding level 5 on the standard scale.

(9) A government department is not liable to prosecution in relation to an offence under paragraph 12 of Schedule 3 to the Act but that offence shall apply to a person in the public service of the Crown and to a person acting on behalf of either House of Parliament or on behalf of the Northern Ireland Assembly as it applies to any other person.

(10) Section 76(1) of the Act (disclosure of information between Commissioner and ombudsmen) shall apply to any information obtained by, or furnished to, the Commissioner under or for the purposes of these Regulations.

Offence of altering records with intent to prevent disclosure

19.—(1) Where—

(a) a request for environmental information has been made to a public authority under regulation 5; and
(b) the applicant would have been entitled (subject to payment of any charge) to that information in accordance with that regulation,

any person to whom this paragraph applies is guilty of an offence if he alters, defaces, blocks, erases, destroys or conceals any record held by the public authority, with the intention of preventing the disclosure by that authority of all, or any part, of the information to which the applicant would have been entitled.

(2) Subject to paragraph (5), paragraph (1) applies to the public authority and to any person who is employed by, is an officer of, or is subject to the direction of, the public authority.

(3) A person guilty of an offence under this regulation is liable on summary conviction to a fine not exceeding level 5 on the standard scale.

(4) No proceedings for an offence under this regulation shall be instituted—

(a) in England and Wales, except by the Commissioner or by or with the consent of the Director of Public Prosecutions; or
(b) in Northern Ireland, except by the Commissioner or by or with the consent of the Director of Public Prosecutions for Northern Ireland.

(5) A government department is not liable to prosecution in relation to an offence under paragraph (1) but that offence shall apply to a person in the public service of the Crown and to a person

acting on behalf of either House of Parliament or on behalf of the Northern Ireland Assembly as it applies to any other person.

Amendment

20.—(1) Section 39 of the Act is amended as follows.

(2) In subsection (1)(a), for 'regulations under section 74' there is substituted 'environmental information regulations'.

(3) After subsection (1) there is inserted—

'(1A) In subsection (1) 'environmental information regulations' means—

(a) regulations made under section 74, or

(b) regulations made under section 2(2) of the European Communities Act 1972 for the purpose of implementing any Community obligation relating to public access to, and the dissemination of, information on the environment.'

Revocation

21. The following are revoked—

(a) The Environmental Information Regulations 1992 and the Environmental Information (Amendment) Regulations 1998 except insofar as these apply to Scottish public authorities; and

(b) The Environmental Information Regulations (Northern Ireland) 1993 and the Environmental Information (Amendment) Regulations (Northern Ireland) 1998.

Margaret Beckett
Secretary of State for Environment, Food and Rural Affairs

21st December 2004

Explanatory Note

(This note is not part of the Regulations)

These Regulations implement Council Directive 2003/4/EC on public access to environmental information and repealing Council Directive 90/313/EEC (OJ No. L 41, 14.2.2003, p.26), except in relation to Scottish public authorities (as specified in section 80(2) of the Freedom of Information Act 2000 and defined in section 3 of the Freedom of Information (Scotland) Act 2002). Separate Regulations will be made by Scottish Ministers to implement this Directive in respect of Scottish public authorities.

Regulation 2 contains definitions of expressions in these Regulations, including the definition of environmental information, which is the same as in Council Directive 2003/4/EC. Except as provided in these definitions, expressions in these Regulations which appear in Council Directive 2003/4/EC have the same meaning in these Regulations as they have in that Directive.

Regulation 3 applies the Regulations to public authorities and makes provision in relation to the environmental information held by public authorities. It also provides that a public authority will not be subject to these Regulations to the extent that it is acting in a judicial or legislative capacity and that the Regulations do not apply to either House of Parliament to the extent required for the purpose of avoiding an infringement of the privileges of either House. And it provides that each Government department is to be treated separately for the purposes of Parts 2, 4 and 5 of the Regulations.

Part 2 of the Regulations contains provisions relating to access to environmental information.

Regulation 4 requires public authorities progressively to make available environmental information to the public by electronic means which are easily accessible. And public authorities must take reasonable steps to organize the environmental information they hold relevant to their functions with a view to the active and systematic dissemination of the information to the public.

Regulation 5 requires a public authority that holds environmental information to make it available on request, as soon as possible and no later than 20 working days after the date of receipt of the request. This requirement is subject to the remaining provisions of Part 2 of the Regulations and Part 3, which include the exceptions to disclosure under regulation 12. Regulation 5 also provides that where environmental information requested includes personal data of which the applicant is the data subject the requirement to make the information available under regulation 5 does not apply to that aspect of the request. Instead, such requests for personal data fall to be dealt with under section 7 of the Data Protection Act 1998.

Regulation 6 provides for the form or format in which information must be provided.

Regulation 7 makes provision for a public authority to extend the time to deal with complex and voluminous requests and to inform the applicant if it intends to rely on such an extension.

Under regulation 8, a public authority may charge applicants for environmental information a reasonable amount for making the information available. Payment in advance may be requested. It provides that no charge can be made for access to public registers or lists held by the authority or for examination of the information requested at the place which the authority makes available for that examination.

Regulation 9 provides for a public authority to give reasonable advice and assistance to an applicant or prospective applicant.

Regulation 10 makes provision in relation to the transfer of requests to another public authority or a Scottish public authority.

Regulation 11 provides that a person who has requested environmental information from a public authority may make representations to the authority if it appears that the authority has not complied with the requirements of these Regulations in relation to the request. These representations must be considered by the authority free of charge. It also provides that a public authority must make a decision on those representations as soon as possible and no later than 40 working days after the date of receipt of the representations.

Part 3 of the Regulations contains provisions relating to exceptions to the duty to disclose environmental information.

Under regulation 12, a public authority may refuse to disclose environmental information if an exception to disclosure applies and the public authority decides that in all the circumstances the public interest in maintaining the exception outweighs the public interest in disclosing the information. In these decisions public authorities must apply a presumption in favour of disclosure. Regulation 12 also provides that where the information requested relates to information on emissions, disclosure of that information cannot be refused under the exceptions listed in paragraphs (5)(d) to (g).

Regulation 13 makes provision for exceptions to the disclosure of environmental information which includes personal data of which the person requesting the information is not the data subject. It provides that the personal data shall not be disclosed if that would breach the data protection principles set out in Part I of Schedule 1 to the Data Protection Act 1998. It also provides that the personal data must not be disclosed if the individual who is the subject of the personal data has properly given notice that disclosure would cause unwarranted substantial damage or distress and there is no overriding public interest in disclosure. It also provides that there must be no disclosure if the individual who is the subject of the personal data would not be entitled to have access to the data under section 7(1) of the Data Protection Act 1998 and there is no overriding public interest in disclosure.

Regulation 14 provides that a decision by a public authority to refuse a request for environmental information must be explained to the applicant as soon as possible and no later than 20 working days after the date of receipt of the request. The applicant must be informed of the right to make representations to the authority under regulation 11 and of the enforcement and appeal provisions of the Act applied by regulation 18, under which he may appeal against the refusal to the Information Commissioner.

Regulation 15 provides that a Minister of the Crown, or a person designated by him, may certify that a refusal to disclose information has been made under regulation 12 on the grounds that disclosure would adversely affect national security and would not be in the public interest.

Part 4 of the Regulations contains provisions relating to a code of practice and historical records.

Regulation 16 provides that the Secretary of State may, after consultation with the Information Commissioner, issue a code of practice providing guidance to public authorities as to the practice for them to follow in connection with the discharge of their functions under these Regulations.

Regulation 17 makes provision for consultation by public authorities in relation to requests for the disclosure of information contained in historical records. And in relation to requests for the disclosure of information contained in transferred public records it makes provision for consultation by appropriate records authorities with responsible authorities.

Part 5 of the Regulations contains provisions relating to enforcement and appeals, offences, amendment and revocation.

Regulation 18 applies the enforcement and appeals provisions of the Freedom of Information Act 2000 for the purposes of the Regulations. A person who has made a request for environmental information from a public authority may complain to the Information Commissioner if he believes that the public authority has not dealt with the request, or representations to the authority about the request, in accordance with the requirements of these Regulations. The Information Commissioner has equivalent powers to enforce the requirements of these Regulations as apply under Part IV of the Freedom of Information Act 2000. These include the powers of entry and inspection and, in respect of the exercise of those powers, the offence of obstruction in Schedule 3 to that Act, as applied to these Regulations. Regulation 18 also provides for rights of appeal to the Information Tribunal equivalent to those under Part V of the Freedom of Information Act 2000. It also provides that for these purposes a Ministerial certificate issued under regulation 15 is equivalent to a certificate issued under section 24 of the Freedom of Information Act 2000.

Regulation 19 provides that an offence will be committed by any person who alters, defaces, blocks, erases, destroys or conceals any record of the public authority with the intention of preventing the disclosure to an applicant of the information that they are entitled to receive under regulation 5. The maximum fine is level 5 on the standard scale. Except for prosecutions brought by the Information Commissioner, prosecutions for the offence require the consent of the Director of Public Prosecutions or, as appropriate, the Director of Public Prosecutions for Northern Ireland.

Regulation 20 amends section 39 of the Freedom of Information Act 2000. The effect of the amendment is that information which can be required to be disclosed to the public under these Regulations (or which could be required to be disclosed but for an exception in these Regulations) is exempt information for the purposes of that Act.

Regulation 21 revokes previous Environmental Information Regulations: S.I. 1992/3240, as amended by S.I. 1998/1447, except insofar as these apply to Scottish public authorities; and the Environmental Information (Northern Ireland) Regulations 1993 (S.R. 1993 No.45) as amended by the Environmental Information (Northern Ireland) Regulations 1998 (S.R. 1998 No.238).

A Transposition Note has been prepared for these Regulations and a copy has been placed in the library of each House of Parliament. Copies of the Transposition Note can be obtained from Information Management Division, DEFRA, Nobel House, 17 Smith Square, London SW1P 3JR.

A Regulatory Impact Assessment has not been prepared in relation to these Regulations.

APPENDIX G3

Code of Practice on the Discharge of the Obligations of Public Authorities under the Environmental Information Regulations 2004 (SI 2004 No 3391)

Issued under Regulation 16 of the Regulations, February 2005

Foreword to the Code of Practice

Introduction

1. The Code of Practice, to which this is a foreword, is prepared in accordance with Regulation 16 of the Environmental Information Regulations 2004 (EIR) and provides guidance to public authorities as to the practice that would be desirable for them to follow in connection with discharging their functions under the EIR. However, if public authorities do not follow the Code's recommendations it will be difficult for them to meet their obligations under the Regulations.

2. The definition of 'public authority' for the purposes of the EIR is wider than that under section 3(1) of the Freedom of Information Act 2000 (FOIA). Those bodies subject to both the FOIA and the EIR will need to consider the Code provisions relevant to the appropriate regime (this Code or the FOIA section 45 Code). Public authorities covered only by the EIR need only consider this Code of Practice on access to information. Recommendations for EIR public

authorities on record keeping, management and destruction are set out in the FOIA section 46 Code of Practice.

3. This Code applies where a request for environmental information is received, as defined in the EIR. Any request for other information should be handled in accordance with the FOIA and other access regimes such as the Data Protection Act as appropriate. Where a request relates to information, part of which is environmental and part of which is not, then each part of the request should be handled in accordance with the relevant legislation.

4. This foreword does not form part of the Code itself.

5. An access to environmental information regime has been in place since 1992, in the form of the Environmental Information Regulations 1992, as amended by the Environmental Information (Amendment) Regulations 1998, and also the Environmental Information Regulations (Northern Ireland) 1993 and 1998. The introduction of replacement Regulations in England, Wales and Northern Ireland (and of similar regulations in Scotland) enables compliance with the UK's commitments under the UNECE Convention on Access to Information, Public Participation in Decision-making, and Access to Justice in Environmental Matters (the 'Aarhus' Convention), and with EU Directive 2003/4/EC. Increased public access to environmental information and the dissemination of such information contribute to a greater awareness of environmental matters, a free exchange of views, more effective participation by the public in environmental decisionmaking and, eventually, to a better environment (Recital 1, Directive 2003/4/EC).

6. The Government is committed to greater openness in the public sector. FOIA and EIR will further this aim by helping to transform the culture of the public sector to one of greater openness, enabling members of the public to scrutinise the decisions of public authorities more closely and ensure that services provided by the public sector are more efficiently and properly delivered. Conformity with the Code will assist this.

7. The Code is a supplement to the provisions in the EIR. It is not a substitute for legislation. Public authorities should seek legal advice as considered necessary on general issues relating to the implementation of the EIR or its application to individual cases. They should also refer to the Government's Guidance on the EIR and to any guidance issued by the Information Commissioner.

8. The provisions of the EIR granting a general right of access came into force on 1st January 2005 and the Commissioner's powers to handle appeals and issue guidance also took effect on 1st January 2005.

9. This code of practice outlines to public authorities the practice that it would, in the opinion of the Secretary of State, be desirable for them to follow in connection with the discharge of their duties under the Environmental Information Regulations 2004 (EIR).

10. The aims of the Code are to:

- —facilitate the disclosure of information under the EIR by setting out good administrative practice that it is desirable for public authorities to follow when handling requests for information including, where appropriate, the transfer of a request to a different authority;
- —to set out good practice in proactive dissemination of environmental information;
- —to protect the interests of applicants by setting out standards of advice and assistance that should be followed as a matter of good practice;
- —to ensure that third party rights are considered and that authorities consider the implications for access to environmental information before agreeing to confidentiality provisions in contracts and accepting information in confidence from a third party;
- —to encourage, as matter of good practice, the development of effective review and appeal procedures of decisions taken under the EIR.

11. Although there is a power under EIR for the Secretary of State to issue the Code, the provisions of the Code are not legislation. However, authorities are expected to abide by the Code unless there

are good reasons, capable of being justified to the Information Commissioner, why it would be inappropriate to do so.

12. The requirements for dealing with requests for environmental information are contained in the EIR and public authorities must comply with these provisions at all times. However, Regulation 16 applies section 47 of the FOIA, which places a duty on the Information Commissioner to promote good practice by public authorities ('good practice' includes compliance with the provisions of the Code), and section 48 of the FOIA which enables the Information Commissioner to issue a 'practice recommendation' to a public authority if it appears to him that the practice of the authority does not conform with that proposed in the Code.

13. Public authorities and others are encouraged to contact the Information Commissioner's Office for advice and assistance about their duties under the Regulations. The Information Commissioner can provide valuable, detailed assistance to help organisations achieve compliance through the development of good practice. Further, Regulation 9 of the EIR places a duty on public authorities to provide advice and assistance to applicants and potential applicants. Authorities will have complied with this duty in any particular case if they have conformed with the Code in relation to the provision of advice or assistance in that case.

Main differences between requirements under the FOIA and EIR that must be reflected in this Code

14. The main differences are:

- i. the range of bodies covered by the EIR is wider to allow for consistency with the EC Directive, and includes public utilities and certain public–private partnerships and private companies, such as those in the water, waste, transport and energy sectors;
- ii. requests for environmental information need not be in writing;
- iii. the information held by a public authority includes holding information held on behalf of any other person;
- iv. the duty to provide advice and assistance requires a public authority to respond within 20 working days when requesting more particulars from the applicant;
- v. the time limits for responding to a request apply to ALL requests including those involving consideration of the public interest. Regulation 7 allows for an extension from 20 to 40 working days for complex and high–volume requests;
- vi. no exception is made for requests that will involve costs in excess of the 'appropriate limit' within the meaning of the Fees Regulations made under sections 9, 12 and 13 of the FOIA. Except in specified limited circumstances, ALL requests must be dealt with and any charges imposed must be reasonable;
- vii. there are differences in the exceptions available under EIR and the exemptions available under FOIA;
- viii the requirement for public authorities to have in place a complaints and reconsideration procedure to deal with representations alleging non-compliance with the EIR is mandatory. Each of these differences is explained in greater detail in the EIR Guidance that can be found at http://www.defra.gov.uk/environment/pubaccess/. The Guidance also explains the scope of environmental information and provides further information on terminology, including 'emissions' and 'held by or for'.

Duty to provide advice and assistance

15. Regulation 9 of the EIR places a duty on public authorities to provide advice and assistance to applicants. A public authority is deemed to have complied with this duty in any particular case if it has conformed with this Code in relation to the provision of advice and assistance in that case. The duty to assist and advise is enforceable by the Information Commissioner. If a public authority fails in its statutory duty, the Commissioner may issue a decision notice under section 50, or an enforcement notice under section 52 of the FOIA.

16. Public Authorities should not forget that other Acts of Parliament may be relevant to the way in which authorities provide advice and assistance to applicants or potential applicants, e.g. the Disability Discrimination Act 1995 and the Race Relations Act 1976 (as amended by the Race Relations (Amendment) Act 2000).

Copyright

17. Public authorities should be aware that information that is disclosed under the EIR might be subject to copyright protection. If an applicant wishes to use any such information in a way that would infringe copyright, for example by making multiple copies, or issuing copies to the public, he or she would require a licence from the copyright holder. HMSO have issued guidance, which is available at http://www.hmso.gov.uk/copyright/managing_copyright.htm or by telephone on 01603 621000.

18. http://www.hmso.gov.uk/copyright/guidance/gn_19.htm explains more fully the distinction between the supply of information held by public authorities under Freedom of Information legislation and the reuse of that information and those circumstances where formal licensing is required.

19. Reports on the environment may be commissioned by public authorities from outside organisations. In general, public authorities should seek to ensure that the copyright of any such reports rests with them. If not, it should be made clear to the outside organisation that under the terms of the EIR, the public authority will likely be making copies of their reports, or parts thereof, available to the public in response to EIR applications, and it may not be solely environmental information contained in reports that will be disclosed.

Practice recommendations

20. The Information Commissioner has a duty to enforce compliance and promote good practice. The following (described in paragraphs 21–24) are the principal tools at his disposal. The Information Commissioner (the Commissioner) is issuing guidance for public authorities on dealing with requests for environmental information, which may be helpful in setting out in more detail the Commissioner's enforcement powers.

21. In accordance with the powers provided in section 74 of the FOIA, Regulation 16(5) of EIR provides that the general functions of the Commissioner under sections 47–49 of the FOIA shall apply under EIR. Under section 47 of the FOIA, the Information Commissioner has a duty to promote the observance of this Code by public authorities. If it appears to the Commissioner that the practice of a public authority in the exercise of its functions under the EIR does not conform with that proposed in the Code of Practice, he may give to the authority a recommendation, under section 48 (known as a 'practice recommendation'), specifying the steps which should, in his opinion, be taken to promote such conformity. Unless the public authority appeals against the decision of the Commissioner the public authority must comply with the recommendation of the Commissioner. There is no statutory time limit for this; it will depend on the circumstances of the case but the Commissioner can specify a particular time limit for compliance in the recommendation in question, and will take into consideration the measurements of Articles 9(1) and 9(4) of the Aarhus Convention in setting any time limit.

22. A practice recommendation must be given in writing and must refer to the particular provisions of the Code of Practice with which, in the Commissioner's opinion, the public authority's practice does not conform. A practice recommendation is simply a recommendation and cannot be directly enforced by the Commissioner. However, a failure to comply with a practice recommendation may lead to a failure to comply with the EIR. Further, a failure to take account of a practice recommendation may lead to an adverse comment in a report to Parliament by the Commissioner.

Information notices

23. Regulation 18 of the EIR applies the enforcement and appeal provisions of FOIA to environmental information. The Information Commissioner determines whether the practice of a public authority conforms to this Code. Where an application has been received under section 50 of the FOIA, under section 51 of the FOIA, he may serve an information notice on the authority requiring it to provide information relating to its conformity with the Code.

24. Under the provisions of section 54 of the FOIA, if a public authority fails to comply with an information notice the Commissioner may certify in writing to the court that the public authority has failed to comply with that notice. The court may then inquire into the matter and, after hearing any witnesses who may be produced against or on behalf of the public authority, and after hearing any statement that may be offered in defence, deal with the authority as if it had committed a contempt of court.

Code of Practice on the Discharge of the Obligations of Public Authorities under the Environmental Information Regulations 2004 (SI 2004 No. 3391)

The Secretary of State, after consulting the Information Commissioner, issues the following Code of Practice pursuant to Regulation 16 of the Environmental Information Regulations 2004. Laid before Parliament on 16 February 2005 pursuant to Regulation 16 of the Environmental Information Regulations.

I Training

1. All communications to a public authority, including those not in writing and those transmitted by electronic means, potentially amount to a request for information within the meaning of the EIR, and if they do they must be dealt with in accordance with the provisions of the EIR. It is therefore essential that everyone working in a public authority who deals with correspondence, or who otherwise may be required to provide information, is familiar with the requirements of the EIR and this Code in addition to the FOIA and the other Codes of Practice issued under its provisions, and takes account of any relevant guidance on good practice issued by the Commissioner. Authorities should also ensure that proper training is provided.

2. Requests for environmental information may come in the form of verbal requests which has specific implications for training provision.

3. In planning and delivering training, authorities should be aware of other provisions affecting the disclosure of information such as the FOIA, the Data Protection Act 1998, and anti-discrimination legislation (such as the Disability Discrimination Act).

II Proactive dissemination of information

4. Under Regulation 4, a public authority has a duty to progressively make the information available to the public by electronic means which are easily accessible, and to take reasonable steps to organize information relevant to its functions with a view to active and systematic dissemination.

5. Consideration should be given to making web sites accessible to all and simple to use, so that information can be readily found, for example by enabling search functions and having an alphabetical directory as well as tree structures. Information should not be 'buried' on a site.

6. Public authorities should consider how to publicise applicants' rights to information, for example as part of general information on services provided by the authority.

7. When public authorities are considering what information to disseminate proactively, they should not restrict themselves to the minimum requirements as listed in the Directive. For example, consideration should be given to disseminating frequently requested information, which will reduce individual requests for such information in the future.

III The provision of advice and assistance to persons making requests for information

8. The provision of advice and assistance to persons making requests for environmental information differs from that provided to those making general requests for information under FOIA:

—requests for environmental information need not be in writing;

—EIR contains no equivalent to the 'appropriate limit' exemption under section 12 of the FOIA; and

—the duty to provide advice and assistance under EIR requires the public authority to request that the applicant provide more particulars within 20 working days of the request where a request is formulated in too general a manner.

9. Every public authority should be ready to provide advice and assistance, including but not necessarily limited to the steps set out below. This advice and assistance should be available to those who propose to make, or have made requests and help them to make good use of the Regulations. The duty on the public authority is to provide advice and assistance 'so far as it would be reasonable to expect the authority to do so'.

10. Appropriate assistance might include:

—providing an outline of the different kinds of information that might meet the terms of the request;

—providing access to detailed catalogues and indexes, where these are available, to help the applicant ascertain the nature and extent of the information held by the authority; and

—providing a general response to the request setting out options for further information that could be provided on request.

—advising the person that another person or agency (such as a Citizens Advice Bureau) may be able to assist them with the application or make the application on their behalf.

11. This list is not exhaustive and public authorities should be flexible in offering advice and assistance most appropriate to the circumstances of the applicant.

12. Public authorities should publish their procedures for dealing with requests for information. These procedures may include what the public authority's usual procedure will be where it does not hold the information requested. (See also VI—'Transferring requests for information'). It may also alert potential applicants to the fact that the public authority may want to consult other public authorities and/or third parties in order to reach a decision on whether the requested information can be released. Potential applicants may wish to be notified before any transfer of request or consultation is made. If this is the case, the published procedure should therefore alert them to say so in their applications. (See also VII—'Consultation with third parties'.) The procedures should include an address or addresses (including an e-mail address where possible) to which applicants may direct requests for information or for assistance. A telephone number should also be provided and where possible the name of an individual who can provide assistance. These procedures should be referred to in the authority's publication scheme where it has one.

13. Public authorities may wish to consider publishing their procedures for reviewing refusals for requests. In addition, public authorities will also wish to consider providing information about other access regimes (where appropriate), provide guidance about frequently requested information, and provide information relating to previous disclosures.

14. Staff in public authorities in contact with the public should bear in mind that not everyone will be aware of the EIR or the FOIA and they should draw the legislation to the attention of potential applicants who appear unaware of them. Any question which cannot be dealt with on the spot should be treated as a request for information.

15. A request for information under the EIR can be in any form and need not be in writing. However, for a response to be made by the public authority it will need contact details to either provide the information or refuse the request. A request in writing includes a request transmitted by electronic means. Where a person finds it difficult to specify very clearly the nature of their request,

the public authority should ensure that appropriate assistance is given to enable that person to make a request for information. For example, if a request is formulated in too general a manner the public authority shall, as soon as possible and not later than 20 working days after receipt of the request, ask the applicant to provide more particulars and shall assist them in doing so. However, Public Authorities should be aware of the dangers of overbureaucratising procedures when responding to requests for routine information.

Clarifying the request

16. Where the applicant does not describe the information sought in a way which would enable the public authority to identify or locate it, or the request is ambiguous, the authority should, as far as practicable, provide assistance to the applicant to enable him or her to describe more clearly the information requested. Authorities should be aware that the aim of providing assistance is to clarify the nature of the information sought, not to determine the aims or motivation of the applicant. Care should be taken not to give the applicant the impression that he or she is obliged to disclose the nature of his or her interest or that he or she will be treated differently if he or she does. It is important that the applicant is contacted as soon as possible, preferably by telephone, fax or e-mail, where more information is needed to clarify what is sought. Public authorities should also be prepared to explain why they are asking for additional information. The 20 day time limit stops running when a request for clarification is issued.

17. In seeking to clarify what is sought, public authorities should bear in mind that applicants cannot reasonably be expected to possess identifiers such as a file reference number, or a description of a particular record, unless this information is made available by the authority for the use of applicants.

18. If, following the provision of such assistance, the applicant is still unable to describe the information requested in a way that would enable the authority to identify and locate it, the authority is not expected to seek further clarification. The authority should disclose any information relating to the application that has been successfully identified and found that it can disclose. It should also explain to the applicant why it cannot take the request any further and provide details of the authority's complaints procedure and where applicable the applicant's rights under section 50 of the FOIA (see 'Complaints Procedure' in section XII below).

19. Where the applicant indicates that he or she is not prepared to pay any charge requested, the authority should consider whether there is any information that may be of interest to the applicant that is available free of charge.

20. There is no EIR equivalent to the 'appropriate limit' under section 12 of the FOIA. A public authority is expected to deal with all requests for environmental information. However, cost may be relevant when considering whether to apply the exceptions relating to 'manifestly unreasonable' or 'too general'. Where the applicant makes a request that is clear but which involves the provision of a very large volume of information, and specifies a cost ceiling, the authority should consider providing an indication of what information could be provided within the cost ceiling.

21. There are no special provisions for dealing with requests that appear to be part of an organised campaign. Such requests are to be expected and dealt with in the usual way. Repeatedly requested information may be best made available by means of a publication scheme. Being part of a campaign does not necessarily make a request 'manifestly unreasonable'.

Form and format

22. Regulation 6 allows for the applicant to be given the information available in a particular form or format unless there is another reasonable approach to supplying the information. A public authority should be flexible, as far as is reasonable, with respect to form and format, taking into account the fact, for example, that some IT users may not be able to read attachments in certain formats, and that some members of the public may prefer paper to electronic copies.

23. Although there is no specific reference in the Regulations to the provision of information in the form of a summary or digest, a request for environmental information may include a request for information to be provided in the form of a digest or summary. This should generally be provided so long as it is reasonably practical to do so, taking into account the cost. Many applicants will find a summary more useful than masses of data, and this should be taken into account when considering proactive dissemination.

IV Timeliness in dealing with requests for information

24. Requests for information must be responded to within 20 working days. The 20 day time limit can be extended to 40 working days if the complexity and volume of the information requested means that the 20 working days deadline cannot be complied with. Unlike FOIA, there is no provision to further extend the time limit for cases where the public interest has to be balanced.

25. Public authorities are required to comply with all requests for information as soon as possible and they must not delay responding until the end of the 20 working day period under Regulation 5(2)(b) if the information could reasonably have been provided earlier.

26. Public authorities must aim to make all decisions as soon as possible and in any case within 20 working days, including in cases where a public authority needs to consider where the public interest lies. However, it is recognised there will be some instances where, because of the complexity and volume of the information requested it will not be possible to deal with an application within 20 working days. In such cases a public authority is expected to inform the applicant of this as soon as possible and within 20 working days, and should, be as specific as possible in their response to the applicant indicating when they will receive the information and the reasons for the delay, The 20 days will halt at the point that the authority issues a request for payment of an advance charge, and commences again at the point payment is received. Authorities must in any case comply with or refuse the request within 40 working days. Authorities may find it helpful to formulate a policy about how to apply the provision on making a time extension.

27. It is of critical importance for the body receiving a request to identify the request for environmental information in the first instance, and then to meet the timetable. Monitoring the timeliness of responses is easiest where requests for information are in writing. Where requests for environmental information are made otherwise than in writing (e.g. by telephone or in person) public authorities will need a system for recording the request. This may, for example, involve making a written note of the request and asking the applicant to confirm its accuracy.

V Charges

28. The EIR does not require charges to be made but public authorities have discretion to make a reasonable charge for environmental information. However, if they are providing access to a public register, or if the applicant examines the information at the offices of the public authority or in a drop-in library or other place which the public authority makes available for that examination, access to the information shall be free of charge. When making a charge, whether for information that is proactively disseminated or provided on request, the charge must not exceed the cost of producing the information unless that public authority is one entitled to levy a market-based charge for the information, such as a trading fund.

29. Where a public authority proposes to make a charge, a schedule of charges should be made available (including, e.g. a price list for publications, or the charge per unit of work which will be incurred to meet a request). When an advance payment is required, the applicant should be notified and the public authority should invite the applicant to say whether they wish to proceed with the request, or their request, or part of it, or whether the request may be met in some other way (for example, by visiting the offices of the public authority to inspect the information or by making use of more easily identifiable data). Where a requirement for advance payment has been notified, the period between the notification and the receipt of payment will be disregarded in determining

the response times for meeting requests (Regulation 8(5)).The request will remain active for up to 60 working days from the date of notification. If no payment is received during this time the request lapses but the applicant may make a new application at any time. When a fee payment is received the public authority should release the information promptly and within the appropriate time limit.

30. Public authorities should ensure that any charges they make are reasonable, and in accordance with the EIR and the guidance. http://www.defra.gov.uk/environment/pubaccess/

VI Transferring requests for information

31. A request whether in writing or received in any other form can only be transferred where a public authority receives a request for environmental information that it does not itself hold and which is not held by any other person on its behalf. If a public authority in receipt of a request holds some of the information requested, a transfer can only be made in respect of the information it does not hold but is held by another public authority.

32. Public authorities should bear in mind that 'holding' environmental information under the EIR includes holding a copy of a record produced or supplied by another person or body and, unlike FOIA, it extends to holding a record on behalf of another person or body. Where information is held on behalf of another person or body it will be appropriate to consult on whether the environmental information requested should be supplied unless the outcome can be predicted with reasonable confidence. (See also VII—Consultation with Third Parties). (Special provisions apply to the National Archives and other public record holding bodies under Regulation 17 including the Public Records Office Northern Ireland).

33. The authority receiving the initial request must always deal with that request in accordance with the EIR. When the authority receiving the original request does not hold all the information requested it must still deal with the request for information it does hold. The authority must also advise the applicant that it does not hold part of the requested information, or all of it, whichever applies. However, before doing this, the authority must be certain as to the extent of information requested that it holds itself. If information is freely available via a third party's public register, an authority may point to that register as part of providing advice and assistance, but this does not alter the authority's responsibility to respond to the request, for example if the applicant requests the information in the format in which it is held by the authority.

34. If the authority to whom the initial request was made believes that some or all of the information requested is held by another public authority, the authority should consider what would be the most helpful and expeditious way of assisting the applicant with his or her request. In most cases this is likely to involve:

—contacting the applicant and informing him or her that the information requested may be held by another public authority;
—suggesting that the applicant re-applies to the authority that is believed to hold the information;
—providing him or her with contact details for that authority;
—if the public authority receiving the request and the authority holding the information are publicly perceived as indelibly linked, explaining to the applicant the difference between the two authorities.

35. However, in some cases the authority to whom the original request is made may consider it to be more appropriate to transfer the request for information that it does not itself hold to another authority. In such cases, the authority should always consult with the other authority with a view to ascertaining whether it does hold the information and, if so, whether it should transfer the request to it. A request (or part of a request) should not be transferred if there is any reason to doubt that the second authority holds the information. When consulting a second authority the identity of the person requesting the information should not be disclosed unless that person has consented.

36. Before transferring a request for information to another authority, the authority should firstly consider whether a transfer is appropriate. If a transfer is appropriate the authority should first

obtain the consent of the applicant who may have valid reasons for not wishing their request to be transferred to a third party. If consent is given the applicant should always be provided with sufficient details concerning the date and destination of transfer.

37. Where a request or part of a request is transferred from one public authority to another, the receiving authority must comply with its obligations under the EIR in the same way as it would for a request that is received direct from an applicant. The time for complying with such a request will be measured from the day that the receiving authority receives the request.

38. All transfers of requests should take place as soon as is practicable, and the applicant should be notified as soon as possible once this has been done by issuing a refusal letter under Regulation 14.

39. Where a public authority is unable either to advise the applicant which public authority holds, or may hold, the requested information or to facilitate the transfer of the request to another authority (or considers it inappropriate to do so) it should consider what advice, if any, it can provide to the applicant to enable him or her to pursue his or her request. In this event the public authority should also issue a refusal letter in accordance with Regulation 14. The refusal letter should explain that the public authority does not hold the information.

VII Consultation with third parties

40. Public authorities must always remember that unless an exception is provided for in the EIR in relation to any particular information, they will be obliged to disclose that information in response to a request. Authorities are not obliged by the EIR to consult in respect of information which may be wholly or jointly owned by third parties, but may make a commitment to do so.

41. All EIR exceptions are subject to the public interest test; unlike FOIA, the EIR contains no 'absolute' exceptions. Moreover, lack of consent of a third party does not necessarily preclude disclosure, as in each case the public interest must be balanced. If the public interest in disclosing the information outweighs the public interest in withholding it, the information must be disclosed. (Information on emissions must be disclosed in accordance with Regulation 12 and personal data must be considered in accordance with DPA requirements).

42. A public authority may consider that consultation is not appropriate where the cost of consulting with third parties would be disproportionate because, for example, many third parties are involved or there has been earlier consultation on the status and sensitivity of the information. It should be noted that in this context 'third party' is specifically a person or body affected by the information that is the subject of the consultation. In such cases the authority should consider what is the most reasonable course of action for it to take in light of the requirements of the EIR, the potential effects of disclosure, and the public interest.

43. Where the consent of a number of third parties may be relevant and those parties have a representative organisation that can express views on behalf of those parties the authority may, if it considers consultation appropriate, consider that it would be sufficient to consult that representative organisation. If there is no representative organisation, the authority may consider that it would be sufficient to consult a representative sample of the third parties in question.

44. The fact that the third party has not responded to consultation does not relieve the authority of its duty to disclose information under the EIR, or its duty to reply within the time specified in the EIR.45. In all cases, it is for the public authority that received the request, not the third party (or representative of the third party) to weigh the public interest and to determine whether or not information should be disclosed under the EIR. A refusal to consent to disclosure by a third party does not in itself mean information should be withheld, although it may indicate interests involved. Note that in the case of public records transferred to a public record office there is a requirement to consult (see Regulation 17).

VIII Environmental information regulations and public sector contracts

46. When entering into contracts public authorities should refuse to include contractual terms that purport to restrict the disclosure of environmental information held by the authority and relating to the contract beyond the restrictions permitted by the EIR. Public authorities cannot 'contract out' of their obligations under the Regulations. This means that they cannot sign a contract that gives an undertaking to a private firm (or anyone else) that they will not comply with their obligations under the Regulations. Unless an exception provided for under the EIR is applicable in relation to any particular information and the balancing of public interest favours refusal, a public authority will be obliged to disclose that information in response to a request, regardless of the terms of any contract. Where personal data is concerned this will be done in accordance with the requirements of Regulation 13 and the Data Protection Act 1998.

47. When entering into contracts with non-public authority contractors, public authorities may be under pressure to accept confidentiality clauses so that information relating to the terms of the contract, its value and performance will be exempt from disclosure. Public authorities should reject such clauses wherever possible and explain the relevance of the public interest test. Where, exceptionally, it is necessary to include non-disclosure provisions in a contract, an option could be to agree with the contractor a schedule of the contract that clearly identifies information that should not be disclosed. But authorities will need to take care when drawing up any such schedule, and be aware that any restrictions on disclosure provided for could potentially be overridden by their obligations under the EIR, as described above.

48. In any event, public authorities should not agree to hold information 'in confidence' which is not in fact confidential in nature. Authorities should be aware that certain exceptions including those for commercial confidentiality, and voluntarily supplied data, are not available when the information requested is about emissions into the environment.

49. Any acceptance of confidentiality provisions must be for good reasons and capable of being justified to the Commissioner.

50. It is for the public authority to disclose information pursuant to the EIR, and not the non-public authority contractor, unless that contractor received the request and is, itself, a body subject to the EIR. However, a public authority may have concerns regarding contractual matters and not wish the contractor to release information without consulting them. In these cases, contracts or other working arrangements should be made to ensure appropriate consultation about the handling of requests for information exchanged between the parties. Any such constraints should be drawn as narrowly as possible and according to the individual circumstances of the case. Apart from such cases, public authorities should not impose terms of secrecy on contractors.

51. With contracts in existence prior to EIR 2004 being enacted, if an authority receives a request for information whose release would mean an actionable breach of confidence, the authority should refer to the guidance issued by the Information Commissioner: http://www.informationcommissioner.gov.uk Public authorities in this position should seek their own legal advice as appropriate.

52. Under the EIR, some contractors, including public utilities that have been privatised, are subject to the requirements of the EIR. http://www.defra.gov.uk/environment/pubaccess/guidance/index.htm

IX Accepting information in confidence from third parties

53. A public authority should only accept information from third parties in confidence if it is essential to obtain that information in connection with the exercise of any of the authority's functions and it would not otherwise be provided. Even in these circumstances it will be necessary to explain the relevance of the public interest test and the fact that there could be circumstances in which the public interest in disclosure equals or outweighs the adverse effects of disclosure on a third party.

In addition, public authorities should not agree to hold information received from third parties 'in confidence' which is not confidential in nature (paragraph 47). Again, acceptance of any confidentiality provisions must be for good reasons, capable of being justified to the Commissioner. (Special provisions apply to archives (paragraph 32).

X Consultation with devolved administrations

54. Public authorities should consult with the relevant devolved administration before disclosing information provided by or directly concerning that administration, except where:

- the views of the devolved administration can have no effect on the decision of the authority (for example where there is no applicable exception so the information must be disclosed under EIR); or
- where the outcome may be predicted with reasonable confidence and in the circumstances, consultation would be too costly or time consuming.

55. Similarly, the devolved administrations should consult with the relevant non-devolved public authority before disclosing information provided by or directly concerning that authority, except where the views of the public authority can have no effect on the decision whether to disclose, or where consultation would be disproportionate in the circumstances.

XI Refusal of request

Advice on withholding of information is covered in Chapter 7 of the Guidance.

56. Where a request for information is refused or partially refused in accordance with an exception, the EIR requires that the authority notify the applicant which exception has been claimed and why that exception applies. Public authorities should not unless the statement would involve the disclosure of information which would itself be withheld in accordance with the EIR merely paraphrase the wording of the exception. They should state clearly in the decision letter the reason why they have decided to apply that exception in the case in question. The EIR also requires authorities, when withholding information, to state the reasons for claiming that the public interest in maintaining the exception outweighs the public interest in disclosure. Public authorities should specify the public interest factors (for and against disclosure) that they have taken into account before reaching the decision (again, unless the statement would involve the disclosure of information which would itself be withheld in accordance with the EIR). They should also include details of the complaints procedure.

57. For monitoring purposes public authorities should keep **a record of all** applications where either all or part of the requested information is withheld, the basis on which it was withheld (including the exception or exceptions which were applied), and, where relevant, a full explanation of how the public interest test was applied and the factors which were considered. Public authorities should also keep copies of redacted information, together with a copy of the information that the applicant actually received in case of a subsequent complaint. Senior managers in each public authority will need this information to determine whether cases are being properly considered and whether the reasons for refusals are sound. The information will also be required if the applicant appeals against the refusal, or refers the case to the Information Commissioner. This could be done by requiring all staff that refuse a request for information to forward the details to a central point in the organisation for collation. Details of information on complaints about applications which have been refused (see XII—'Complaints procedure') could be collected at the same central point.

XII Review and complaints procedures

58. Each public authority must have a review procedure in place. This procedure may be used by any person who considers that their request has not been properly handled or who are otherwise dissatisfied with the outcome of the consideration of their request and where the issue is such that it cannot be resolved informally in discussion with the official dealing with the request. Information relating to the complaints procedure should be included in an authority's publication scheme if it

has one, or made readily available elsewhere. Under Regulation 18, the enforcement and appeal provisions of the FOIA will apply in respect of a complaint made after 1st January 2005.

59. Any decision made in relation to a request under the EIR that contains a refusal must be in writing and public authorities are obliged under Regulations 14 (5) to notify the applicant of his or her right of complaint. They should provide details of their own complaints procedure, including how to make a complaint and inform the applicant of the right to complain to the Commissioner under section 50 of the FOIA if he or she is still dissatisfied following the authority's review. However, as a matter of good practice authorities should provide details of their complaints procedure when responding to all requests. It is for the applicant to decide whether they are content with the response they receive; they may have concerns that they wish to pursue in circumstances where the public authority claims to have fully complied with their request.

60. Any written reply from the applicant (including one transmitted electronically) expressing dissatisfaction with an authority's response to a valid request for information should be treated as a complaint, as should any written communication from a person who perceives the authority is not complying with its publication scheme where it has one. These communications should be handled in accordance with the authority's review procedure pursuant to Regulation 11, even if the applicant does not state his or her desire for the authority to review their decision or the handling of their application.

61. The complaints procedure should be a fair and impartial means of dealing with handling problems and reviewing decisions taken pursuant to the EIR, including decisions taken about where the public interest lies. It should be possible to reverse or otherwise amend decisions previously taken. Complaints procedures should be clear and not unnecessarily bureaucratic. They should be capable of producing a prompt determination of the complaint.

62. In all cases, complaints should be acknowledged and the complainant should be informed of the authority's target date for determining the complaint. Where it is apparent that determination of the complaint will take longer than the target time (for example because of the complexity of the particular case), the authority should inform the applicant and explain the reason for the delay. The complainant should always be informed of the outcome of his or her complaint.

63. Authorities must consider each complaint, decide whether they have complied with their requirements under EIR and respond to the complainant within 40 working days from the time when the complaint was received.

64. Records should be kept of all complaints and of their outcome. Authorities should have procedures in place for monitoring complaints and for reviewing, and if necessary amending procedures for dealing with requests for information where such action is indicated by more than occasional reversals of initial decisions.

65. Where the outcome of a complaint is that information should be disclosed which was previously withheld, the information in question should be disclosed with immediate effect.

66. Where the outcome of a complaint is that the procedures within an authority have not been properly followed by the authority's staff, the authority should apologise to the applicant. The authority should also take appropriate steps to prevent similar errors occurring in future.

67. Where the outcome of a complaint is that an initial decision to withhold information is upheld or is otherwise in the authority's favour, the applicant should be informed of his or her right to apply to the Commissioner and be given details of how to make an application for a decision on whether the request for information has been dealt with in accordance with the requirements of the EIR. As failure to deal with a complaint promptly may be grounds for complaint to the Information Commissioner, authorities should set out details of the timescale for dealing with complaints in their complaints procedure, which should be made readily available.

APPENDIX J1

Freedom of Information and Data Protection (Appropriate Limit and Fees) Regulations 2004 (SI 2004 No 3244)

Made	*7th December 2004*
Laid before Parliament	*9th December 2004*
Coming into force	*1st January 2005*

The Secretary of State, in exercise of the powers conferred upon him by sections 9(3) and (4), 12(3), (4) and (5), and 13(1) and (2) of the Freedom of Information Act 2000, and by sections 9A(5) and 67(2) of the Data Protection Act 1998, and having consulted the Information Commissioner in accordance with section 67(3) of the Data Protection Act 1998, hereby makes the following Regulations:

Citation and commencement

1. These Regulations may be cited as the Freedom of Information and Data Protection (Appropriate Limit and Fees) Regulations 2004 and come into force on 1st January 2005.

Interpretation

2. In these Regulations—

'the 2000 Act' means the Freedom of Information Act 2000;
'the 1998 Act' means the Data Protection Act 1998; and
'the appropriate limit' is to be construed in accordance with the provision made in regulation 3.

The appropriate limit

3.—(1) This regulation has effect to prescribe the appropriate limit referred to in section 9A(3) and (4) of the 1998 Act and the appropriate limit referred to in section 12(1) and (2) of the 2000 Act.

(2) In the case of a public authority which is listed in Part I of Schedule 1 to the 2000 Act, the appropriate limit is £600.

(3) In the case of any other public authority, the appropriate limit is £450.

Estimating the cost of complying with a request—general

4.—(1) This regulation has effect in any case in which a public authority proposes to estimate whether the cost of complying with a relevant request would exceed the appropriate limit.

(2) A relevant request is any request to the extent that it is a request—

(a) for unstructured personal data within the meaning of section 9A(1) of the 1998 Act, and to which section 7(1) of that Act would, apart from the appropriate limit, to any extent apply, or
(b) information to which section 1(1) of the 2000 Act would, apart from the appropriate limit, to any extent apply.

(3) In a case in which this regulation has effect, a public authority may, for the purpose of its estimate, take account only of the costs it reasonably expects to incur in relation to the request in–

(a) determining whether it holds the information,
(b) locating the information, or a document which may contain the information,

(c) retrieving the information, or a document which may contain the information, and
(d) extracting the information from a document containing it.

(4) To the extent to which any of the costs which a public authority takes into account are attributable to the time which persons undertaking any of the activities mentioned in paragraph (3) on behalf of the authority are expected to spend on those activities, those costs are to be estimated at a rate of £25 per person per hour.

Estimating the cost of complying with a request—aggregation of related requests

5.—(1) In circumstances in which this regulation applies, where two or more requests for information to which section 1(1) of the 2000 Act would, apart from the appropriate limit, to any extent apply, are made to a public authority —

(a) by one person, or
(b) by different persons who appear to the public authority to be acting in concert or in pursuance of a campaign,

the estimated cost of complying with any of the requests is to be taken to be the total costs which may be taken into account by the authority, under regulation 4, of complying with all of them.

(2) This regulation applies in circumstances in which—

(a) the two or more requests referred to in paragraph (1) relate, to any extent, to the same or similar information, and
(b) those requests are received by the public authority within any period of sixty consecutive working days.

(3) In this regulation, 'working day' means any day other than a Saturday, a Sunday, Christmas Day, Good Friday or a day which is a bank holiday under the Banking and Financial Dealings Act 1971 in any part of the United Kingdom.

Maximum fee for complying with section 1(1) of the 2000 Act

6.—(1) Any fee to be charged under section 9 of the 2000 Act by a public authority to whom a request for information is made is not to exceed the maximum determined by the public authority in accordance with this regulation.

(2) Subject to paragraph (4), the maximum fee is a sum equivalent to the total costs the public authority reasonably expects to incur in relation to the request in–

(a) informing the person making the request whether it holds the information, and
(b) communicating the information to the person making the request.

(3) Costs which may be taken into account by a public authority for the purposes of this regulation include, but are not limited to, the costs of–

(a) complying with any obligation under section 11(1) of the 2000 Act as to the means or form of communicating the information,
(b) reproducing any document containing the information, and
(c) postage and other forms of transmitting the information.

(4) But a public authority may not take into account for the purposes of this regulation any costs which are attributable to the time which persons undertaking activities mentioned in paragraph (2) on behalf of the authority are expected to spend on those activities.

Maximum fee for communication of information under section 13 of the 2000 Act

7.—(1) Any fee to be charged under section 13 of the 2000 Act by a public authority to whom a request for information is made is not to exceed the maximum determined by a public authority in accordance with this regulation.

(2) The maximum fee is a sum equivalent to the total of–

(a) the costs which the public authority may take into account under regulation 4 in relation to that request, and

(b) the costs it reasonably expects to incur in relation to the request in–

(i) informing the person making the request whether it holds the information, and

(ii) communicating the information to the person making the request.

(3) But a public authority is to disregard, for the purposes of paragraph(2)(a), any costs which it may take into account under regulation 4 solely by virtue of the provision made by regulation 5.

(4) Costs which may be taken into account by a public authority for the purposes of paragraph (2)(b) include, but are not limited to, the costs of–

(a) giving effect to any preference expressed by the person making the request as to the means or form of communicating the information,

(b) reproducing any document containing the information, and

(c) postage and other forms of transmitting the information.

(5) For the purposes of this regulation, the provision for the estimation of costs made by regulation 4(4) is to be taken to apply to the costs mentioned in paragraph (2)(b) as it does to the costs mentioned in regulation 4(3).

Baroness C Ashton

Parliamentary Under Secretary of State Department for Constitutional Affairs

Date 7th December 2004

Explanatory Note

(This note is not part of the Order)

These Regulations prescribe 'the appropriate amount' for the purposes of section 9A of the Data Protection Act 1998 and section 12 of the Freedom of Information Act 2000. If a public authority estimates that the cost of complying with a request for the information to which either of those provisions applies would exceed the appropriate amount, then the obligations which would otherwise be imposed by section 7 of the 1998 Act and section 1 of the 2000 Act in respect of such requests for information do not apply.

Regulation 3 prescribes an appropriate limit of £600 in the case of the public bodies listed in Part I of Schedule 1 to the 2000 Act (including government departments). An appropriate limit of £450 is prescribed in relation to all other public authorities.

Regulation 4 makes provision as to the costs to be estimated, and as to the manner in which they are to be estimated, for the purpose of estimating whether the cost of complying with a request would exceed the appropriate limit. The costs which may be taken into account are limited to those which the public authority reasonably expects to incur in undertaking certain specified activities in response to the request. Regulation 5 makes supplementary provision as to the estimation of costs in cases to which the 2000 Act applies. It provides that in relation to multiple requests which are related in specified ways by reference to those making the requests, the information to which the requests relate, and the timing of the requests, the estimated costs of complying with any single request is to be taken to be the aggregate estimated costs of complying with them all.

Regulation 6 makes provision as to the maximum fee that a public authority may specify in a fees notice under section 9 of the 2000 Act as a charge for complying with its duty under section 1(1) of the Act. The maximum is to be calculated by reference to specified limited aspects of the costs of informing the requester whether it holds the information and, if so, of communicating it to the requester.

Section 13 of the 2000 Act makes new provision for public authorities to be able to charge for the communication of information whose communication is not required because of the effect of the appropriate limit and is not otherwise required by law. Regulation 7 makes provision as to the maximum fee that a public authority may charge for the communication of information in the exercise of that power. The maximum is to be calculated by reference to the total costs which may be taken into account in estimating whether the cost of complying with the request would exceed the appropriate limit (excluding any costs 'aggregated' from other requests), together with the full costs of informing the requester whether the information is held, and, if so, of communicating it to the requester.

APPENDIX L

Department for Constitutional Affairs
Justice, rights and democracy

Freedom of Information

Memorandum of Understanding (signed 24 February 2005)

Memorandum of Understanding (MoU) between the Secretary of State for Constitutional Affairs (on behalf of government Departments) and the Information Commissioner, on co-operation between government Departments and the Information Commissioner in relation to sections 50 and 51 of the Freedom of Information Act 2000 (the 'FOI Act') (including ss.50 and 51 as applied, as amended, by Regulation 18 of the Environmental Information Regulations 2004).

Roles of the Information Commissioner and government Departments under the FOI Act and the Environmental Information Regulations 2004 (EIRs).

Purpose of the MoU

1. The purpose of this Memorandum of Understanding is to promote good standards of co-operation between Departments and the Commissioner:

   (a) in dealing with applications made to the Commissioner for a decision under section 50 of the FOI Act; and

   (b) where the Commissioner is considering serving a notice under section 51 of the FOI Act.

2. This MoU does not apply in situations in which an exemption under one or any of sections 23 or 24 of the FOI Act, or the exception in regulation 12(5)(a) (insofar as that regulation relates to national security) of the EIRs is engaged. Such situations are dealt with at Annex 2 to this MoU.

3. The Definitions in Annex 1 apply to this MoU. The respective roles and responsibilities of the ICO and DCA under the FOI Act and the EIRs will be summarised in a separate document, to which this document is subject. This MoU sets out guideline procedures designed to apply in the majority of cases. It is recognised that, because of unusual complexity or sensitivity, or where the information is voluminous, there may be some exceptions to these procedures. Departments may need to consider procedural issues on a case by case basis in the particular circumstances arising, but will continue to have regard to the procedures set out in the MoU as far as possible.

4. This MoU takes effect subject to the FOI Act, the EIRs and any other relevant legal provisions. For the avoidance of doubt nothing in this MoU shall operate to restrict or otherwise inhibit the exercise of the Commissioner's or Department's powers and duties under the FOI Act or the EIRs.

5. This MoU seeks to minimise the costs of complying with the FOI Act and to promote the efficient administration of its requirements within Departments and the Commissioner's office.

Steps to be taken where an application is made for a Decision under s.50 of the FOIA

6. The Commissioner will contact the relevant Department(s) (via nominated contact, where known) when he receives an application under section 50 of the FOI Act, as soon as practicable and in any event within 10 working days of such receipt. At this time he will:

- provide the Department with details of the Complainant's application;
- request the Department to provide all information relevant to the application; and
- invite the nominated contact to comment on the case;
- aim to establish a single channel of communication.

7. The Department will:

- provide all relevant information requested as quickly as possible and in any event within 20 working days of being contacted by the Commissioner, unless the Commissioner otherwise agrees;
- provide any additional relevant information subsequently requested by the Commissioner as quickly as possible and in any event within 10 working days of it being requested;
- provide all the information requested, including any information that has been redacted;
- inform the Commissioner, giving reasons, where it is not able to provide the information within the time periods set out in this paragraph and provide an indication of when it expects to be able to do so.

Information notices

8. The Commissioner will not normally serve an Information Notice under section 51 of the FOI Act on any government Department unless he believes that relevant information is being withheld from him or that there has been undue delay in providing the information requested. Where the Information Commissioner intends to serve an Information Notice, wherever possible he will inform the Department in advance.

Obligations in relation to information provided in accordance with this MoU

9. The Commissioner will not disclose to the Complainant or to any third party any information provided to him by a government Department either under the terms of this MoU, or as a result of serving a notice under section 50 or 51 of the FOI Act unless:

- the Department consents to the disclosure; or
- subject to paragraph 26, all appeal proceedings have been exhausted.

10. Where a request is made to the Commissioner (whether under the FOI Act or otherwise) for information that has been supplied to him in accordance with this MoU, or where release of such information seems to the Commissioner to be necessary under or in connection with any enactment, Community obligation, proceedings or otherwise, the Commissioner shall inform the Department as soon as possible.

11. Where the circumstances mentioned in para 10 arise, the Commissioner acknowledges that he will resist release of the information, where in all the circumstances it is reasonable to do so, and by all reasonable means including the use of any appeals processes.

12. Where a Department relies upon an exemption from the duty to confirm or deny whether it holds the information of the description specified in the request, the Commissioner will not seek access to that information where it is possible to judge the strength of a decision neither to confirm or deny the holding of information without inspecting such information as may actually be held by the Department.

13. The Commissioner will not hold information provided to him under this MoU for longer than is necessary for the discharge of his statutory functions. The Commissioner shall, in consultation with the Department, arrange for the return or other disposal of the information, where necessary.

14. The Commissioner will ensure that any information that is protectively marked will be kept under the conditions of security required by the Manual of Protective Security for as long as he retains the information.

15. The Commissioner agrees to inspect in situ papers which are particularly sensitive and therefore would not be circulated beyond the offices of the Department in question.

16. Where stringent security or similar consideration so demand, the Department may indicate that it would, in their view, be more appropriate for the Commissioner himself, or nominated members of staff, to inspect the information, rather than be provided with it. The Commissioner will take full account of such a view and not refuse any such representations unless there are overriding reasons why provision of the information to or inspection by other staff would significantly obstruct the discharge of his statutory functions.

17. Inspection of the information may also be agreed in other cases where to do so would be in the mutual interests of the Commissioner and the Department, for instance where the information involved is voluminous, or where it would be helpful to have matters of a technical nature explained to a member of the Commissioner's staff.

Processes on whether to issue a Decision Notice

18. The Commissioner will consider all information provided to him in reaching a decision whether to serve either a Decision Notice or an Information Notice on the Department.

19. The Commissioner will contact both the Department and the Complainant, whenever appropriate, throughout his consideration of a complaint and, in any event, will normally provide progress reports every 28 days.

20. Wherever practicable, the Commissioner will explore the scope for a settlement of the complaint, which would be acceptable to the Complainant and to the Department. Where such settlement can be achieved—for example, by disclosure of some of the information requested—he will invite the Complainant to withdraw the complaint.

Preliminary Decision Notices

21. Before serving a Decision Notice, the Commissioner will consider issuing a (non-statutory) Preliminary Decision Notice and invite the Department to comment on it within 28 working days. The Commissioner undertakes to consider any such comments before deciding to serve a Decision Notice under section 50 of the Act. The decision as to whether to serve either a Preliminary Decision Notice or a Decision Notice shall be informed by the policy set out in Annex 2 of the Commissioner's paper 'Regulation under the Freedom of Information Act 2000 and the Environmental Information Regulations 2004 which, for convenience, is attached at Annex C of this MoU.

22. Where a Department does not agree to the steps suggested in the Preliminary Decision Notice, it will inform the Commissioner accordingly, setting out its reasons. Efforts will be made between the Commissioner and the Department in question to understand why the Preliminary Decision Notice has not been accepted and to explore alternatives.

Decision Notices

23. If the Commissioner decides to issue a formal Decision Notice under section 50(3)(b) of the Act, he shall serve the Notice on the Department and the Complainant simultaneously. He will give both Departments and complainants a reasonable period of time to digest the Notice before himself making the Decision Notice publicly available.

24. Where the Department proposes to serve a certificate under section 53 of the FOI Act, it will, wherever possible, inform the Commissioner in advance.

25. The Commissioner shall not serve a Decision Notice, which may reveal or refer to 'market sensitive' information, without first being satisfied as to the relevant regulatory requirements.

26. The Commissioner will only publish complaint case summaries after the period for appeal to the Information Tribunal has passed, or otherwise following the conclusion of any appeal proceedings. He may, however, comment upon Decision Notices once these have been made public without, of course, revealing any information which might be subject to an appeal. Any complaint case summaries will not reveal information which may be exempt under the FOI Act or the EIRs.

General

27. Wherever possible, the Commissioner and Departments shall communicate by means of electronic communication.

28. This MoU shall be kept under review and will be amended, as necessary, in the light of experience.

29. The Department for Constitutional Affairs shall ensure that this MoU is widely disseminated within government and shall encourage compliance with it.

30. The Commissioner and the Secretary of State for Constitutional Affairs shall place copies of this MoU on their respective websites.

Annex 1: Definitions

In this Memorandum of Understanding:

'the DCA' means the Department for Constitutional Affairs

'The Commissioner' means the Information Commissioner

'MoU' means Memorandum of Understanding

'Department' means—

a) where the information to which the request relates is governed by the Freedom of Information Act 2000, a government department as defined in that Act. In the case of the Ministry of Defence, the term includes armed forces of the Crown (except the special forces and units assisting GCHQ), and the Ministry of Defence Police;
b) where the information to which the request relates is governed by the Environmental Information Regulations 2004, a government department as defined in those Regulations. In the case of the Ministry of Defence, the term includes armed forces of the Crown and the Ministry of Defence police.

'The FOI Act' means the Freedom of Information Act 2000 and references to the Act include, where the context so requires, the Act as amended by the Environmental Information Regulations.

'The EIRs' means the Environmental Information Regulations 2004.

'The Tribunal' means the Information Tribunal.

'Complainant' means a person who has applied to the Commissioner for a decision, under section 50 of the FOI Act.

'Information Notice' and 'Decision Notice' have the meanings assigned to them in the FOI Act.

Annex 2: Information to which s.23 and s.24 FOI Act and regulation 12(5)(a)EIRs apply

1. It is recognised that cases involving information relating to, or obtained from, the bodies specified in section 23 of the FOI Act and those where information has been withheld on national

security grounds (section 24 of the FOI Act/ regulation 12 (5) (a) of the EIRs), are likely to be particularly sensitive. It is also accepted that the sensitivity of such cases means that there is likely to be a need for greater dialogue between the Commissioner and Departments before reaching any final conclusions.

2. Wherever practicable, the Commissioner will explore the scope for a settlement of the complaint which would be acceptable to the Complainant and to the Department. Where such settlement can be achieved, the Commissioner will invite the Complainant to withdraw the complaint.

3. It is envisaged that, in most cases, the issue will be resolved by dialogue between the Commissioner and the relevant Department(s). This will include discussion of the reasons and justification for relying on the exemptions under section 23 or 24 (or regulation 12(5)(a)) in a particular case).

4. Where the Commissioner requests access to information which has been withheld on the basis of the exemption in section 23 or 24 FOI Act (or regulation 12(5)(a)), the relevant Department does not commit itself to providing the withheld information to the Commissioner, but will consider any request to do so on a case by case basis.

5. It is envisaged that Departments will only seek a Ministerial Certificate under section 23 or 24 (or under regulation 12(5)(a) of the EIRs) where (i) the individual whose request for information has been refused complains to the Commissioner, and (ii) the Commissioner indicates that he is minded to pursue the complaint and embark on the enforcement procedure under the FOI Act.

6. With this in mind, where the Information Commissioner intends to serve an Information Notice, wherever possible he will inform the relevant Department in advance.

7. By the same token, where the relevant Department proposes to serve a certificate under section 23 or 24 of the FOI Act or under regulation 15 of the EIRs, wherever possible it will inform the Commissioner in advance.

Annex 3: Annex 2 of the Commissioner's paper 'Regulation under the Freedom of Information Act 2000 and the Environmental Information Regulations 2004' (Preliminary Notices)

General Policy

1. The Commissioner may serve three legally binding notices. These are Decision Notices, Enforcement Notices and Information Notices. The Council on Tribunals has previously advised that in serving Enforcement Notices under the Data Protection Act it is good practice to first serve Preliminary Notices. The Commissioner's policy in relation to Preliminary Notices under the FOI Act and EIRs builds upon this approach.

2. The purpose of a preliminary stage is not to layer an additional bureaucratic procedure onto the enforcement process, but rather to reduce the number of appeals to the Information Tribunal by allowing all parties, the public authority, the applicant (where applicable) and the Information Commissioner, to reach agreed solutions without the expense, effort and delay which appeals inevitably entail.

3. The governing principle which will be followed is that Preliminary Notices will be served in those cases where the Commissioner judges that this is likely to lead to a swifter and more equitable outcome both for applicants and public authorities.

4. In the final analysis the decision as to whether to serve a Preliminary Notice is a matter of judgement. However, the Commissioner will be guided by the following general 'rules of thumb'. Except in most clear-cut cases, for instance when an organisation clearly falling within the definition of public authority denies any obligations under the Act, the Commissioner will make an informal approach to a public authority suspected of failure to meet its obligations in order to establish basic facts before serving either a Preliminary or a Final Notice.

Preliminary Decision Notices

5. The following is a series of general scenarios ranging from cases where a preliminary stage would be unlikely through to ones in which it would be probable.

- The Commissioner does not consider that it would be appropriate to specify any steps to be taken by a public authority. A complaint may be clearly unjustified, for instance if it is obvious that the authority can legitimately rely upon an absolute exemption. In other cases, complaints may be justified. For instance there may have been a delay in supplying information. However, once the information has now been provided, there will be no steps that can be usefully specified in a Decision Notice adverse to the public authority. It is unlikely that he will issue Preliminary Decision Notices in these cases.
- The issues raised in a complaint are simply of a procedural nature. For instance the Commissioner does not consider that a proper refusal notice has been issued or it seems to him that it would be reasonable for the authority to have provided further advice and assistance to the applicant. These cases would be unlikely to merit a Preliminary Decision Notice.
- A public authority has failed to identify a relevant exemption in refusing a request. In this case, the Commissioner is more likely than not to issue a Decision Notice, either ordering the disclosure or information or requiring the authority to reconsider, perhaps relying upon a more appropriate exemption. Such cases are less clear cut than the earlier ones.
- An authority has identified a relevant exemption but has refused information having applied the public interest test. The Commissioner will generally issue a Preliminary Decision Notice unless the Information Tribunal has previously ruled in similar cases that information should be disclosed on public interest grounds.
- The investigation of a complaint has suggested other exemptions upon which the public authority could credibly rely or other public interest arguments for or against disclosure have transpired. Such cases are likely to be more complex involving large quantities of information and requiring careful judgement by the public authority, including decisions about the detailed redaction of documents. Preliminary Decision Notices are likely to be served in these cases.

INDEX